Bird in a Banyan Tree

Bird in a Banyan Tree

My Story

BINA RAMANI

RAINLIGHT

RUPA

Published in Rainlight by Rupa Publications India Pvt. Ltd 2013
7/16, Ansari Road, Daryaganj
New Delhi 110002

Sales centres:
Allahabad Bengaluru Chennai
Hyderabad Jaipur Kathmandu
Kolkata Mumbai

ISBN: 978-81-291-2912-3

First impression 2013

10 9 8 7 6 5 4 3 2 1

The moral right of the author has been asserted.

Printed at Replika Press Pvt. Ltd., India

To my beloved grandchildren, Kai and Kaspian, the blessed inheritors of the magnificent banyan tree, who will continue the legacy in times of peace...I hope.

Contents

Prologue

I HAD SPENT SEVEN traumatic days and nights in police custody. The police had found nothing more to hold against me. In fact, they did not interrogate me even once during those seven days. Yet, their daily bulletins to the media claimed, 'Bina Ramani is not cooperating' offering no other detail. Now the police had issued a non-bailable warrant against me, and I was going to jail! Jail! Unthinkable! Why?

Finally, the media were demanding explanations. They were asking the same questions we were: why was the key witness in the Jessica Lal murder trial being arrested?

In 2006, the retrial of the Jessica Lal murder case had been announced due to unprecedented public and media pressure. An elite Special Investigation Team (SIT), under the watchful eye of then Delhi Police Commissioner K.K. Paul, had been hastily appointed. We had heartily welcomed the move. Among the few witnesses remaining in the seven-year-long sensational case, in which our role had been frequently derailed by the powerful lobby of the accused, we hoped finally to vindicate our stand and help achieve 'Justice for Jessica'. That slogan was being chanted by millions who had been unanimously roused when the six accused were mysteriously acquitted of the 1999 crime.

Then, in an early step in the new investigation, the SIT, riding the wave of heightened emotion throughout the nation, issued statements to the media that 'The Ramanis'—my daughter Malini, my husband Georges Mailhot and myself—'have been put on an international "lookout notice"'. I had played a critical role in confronting the murderer on the night of the shooting in April 1999. We had reported the crime, grappled with the murderer and taken Jessica to a hospital. We were determined to cooperate with the police team in their investigation. But throughout, we had to stoically stand up to the mounting pressure to cave in and change our statements, as most of the other witnesses had done.

Now here I was, seven years after the incident, and instead of watching justice take its course I sat on a bench alone, in the centre of a big godown-like hall in the Patiala House Court Complex. On either side of me were packed cages, each holding dozens of men and women prisoners of the day. They were to be transported to Tihar Jail at 5.30 p.m. It was now about 3 p.m. Numb with shock, I was trying to take stock of what had transpired in the last hour.

The atmosphere around me was totally alien. This hall felt like a different world. Today, the authorities had brought me to court before 2 p.m., almost two hours earlier than the routine appointed time. During my seven days in captivity they had taken me to court daily at 3.30 p.m., where my lawyers, family and friends would appear to rally for my freedom. Each day, however, my custody would be extended, thanks to yet another delay tactic successfully set before the magistrate, Kamini Lau.

On this seventh day of my custody, I craved my freedom. The two policewomen who always accompanied me had cheered me up, saying, 'Try and be happy today, we think you will go home.' They had smiles on their faces, which I had never seen before. One of them pressed a tika on my forehead for good measure. I could feel her sincerity.

The magistrate had not yet arrived, and the courtroom was almost empty. I spotted Nafisa Ali, my true and loyal friend, who had always been the first to arrive in court. I gave her a warm smile, feeling euphoric at the prospect of being freed from the nightmarish police custody.

As soon as the magistrate arrived, one of the police personnel accompanying me, a senior cop, walked up to her desk with a sheaf of papers. They engaged in a five-minute discussion, turned towards me, and all of a sudden I was being hurriedly led out of the courtroom. It all seemed so ominous. I was gripped with fear. I grabbed Nafisa's arm as we passed her seat and pulled her along with me, resisting the pressure my guards were using to separate us. Nafisa looked into my eyes momentarily and, like a mother to a child, whispered, 'Bina, be brave. I think they are taking you to Tihar, and it will only be for one night. They have already announced it to the media.'

The media had fallen for every fabricated bulletin the authorities fed them, sensationalizing my so-call misdeeds. Now, as we stepped out of the courtroom, I could not believe my eyes. The empty lane from which we had entered was choked with scores of photographers and journalists, all falling over themselves to see Bina Ramani being led away into the hall reserved for convicts of the day, to be transported to the notorious Tihar Jail!

I had no idea what exactly I was being accused of, but I was forced away by a police cordon amidst the jostling crowds, crying out for my fundamental rights and demanding that my lawyers be given a chance to hear the verdict. It was shocking. I lost Nafisa along the way. Everywhere I looked, I saw cameras and eager bystanders squeezing for a glimpse. A tall, burly uniformed man suddenly materialized as the narrow lane took a turn towards an enclosure with heavy barbed wire for a boundary wall. A doorway from there led us to a big iron gate that opened to receive us. The posse of police parted ways with me, as did the others who had taken me to court. The gate to this large hall was pulled shut and the burly man opened a closet near the entrance, pulled out a bunch of the largest keys I had ever seen and motioned me to follow him.

With nothing more than a bottle of water and my asthma inhaler in my hands, I simply surrendered to my fate, numbed my senses and tried to forget 'me'. The burly man, his large keys now thrown menacingly over his left shoulder, led me towards a dark cell. Behind several iron bars, I saw dozens of scrawny, bedraggled and helpless women with desperation in their eyes. They rushed forward, clutching at the iron bars to get a glimpse of their newest cellmate. I was flabbergasted at the sight, but luckily, rose to the occasion and found my voice. 'I am not going in there; I am not a prisoner.'

I glared up at him. He looked at me in shock for having dared to challenge his authority. I refused to buckle, and raised my hand. 'Do you see this—it is my asthma inhaler.' I waved it in his face. The other convicts silently watched our confrontation. I continued, 'Do you know I am a serious asthma patient?'

The man now showed his wrath, taking a deep breath, ignoring my plea, and started to unlock the door with one of his giant keys.

I was paralysed with fear. I had to win this battle of wills. Diving into my deepest reserve, I gave it one more shot, hoping I would either intimidate him or reach his human side. 'Okay,' I offered, 'take me in. Just remember, if I drop dead there in the next ten minutes,' you will be responsible for it.' I looked into his eyes with a cold stare.

The man hesitated for a moment, then shut the iron door, and again threw the bunch of keys over his shoulder. Irritation clouded his face. He walked me around the corner to a tiny room where they kept the cooling machinery. It was equally bad, if not worse than the cells, being no bigger than a closet and covered with dust. I was horrified. Now I reacted fiercely. 'Oh no, I'm not going in there. I will die here even faster! There's no standing room and it's filled with dust!' I ranted, waving my inhaler in his face again. I spoke in English, knowing it gave me a better chance of intimidating and challenging him.

I saw an annoyed resignation creep into his eyes. A young uniformed woman, who seemed to be in charge of this space, also looked at me in scorn for challenging such a senior officer. My mind ticked at high speed as a defence measure. It was all happening so fast.

The burly man now looked at me as if he were weighing whether to bash me up. It certainly would not have been the first time for him; he seemed to enjoy his job. Wordlessly, with a motion of his hand, he walked me over to the centre of the big shed where there were three long, worn benches, all empty. He pointed to the benches and said, 'Go sit there.' He seemed eager to disappear from my sight.

I chose the furthest of the three benches, which offered a minimal view of the caged prisoners. Numerous official-looking men walked along two open corridors on either side of the benches. I was suddenly gripped with the reality of my situation. My mind reeled with a thousand questions.

Who were all these people? How many were victims of a conspiracy, perhaps like me? What had they done to be locked up? Had they actually committed the offences they were being charged with? What sad and tragic stories could they tell? Would I be with them long enough to get to know their personal stories? Those thoughts filled me with a dreadful sinking feeling. I looked up, hoping to receive an embrace from the sky or something. I saw a dusty, sagging, water-stained asbestos ceiling. Thankful for my tinted glasses, I let my tears flow, wondering for the umpteenth time how and why I was in this mess. How could my life have gone so wrong?

Suddenly, I sensed someone standing next to me. I snapped back into the present, quickly brushed away my tears, adjusted my glasses and looked up. A tall, authoritative-looking man was staring at me. He looked elegant in his crisp white shirt, starched white pants and tan loafers. His incongruous appearance, seemingly out of nowhere, baffled me. Seeing my tear-stained face, he offered me some tea. Even as I accepted his offer, he sat down next to me and gestured to a man who had been standing behind him to bring two cups of tea.

Startled as I was, his presence somehow put me at ease. He introduced himself but I did not register his name. Feeling embarrassed to ask him to repeat it, I simply sat there, alert to whatever news he was about to deliver. Even though his appearance had bewildered me, I felt he was a good omen. It seemed like a mirage.

Taking a sip from his cup, he looked around to ensure there was no one within earshot. I observed that a pall of silence had blanketed us. Everyone kept a respectful distance, indicating that he must be a very important official. Then, in a kind but matter-of-fact voice, he started to speak. 'You must not be afraid. There are some people in high places watching over you, and you can rest assured that no harm will come to you. We are proud of the way you have handled yourself. Please continue to be brave. You will not be let down. Many crores have been spent to destroy justice in this case and keep Manu Sharma out of jail, but as long as you stick to the truth no harm will come to you. We are watching. You have a key role to play. Just have patience for another day or two. You will be safe in Tihar; you are protected.' He reached the end of his narration and placed his empty cup and saucer on the bench at the same time. It was over as swiftly as it had started.

I took a deep breath as I tried to digest what I had just heard from this mystery man. Even as I framed a question for him, he got up to take his leave. 'Please tell me your name again,' I asked, as I thanked him. It was all too much to absorb—was I supposed to have blind faith in what I had just heard?

It was clear that he didn't want to reveal his identity to me, as he mumbled his name incoherently for the second time. It made no sense. I wished he would simply take me away to wherever he was going. Then, desperately clinging to the moment and trying to stretch it, I asked, 'Will the truth finally surface or not? When will the public know about this terrible injustice I am being put through?' He just raised his hand, offering a comforting assurance, and repeated, 'Don't worry, you are being watched and protected by good people who are on your side.' He paused for a moment, then before parting, said, 'It's only a matter of days, the truth *will* be out. Justice will be delivered.' Giving me a reassuring smile, he hurriedly left the hall. Whoosh—he was gone in an instant. A surge of relief ran through me, like a balm for my broken spirit. It lasted only too briefly, then the dreadful reality sunk in again. Feeling intensely alone, resigned hopelessly to my fate, I was fighting back tears. What was I doing in this dust-filled, asbestos-roofed enclosure, surrounded by a living scene of Kalyug at its worst? How had I come to this? I wondered. Suddenly, an old memory in the form of my mother's voice awakened my spirit: 'One must learn to separate the "me" from the "self"'. She used to quote this line from Guru Nanak's teachings. It was just the wisdom I needed at that moment to ease the anguish I was feeling. She would explain that the 'self' is the permanence, the God within you that would never let you down if you put your faith in it. The 'me' is the ego that has been created by the illusion of earthly wants and needs. 'Learn to count on your self,' she seemed to be reminding me now. I felt like a child again, reflecting on my mother's words.

1

Dadar and Breach Candy

A NINE-YEAR-OLD GIRL RECLINES on her favourite black rock. It is flattened out at the top, just for her, so she can sit and stare out at the vast expanse of the Arabian Sea in Bombay. Each day that rock seems to await her arrival with as much delight as she feels for it. This is her haven of privacy, an ally in building her dreams. The young girl's life lies before her, an empty canvas. The sea offers a palette of colours, and with the finest brush of imagination she paints her dreams...

I was that girl. And that rock was where I first began to discover who I was and who I might become. It was the refuge I would escape to as often as I could, whether for two hours or just fifteen minutes. I would slip out of our family apartment across the road whenever I was sure I wouldn't be missed. My beloved rock, the endless frothy waves, the shells and snails at low tide—for the first time, they opened a window to the miracle of God's nature and my place within it.

■

We arrived at our new apartment in Bombay, opposite the sea, in 1951, after spending four years in a crowded makeshift haveli in Dadar, to which we had fled from post-Partition Karachi in 1947. I was captured by the endless horizon and the majestic sounds of the ocean, drawing its smell deep into my lungs. The vastness of what I saw made me feel insignificant, but it also gave me a sense of security and awakened in me a longing for escape, for adventure. The thought of being able to access it just by crossing the road, anytime I wished, was exciting.

I grew up in a large, very social and rather religious Sikh household, the youngest of twelve brothers and sisters, the child of two doting parents. As if that wasn't enough, there were numerous nieces, nephews, cousins, acquaintances and neighbours always milling around in our pre-Partition Karachi home, where the doors were always open. My family had converted to Sikhism after two of my brothers started following a Sikh guru, well before I was born. Both these brothers succumbed to a typhoid epidemic at the ages of thirteen and fifteen; a third brother, too, died of the same malady soon after, at the tender age of ten months, leaving my mother heartbroken. My father, the second of nine siblings, ran a successful pharmaceutical business and supported his younger brothers and their families, while his elder brother was a renowned doctor. We led a comfortable, though unostentatious life. My mother was a much-loved woman, whose main joy in life lay in doling out happiness. Everyone agrees that as the youngest, I was my father's favourite.

Then, on 15 August 1947, came Independence and Partition. In a complicated pact between the departing British rulers and the Muslim and Hindu leaders, undivided India gave birth to a new nation called Pakistan. The majority of Muslims from India made their way to their new motherland, and the Hindus left Pakistan and departed for India, giving rise to one of the greatest mass migrations in human history. The first few weeks after Partition were brutal and barbaric. People on both sides of the border spewed violent rage against each other, killing, raping, looting and burning. Millions became homeless, having left behind fortunes as they fled for their lives. I was then four years old.

We were more fortunate in our uprooting, even though we arrived in Bombay with little more than the clothes on our backs. We were able to avoid the murderous overland route through the Punjab, travelling instead by ship from Karachi. My father's pharmaceutical business had often brought him to Bombay, and among his business associates in the city was an agreeable and wealthy Muslim merchant who saw his future in Pakistan. Over a handshake, they agreed to an exchange of homes. The merchant took possession of our house in Clifton, a fashionable part of Karachi, while we got his house, Chandiwala Mansion in Dadar, then an upscale residential area. Our new palatial home was located opposite the famous film studio Filmistan and we found, to our delight, that many hit Hindi movies had been shot there.

My father's acquaintance had been a silver merchant from the royal state of Hyderabad. His vision had stretched beyond the feudal society of his native place and, at the age of twenty-one, he had left to make his fortune. He studied in England and hobnobbed with British aristocrats and merchants, who became his business partners. His taste for the high life was amply on display in the mansion. The British influence was evident in his choice of décor, furniture and even in the clothes stacked neatly in the armoires. His fate would have reflected ours across the new border, as he, too, had hurriedly fled with little more than important personal documents and jewels.

My earliest memory of living in that sprawling mansion in Bombay is of running up the crescent-shaped grand wooden staircases and sliding down the wide banisters. Wide verandas wrapped around every room, allowing cool breezes to waft in from the large central courtyard. Several areas of the mansion had coloured-glass windows and the bathrooms had glass doors with lotus patterns etched on them. The floors had intricate geometric patterns in fine terrazzo tiles, inlaid here and there with granite and marble. One of the several corridors led to what could be best described as a modern-day penthouse. The languid luxury and grandeur of that master suite bespoke a princely lifestyle and it was called the 'Sheesh Mahal', encased as it was in colourful stained glass on three sides. The end wall had a pale blue satin canopy with a matching satin bed underneath, ruffled skirting all around and heaps of pillows upon the bed. In the centre of the room hung a beautiful chandelier that sparkled like a thousand prisms when the rays of the sun kissed it. A couple of years after we had moved to Bombay, my eldest brother, Joginder, married a beautiful girl named Kamla; they became the privileged occupants of this 'glass palace'.

I spent wonder-filled days in the house, rummaging through numerous closets and chests of drawers, uncovering surprises and things of beauty. The chests were full of beautiful saris, silk and lace gloves and high-heeled shoes that I wore at will, strutting noisily up and down the grand wooden stairs. No one stopped me from my forays into these secret spaces; I was a five-year-old let loose in a fantasy land. The mansion held treasures for each one of us—my older siblings, who usually kept a censorious eye on what I was doing, had as much fun as I did. We reacted to this new residence somewhat like the 'Beverly Hillbillies' of later TV fame, marvelling at the frescoed walls, etched glass doors and windows, the elaborate cornices along the ceilings and chandeliers. We had not been accustomed to this sort of elegant European grandeur. The romantic garden, with its dazzling Romanesque marble statues, winding pathways and a fountain in the shape of a multi-petalled lotus, offered its own irresistible adventures. I would repeatedly try to climb into the fountain, despite falling many times and being thoroughly scolded for it, and injuring my legs and arms. I was Bina in Wonderland.

The elders in the family had very little time to keep track of what we children were up to. They were preoccupied with assessing the political changes of the time, planning for our education, gathering information on missing relatives and accounting for the possessions that had been left behind. Many of our uncles, aunts and cousins had gone missing; for my parents, the incredible gift of this palatial mansion could not compensate for these losses.

■

My idyllic life didn't last long. Within the next four years, our beautiful haveli was transformed into a boarding house for refugees. Every few weeks, families would arrive at our doorstep, relatives from my mother's or father's side. Times, and our general inclinations, were such that giving refuge to whoever landed at our house was almost mandatory. Consequently, word that our haveli was open to all must have spread like wildfire. The inflow was constant and, as each new family arrived, we were forced to constrict ourselves into smaller spaces, until all nine siblings were living in one room, just like every other family in the haveli, except that we had the largest room with the colourful glass windows. The room was crammed with beds of every size, leaving just enough space for us to circulate between them. During the daytime, the smaller beds would be rolled under the bigger beds and the pretty terrazzo floors would be revealed again as the bedroom transformed into the drawing room. We took turns sharing one bathroom, while the kitchen was shared by two other families.

To this day, no one has been able to state with certainty the exact number of residents that occupied the once-grand mansion at that time. Four makeshift kitchens had been set up in various parts of the house, and the garden, shorn of its beautiful hedges and statues, had become just a big playground. I played gilli-danda and flew kites with my male cousins; the girls played with dolls and toys that held no interest for me.

I had grown up meeting new cousins of every age and size, but I got along best with cousins of my age. The adventurous Maya and the reticent Chiman became close friends. Gulab, my nephew, just two months younger than me and a bundle of trouble, was my partner in climbing trees and other such forays. He and his sister, Miroo, were the children of my eldest sister, Kiki, who had married before Partition and lived in Delhi with her professor husband; they visited us during their vacations and were my best friends.

One winter, when I was about seven years old, a circus-cum-fun-fair set up camp for a week in our neighbourhood. Unable to resist the temptation of seeing it from the inside, and fully aware that it would never be permitted by the family elders, I incited Maya into being my accomplice to secretly explore this source of flashing bright lights and catchy music. Before we snuck away, we managed to extract a five-rupee note from one of the closets. Our hearts pounding with excitement and tinged with fear, we set out on our daring mission.

The gatekeeper at the campground took one look at us and asked where our parents were. 'You are too young to go in by yourselves,' he said, barring our entry.

But we weren't prepared to be turned away. I pointed behind us and told him, 'Our home is next door.' I then flashed the five-rupee note at him. He stared suspiciously, then took the note and gave us smaller change in return. In we ran, feeling victorious, like two little thieves who had hit a jackpot.

The next two hours were enchanting. After thrilling rides on the Ferris wheel and the merry-go-round, we feasted on candy floss, ice lollies and sweet and savoury snacks until we could eat no more. We watched films on a basic bioscope, peering through two peepholes into a colourful, multilayered tin box, where various scenes were set to the latest film music. There were magicians, clowns, monkeys and elephants, all seeming to put out their best performance, just for us. What fun!

We did not want our adventure to end, but it was starting to get dark. Time to go home. We both agreed that we had had the best day of our lives, split the leftover booty equally—even after trying every ride and eating our fill, we had some money left—and swore never to reveal our secret to anyone, no matter what. On our way back, we came up with a flimsy cover story in case we were questioned—which we were.

Clearly, we had been missing for far too long. Even though our parents had not noticed our absence, several of my siblings had. They knew about our propensity to explore the forbidden and had set the alarm bells ringing in the family quarters.

Everyone's eyes were focused on me when I entered the house. This was not a totally unfamiliar feeling, and the more restricted I felt under their watchful gaze, the more rebellious my escapades became. But at that moment, standing before my family, my euphoria vanished, assisted by a few slaps across my face. Several pairs of eyes glared at me, and I blurted out the whole story. I pulled out the remaining coins from my pocket and placed them on the table. I was severely reprimanded for my actions.

Days of isolation and being treated like a pariah by my cousins followed. I didn't have a single regret, though—taking the money had been key to the joy and adventure of that afternoon. However, I had been taught a lesson in integrity by my parents. The only reason they had forgiven me, they explained, was that I had revealed the truth and made the right choice: to not lie. In the end, not only had I accrued an unforgettable and thrilling memory, I had also learnt something important—a few slaps and pangs of fear were a small price to pay for these.

■

Because of the age difference, Kiki was more of a mother than a sister to me. The next two in line, my brother Joginder and my sister Rani, got married while we were living in Dadar. The carefree days at Chandiwala Mansion soon came to an end as the remaining six siblings were separated and sent to different schools. My two older sisters, Mohini and Pushpa, and I were sent as boarders to St Joseph's Convent, a Catholic boarding school in Panchgani, some ten hours' drive west of Bombay. So, at the age of seven, I got my first taste of the Catholic religion. It was, in hindsight, a good decision on my parents' part, though I resented it greatly at the time. The prospect of obtaining a proper day-school education within the chaos of our Dadar house had been dismal. I felt very secure in the attentive care of the nuns, and my exposure to the English language and Western music started there. The strict regimen of prayer time, even though it was lighter for non-Catholics like us, was the kind of discipline I had grown up with in our own home.

However, the boarding school experience came to an abrupt end in less than two years. I developed an infestation of the scalp in school and, consequently, a large part of my hair had to be shaved off. I had no say in the matter. When I returned home for vacation soon after, my parents were horrified to see my partly shaved head. They took it as an affront, because Sikhism forbids the cutting of hair. This sealed our fate—instead of returning to the convent, we had to shuffle through two or three schools in Bombay, owing to the shortage of good schools and the long wait lists for admission.

Meanwhile, we had been driven out of even our one-room accommodation by the continuing influx of refugees. By the time I was nine years old, we had moved into the lovely neighbourhood of Breach Candy. It was one of Bombay's most beautiful areas, where royalty and the elite lived in sprawling mansions that rivalled each other in their splendour. Our new apartment was on a tree-lined boulevard, with an uninterrupted view of the sea across the road. A smart Sindhi builder with great vision, R.J. Advani, had built three upscale six-storey buildings exclusively for a select few Sindhi families who had been uprooted from the Sind state, which was now in Pakistan. We were among the lucky ones who fitted his requirements and my father picked the largest three-bedroom apartment out of them, on the ground floor. It was barely big enough for our large family, but a vast improvement on what we had been reduced to in our former palatial mansion.

I would spend most of my time at the windows, gazing out at the occasional elegant four-horse carriage strutting along the seafront, carrying the gentry through ornamental gates into wide, circular driveways. It was a pristine neighbourhood, quite the opposite of the crowded one we had moved from. The apartments of the kind we were living in were eyesores, comparatively speaking, set as they were amidst stately mansions. Soon, with the burgeoning flow of new arrivals seeking prime locations, many more apartment buildings popped up, sometimes three or four of them replacing one elegant mansion. Being the tallest buildings of the time, they were considered skyscrapers, even though none were more than six storeys high. Soon, we moved into a larger three-bedroom apartment in one of these buildings, with a spacious terrace that had been enclosed to add yet another room.

It was there, with the ocean beckoning to me from across the street, that I formed my special relationship with my rock. I could escape from the bewilderment of my preadolescent years, fantasizing that my troubles could be tossed into the surf and carried away by the retreating waves. I pictured myself as the mermaid from Hans Christian Andersen's tale, 'The Little Mermaid'—I was sure that my dialogue with the sea was filled with the same mysterious emotions as those of the mermaid. She was a soul sister, helping me become familiar with my feminine side and guiding my evolution from tomboy to woman.

This transition into my teens was not an easy one. No one at home had time to answer the thousands of questions that crowded my mind. I was the most restless of the three sisters going through adolescence, and I began to sense that I was somehow different. I needed to spin dreams and feel the reassuring touch of that shore, to breathe in the fragrant air of the sea, to listen to the symphonic sound of the waves. And it was there that I discovered and began to claim my need for solitude. Knowing that life would be beautiful as long as I could maintain frequent touch with my secret rock. Even as a metaphor.

Having grown up surrounded by a multitude of relatives, my personality was usually that of an extroverted, happy-go-lucky girl, with plenty of familial stability and financial security. But what I didn't have, and missed terribly, was freedom. I had a somewhat formal relationship with most of my elder siblings and sensed constant disapproval from them. Almost a generation older than me, they always watched over me and told me how to behave. And with my freewheeling visits to the rooms of the numerous families who had resided with us in Dadar no longer an option, I felt stifled.

I began to get glimpses of the woman within me when I developed a crush on our handsome neighbour, Nari Hira. He lived on the floor above us, was a little older than my eleven years and was a friend of my brother Gulu. This blushing infatuation remained my secret, and all I ever got from Nari was a brotherly slap on the back. But it was enough for me to just catch a glimpse of him every evening, during sunset walks along the beach. I was a tomboy in my denim pedal pushers and T-shirt, with a swaying ponytail, always blowing the largest bubbles with my bubblegum! Taller by a head than my girlfriends, I was hardly the type that older boys would notice.

2

The Banyan Tree

GOING TO SCHOOL offered me the first opportunity to make friends with a cross-section of children who came from different communities, not just the Sindhi clan that had sheltered me during my earliest years. Despite the abundant love and affection I enjoyed in my large family, I sometimes fantasized about being an only child in some other household. I envied my friends who had just one sibling, or none.

My father used to travel to England by sea on long business voyages; the happiest moments of my childhood were those when we would await his return at the port in Bombay. The hours of waiting would gradually turn into minutes, and then would begin the game of 'Who will be the first to spot him on the deck?' Our excitement would build, moment by moment, and reach its pinnacle when one of us spotted him. Then a dozen pairs of arms would fly in the air, the younger ones jumping up and down, waving little tricolour flags. Of course, everyone claimed that he or she had been the first to spot him, as if vying for some grand prize, as we watched him walk down the sloping ramp to the port. My heart would almost leap out of my body in delight—he was the world's greatest dad, and he was returning just for me. He would whisk me off my feet and into the air, and give me a loving hug. The greatest taste I had known in my life at that time was the marzipan-filled chocolate he would then put into my mouth. I vividly recall that taste to this day, and a bite of marzipan-filled chocolate can still transport me to those moments of childhood bliss.

In the days following my father's return, we would all sit in rapt silence around him at mealtimes as he regaled us with marvellous tales of his trip. Just as he had told us heroic stories of other times, when he and his elder brother had risked their lives in support of Mahatma Gandhi's call for self-sacrifice and participated in the civil disobedience protest marches in pre-Independence India. I would always feel immense pride when listening to stories of his role in the freedom struggle—a struggle that, ironically, had resulted in our being uprooted and having to flee to a new homeland.

I still remember the Diwali when I was ten years old. Amidst the pujas, rituals and celebrations, trays of sweets and boxes of gifts were exchanged with everyone who visited. The part I enjoyed the most was my father taking Pushpa and me—all dressed up in our newest fluffy silk frocks, with shiny shoes and matching ribbons in our long braids—on rounds of visits to his business associates in the commercial sector of Bombay. We made stops at some fifteen different stores that stocked goods from my father's pharmaceutical company. While my father exchanged pleasantries and handed out beautiful boxes of chocolates to each merchant, Pushpa and I received hearty pats on the back or fond squeezes on the cheek. We were then asked to stretch out our hands to receive a gold or silver coin each. We came away from those trips feeling rich and sat in the car and counted the booty. Those were prosperous times for a country that was just learning to crawl on its own after its hard-earned freedom from 250 years of colonial rule.

We all grew up enjoying great security under the steady, watchful eye of my mother. She was like the Universal Mother, with a large heart, and was extraordinarily generous and kind. She reminded me of a banyan tree that extends its sturdy, sacred root-branches in every direction, providing food, shelter and comfort to all. I first saw a banyan tree at the age of thirteen, while on a family pilgrimage of temples across India, and was amazed at its expanse—from the imposing roots to the meandering branches that seemed to claim both earth and sky. I loved the uncontrollable, loving spread of it—it was at that moment that I likened it to my mother's largesse. She was our mother earth, deeply rooted, with her arms spread out towards one and all, like the beautiful multiple branches of the grand banyan tree. I imagined myself as a bird flitting through her many strong branches, with my wings seeking further horizons.

Sometimes I wondered if my mother loved her grandchildren more than me. Gulab and Miroo, my niece and nephew, were about the same age as me, and new grandchildren arrived every year. I was torn between envy—as they received more visible affection—and joy at the prospect of new playmates when they came.

Mama, as we called my mother, was always draped in a crisp white cotton sari. By the time she was thirty-six, well before I was born to her (at the age of forty-three), she had already lost three sons to typhoid. Grief-stricken and enveloped in gloom, she shed her worldly desires and material comforts in pursuit of a spiritual and humble way of life. Her hair turned prematurely grey and she took to wearing white, the colour of purity and of mourning. I never saw her wear any other colour. I sometimes teased her about looking like a grandmother, since most of them tended to wear white, but she always dismissed it.

Mama was forever busy, with rarely any time for her own needs. As if she didn't have enough members in the immediate family to tend to, aunts and uncles, cousins and acquaintances would drop by, not just for a visit or a meal but also to seek advice or a handout. These could range from an envelope stuffed with money to blankets, clothes, prayer books or sweets. No one left without something, no matter how small or big.

Even thirty-five years after her passing, I can still hear her say, 'Shukra hai, bhagwan'. She suffered from agonizing rheumatic arthritic pain in her knees, which were always bound in wide elastic bandages. Whenever she stood up or bent her knees to sit, she would utter these words as she grimaced in pain.

'Mama, why do you keep thanking God all the time?' I would ask. 'He has given you so much pain.'

'Just think how much worse it could be. The pain is only in my knees. I am grateful that my other limbs are fine,' she would answer, dismissing my ignorance of God's grace.

In the first week of each month, when my father would hand her a bundle of cash for household expenses, one of the first tasks Mama methodically performed was to count out two smaller bundles and place them in two envelopes. The family driver would then drive her to my father's sister and her own widowed sister. They had suffered the ravages of Partition and had escaped to India with eight children each, leaving a lifetime of possessions behind. They needed a lot more than just financial support, and Mama's visits to their homes brought joy and light into their gloomy lives. I often went along with her on these visits. We would stop on the way to buy baskets of fruits and vegetables and a variety of sweets, in addition to what Mama had already packed from home. Some of our clothes, shoes, blankets and books would be distributed in the crowded, tin-roofed 'camp' home of my cousins. I looked forward to these visits with Maya, my partner in crime in those days, and Mama and I were always greeted with a delighted chorus of welcome.

Until my mother was quite old, she would personally see off every guest who came to our home at the door and hand them some gift or the other to express her joy that they had come. When her closet overflowed with gift packs of every size and kind that we had helped wrap, she took to tucking them away under her bed. And when she could bend down no longer, one of us would have to run to her room and pull out the 'lucky dip' for a departing guest. She loved going on shopping expeditions and God forbid if any vendor found his way past our front door—Mama would buy almost everything she saw and justify it as part of her 'pay it forward' approach to charity.

My parents placed enormous value on sharing, so there was never any shortage or sibling rivalry. The spirit of generosity ran very strong in the family, and we were renowned for it in our community. Our doors were always open—people could come and share our meals or stay in our home. The tradition in our family was that 10 per cent of everything that came to us had to be given to charity, and my siblings and I continue to follow this till today. There was also a strong emphasis on saving—any type of 'piggy bank' was encouraged and applauded. Our comfortable and affluent way of life was a contrast to the harsh realities that existed elsewhere, and I understood at a very young age that detachment from material belongings and generosity to others were most important. I believe that my childhood experiences sowed the seeds of my inner drive to pursue social work, which I am passionate about.

■

As we were growing up, I was often partnered with Pushpa, my sister who was older by eighteen months. We were sent to the same school, made to wear identical clothes and shoes, and even our hair was similarly braided. Until we were twelve and thirteen years old respectively, people often asked if we were twins. But once I turned thirteen, I experienced a sudden growth spurt. Within a year, I was four inches taller than Pushpa and then added another inch or two the following year. This increase in height, which caused me to tower over her, did nothing to increase my power over her, though.

Pushpa and I had very different interests, friends and talents. She was better at academics, while I excelled at sports. She was neat and methodical, while I was quite the opposite. I did not enjoy growing up under her ever-watchful eye. Increasingly, I became a bit of a rebel and an escape artist. This attitude attracted stern attention from the other elders in the family, reigniting my wish that I had been born in a home with only one or two kids. I often let this be known at our dinner table, where we assembled every evening. Because of our very different temperaments and her role as my watchful nemesis, I had many occasions to resent Pushpa in my adolescent years. Today, however, I can confidently say that she has been one of my best friends and travelling companions. We now spend hours reminiscing about past events, howling with laughter at the absurdity of it all.

In Bombay, prior to dinner, just before sunset, every member of our family, including any guests who were with us, would assemble in our large drawing room for a prayer hour. We would all sit in our favourite spots and the Rehras Sahib would be recited by my father. Every member also took turns to recite a select verse, and I too had to memorize a short one. Being home by sunset in time for the evening prayer, as specified by the fifth guru of the Sikhs, was sacred. It was an esoteric form of thanksgiving from the Sikh holy book, the Guru Granth Sahib.

The following hour or two was a sacrosanct dinner tradition: we would all gather for laughter and conversation over the evening meal, cementing the bonds of love and affection between the family members. Those bonds remain strong to this day. There were never any conflicts amongst us, nor did I ever witness an argument between my parents or other family members—it just wasn't done.

We had a long carved teak dining table, where members of the family, usually numbering up to a dozen, would sit together for delicious meals. Mutton and fish were always popular items on the menu. There was plenty of teasing, and I was often the target of jokes because of my often-expressed wish to be an only child. A frequent topic was my prospects for adoption by a childless couple who longed for a girl. My family would come up with new and imaginative variations on this theme, some of which I took quite seriously.

One particular version was popular for several months. My family convinced me that the ideal couple had been found, and that they were looking forward to adopting me. The arrangements were being made for my very own room in a new home. My 'new parents' were travelling abroad, and the formalities would be completed as soon as they returned. I anxiously waited for the day I would become their daughter. I was beside myself with joy, expecting to be a princess who would have everyone's undivided attention, her exclusive bedroom and, above all else, freedom. I even held several conversations in my mind with my new parents. The yarn my family was spinning grew more elaborate with each dinner, and it took a while to dawn on me that it was all a big joke. Needless to say, I was heartbroken, for I had grown deeply attached to my (imaginary) young and stylish mom and dad.

Even though I felt very fortunate to be growing up amidst so much abundance, I hungered deeply for the liberties I saw my friends from smaller families take for granted. I longed to be able to travel to faraway places, even open a boutique or a beauty parlour when I grew up. My imagination ran wild with these dreams. Alas, they had to remain dreams, lest I brought dishonour to my family by deviating from the carefully laid out tradition of grooming all girls in the family into ideal 'homemakers' for their future husbands. There were separate sets of rules for the boys and the girls. The boys were sent to schools and colleges of their choice to pursue either pharmaceuticals, commerce or electronics, thus preparing them to take on the family businesses; the girls were sent to good schools but discouraged from pursuing professional degrees—college or a career was not an option for us. As a result, I grew up in a constant state of conflict between the traditions of a strict Sikh upbringing and my rebellious urges. I began to believe that I would gladly shun any amount of wealth, or even trade my large and affectionate family, for my freedom.

I didn't shine academically, but I made up for it in athletics. I was a high jump champion and represented my school and the state of Maharashtra in the Indian National Games for three consecutive years. I was even considered to have Olympics potential and was introduced to sports legends such as Jesse Owens and Emil Zátopek when they came to India. But that prospect ended when I hit puberty, since my parents felt it was inappropriate for me to be wearing shorts and going to training camps with other girls and boys. This was a crushing blow for me and affected my self-esteem for a long time. Until then, I had lived and breathed sports. Now, my one possible route to the freedom I longed for had been cruelly cut off.

With my brother Kartar—my hero at the time, who had enthusiastically backed my pursuit of athletics—in Germany, studying for a doctorate, and my other brothers studying in England, my parents and sisters made my choices for me. I ended my formal education at Queen Mary High in Bombay at the age of sixteen, while my peers at school went on their way to higher education in medicine, literature, the arts or business studies—whatever suited them.

I was inconsolable and took to brooding, which only strengthened the rebellious streak that had long taken root. A part of me was now always in flight in some fantasy or the other that provided balm to my wounded soul.

3

London

Parents like mine, who wished their daughters to acquire 'polish' so they would shine on the social scene and become ideal wives in a suitable marriage, sent them to Lady Irwin College (LIC) in Delhi. To obtain a degree from LIC was a matter of pride—akin to having a plump dowry—and I was enrolled in the three-year domestic science programme. My course covered a wide range of subjects, from science to literature, art history and geography, in addition to several practical lessons in sewing, designing, cooking, decorating and entertaining. Had I been given a choice, I would have opted for a degree in architecture, but that would, naturally, not have assured me of the skills needed to run a good home.

In Delhi, I moved into Kiki's apartment. Miroo was in school and Gulab was going to college. Among my fellow students at LIC were girls from nearby countries like Ceylon (Sri Lanka), Malaysia and Nepal. Several were from royal families, some were debutantes and most were from traditional upper-class homes. Being an Irwinite was nothing short of membership in an elitist club.

One of the key skills promoted at LIC was the art of making a 'poor man's home feel like a rich man's'. In other words, we were taught how to enjoy a perfectly comfortable way of life, even with a meagre income, by pursuing creative economizing in unusual ways that only frugal ladies of wisdom understood. This was an eye-opener for me. One trick that I learnt, and which I still use, is the old-fashioned method of cleaning glass surfaces with just a simple old newspaper, torn into halves and crumpled into two balls. It does the trick better than any detergent. By wetting one ball with plain water and running it over the surface, then immediately scrubbing the area with the dry ball, an instant, miraculous sparkle can be achieved.

I also learnt the art of dressing like a lady. Displaying my customary exuberance was a strict no-no and I had to tone down my tomboyish ways. I soon took to wearing the sari to college every day, in the fashionable style of the time, with matching jewellery, sandals and accessories. Using inventive ways of painting the bindi on the forehead became a temporary passion. Looking ethnic with panache was the order of the day. Irwinites were not only supposed to be intelligent but also pretty and stylish, besides being experts at all household skills.

What I learnt at LIC has held me in good stead through bumpy patches over the years. Unfortunately, this education of mine was rather short-lived; I had to drop out of the college in the first year because my family decided to emigrate to London. I was seventeen years old.

■

My father had sold a part of his thriving pharmaceutical business in India, leaving the rest to my eldest brother, Joginder. He then took over the small electronics business that my brothers Partap and Gulu had started in England after graduating from college. He felt that they were expanding too fast and it was time to balance the growth with his knowledge and experience, in order to give the business a sturdy foundation.

Consumer electronics were manufactured in Hong Kong to Gulu's specifications. They were then imported to England, where Pratap handled the sales and marketing. England was eager to catch up with America's fast-growing appetite for electronics, and my brothers had stumbled upon the ideal business opportunity. They had devised a winning formula by combining affordable products with smart design and packaging, and worked long hours trying to keep up with the growing demand for their goods. With this newfound success, their desire for greater comfort and luxury also grew. We changed homes for better and bigger ones three times in a span of eight years; the business premises moved from a small warehouse and office to a large building that occupied an entire block and had about 100,000 square feet of space; and there were luxury cars for every member of the family.

On a whim, Gulu, during one of his trips to Hong Kong, decided to name a transistor clock radio after me and sent it to me as a birthday present. We shared a birthdate and usually pulled off a raucous joint celebration. This time, since he was not in London, he surprised me with a 'Binatone' gift. My father liked the sound of it and suggested they bring in that design in my name. By a stroke of luck, not only did that model go on to become their bestselling product, but was also picked by the prestigious *Consumer Reports* magazine as the best product in its category across the United Kingdom. My father and brothers decided to change the name of their business from J. Parkar & Company to Binatone International. The name-change gamble paid off—business boomed and the company started selling internationally.

Meanwhile, I was discouraged from pursuing a formal college education. So I signed up for the odd courses in the home sciences, which included cooking, stitching, gardening, designing and so on. My day consisted of attending classes in the morning, going to the Binatone office in the afternoon or running family errands in the Mercedes I had received for my birthday. I also had to ferry my mother around town whenever she needed. Making English friends was discouraged, but I had several Indian girlfriends whom I could visit or catch a movie with. Eight in the evening was my curfew.

Even though we entertained frequently, I felt as if I was trapped in a gilded cage. Imagining myself sharing a flat with a few girlfriends was a frequent dream, even though I knew full well it could never be achieved. To my conservative existence was added a constant stream of young Sikh and Sindhi suitors who were being sized up as potential husbands for my sisters Mohini and Pushpa. I knew that sooner rather than later, it would be my turn.

Mama would take us on shopping sprees to buy saris, jewellery, china, silverware and crystal, building up lavish trousseaus for the big day. This conditioning ritual was standard practice in most traditional Indian families at that time, grooming daughters for the infamous 'arranged marriage'. I, too, fell under its spell and developed a mental image of a suitable groom with whom I would spend the rest of my life in wedded bliss after, hopefully, falling in love on the day of our marriage. Failing that, love could come later—I had seen it happen with my older siblings, relatives and friends.

My fertile mind pictured a suitable boy somewhere—who was presumably being similarly conditioned by his family—to become my life partner. It was understood that he, too, would fall in love with me at the same time. The horoscopes would be consulted at a certain stage and, inexplicably, our destinies would be revealed as intertwined by those charts. (Of course, all of this would have to take place by the time I turned twenty-five, for, in those days, beyond that age a girl was considered practically out of the matrimonial game.) I would conjure up visions of running a beautiful home using the new exquisitely decorated silver and crystalware, playing the role of trophy wife to someone who would soar to dizzying heights in his career because of my ability to give him the flawless support that every potentially great man needs from his wife. I felt a tremendous rush in imagining myself next to a dashing, intelligent man, with a personality to match, because I felt I had been honed with the qualities required to complement such a person. My brainwashing was complete, as was that of each one of my siblings before me. At times like these, Pushpa and I were in harmony. The shopping expeditions were among the few occasions when we enjoyed each other's company then. We teased each other, laughed and shared a vision.

My fantasies grew more beautiful and detailed with each passing year, with the occasional conflicting flashes of being swept away by some dashing hero who would have neither pedigree nor the right horoscope, but would steal my heart away.

Music had always been an important aspect of our family life. Music is the essence of Sikhism—the Granth Sahib is written in verse, based on numerous ragas. There were frequent religious programmes at home over the years, where groups of singers, called raagis, who were trained only to sing religious verses, would enthral the congregation—which would number from forty to a hundred people at any given time. The sacred langar dinner would be served to everyone after every such two- to three-hour service. Pushpa and I were trained by one such raagi, around the time when we were twelve and ten years old, respectively, to play the harmonium. We could both sing certain bhajans in harmony. It was a matter of great pride to perform at those events.

Though I never developed much enthusiasm for the hymns and only sang them to please the elders, my love for Western music knew no bounds. By the time we moved to London, singing popular Western songs was one of my passions. I was routinely asked by family and friends to sing the latest hits after dinner at our frequent parties. I readily complied and earned praises from all. Thus began another fantasy, this time about becoming a professional singer. Soon, the fantasy became a deep yearning.

I had heard about a school in Baker Street, where Cliff Richard had learnt to sing and perform. He was then the rage in England, second only to my heart-throb, Elvis Presley. It was a well-known fact that Cliff Richard had been born in India—for some strange reason, it gave me hope that I, too, could become an émigré singing star. So, having saved up most of my pocket money over a twelve-month period, I covertly made my way to Baker Street, with a great deal of trepidation.

The school was a posh five- or six-room studio on one of the side lanes off Baker Street. There was a bustle of people in the large reception area. I felt them looking at me as if I had lost my way and turned up at the wrong address; I became conscious of my Indian attire and ethnic appearance, with my hip-length braided hair that I had brought forward over my right shoulder, something I did when I needed an extra dose of confidence. I felt out of place, totally unsuited to the fast-paced pop music ambience that surrounded me. It took all my courage to quiet my thumping heart and inform them that I had been given an appointment by phone a week earlier. With seeming reluctance, they sent me to one of the rooms to be interviewed by the manager. I had to draw on all my reserves of confidence to convince him that I was serious about training in Western pop music. To my relief, he was a kind and sensitive man who tried to ease my discomfort and anxiety and decided to give me a chance. Within ten minutes, he had me singing some of my favourite songs.

I was into my second song, executing what I thought was a perfect imitation of The Everly Brothers' hit 'Bye Bye Love', when he raised his hand. His words stopped me in my tracks, embarrassing me deeply: 'I asked you to impress me with your singing, not The Everly Brothers'.'

The manager then sat me down and, with a satisfied smile, told me that he was impressed by my talent, that he could see I had an ear for music and that, with some direction, I could train my voice and develop a personal style. 'This studio is known for discovering and developing the students' personal style in singing,' he said encouragingly. 'You ought to opt for training in the jazz and blues style. Your voice would suit that genre.'

It was an unexpected suggestion and left me dazed, but I just nodded, speechless, grateful for his advice. I immediately signed up for one semester, which was all I could afford with my savings.

I would reach the studio every other day for my 4 p.m. slot. I got to listen to plenty of Ella Fitzgerald, which they felt suited my singing style. I learnt breathing techniques and voice training. A whole new world of music opened up for me. I began to notice that my ethnic background, which I had earlier seen as a hindrance, was somehow becoming an advantage over the other students, judging by the attention I was getting from the faculty members.

At the end of the semester, when I had finally perfected 'Summertime' from *Porgy and Bess* to a piano accompaniment, they recorded it and played it for the producer of a record company that they were associated with. To my astonishment, they all complimented me on my voice and singing style. My appearance was considered exotic, rather than ethnic—a positive attribute in the business, it appeared. I overheard them discussing how they would make me a singing sensation by marketing me on the most popular television entertainment show of the time. They could style and reinvent me using my long hair to advantage, they said. The names of some of my favourite singers were mentioned—Peggy Lee, Dionne Warwick—people whose voices, they thought, mine could rival, with diligent training.

I could not believe my ears. I was overcome by a strange combination of fear and joy that day when I left the studio. Was I merely being sold a second semester?

On my way home, I decided to reveal my secret to the family. I would wait until dinner, the reserved time for family camaraderie, to make my announcement. I felt particularly mature for my age—almost nineteen then—because I was going to make my family proud. I could almost feel their excitement at having a singing sensation among them. I had visions of myself on stage, performing to applauding audiences; recording contracts would soon follow. I felt an immense sense of power thanks to the validation of my singing talent that day.

At the table, I waited for the right moment to announce my good news. We were having pudding and the black-and-white TV was broadcasting the 9 p.m. prime-time show. Finally, with all the exuberance of someone who had brought home a trophy, choosing every word carefully, I announced: 'I have a nice surprise for everyone tonight.'

All eyes turned to me, loaded with expectation.

'Well,' I said with a tremor in my voice, barely able to breathe, 'you all know how much I love singing. And everyone who has heard me sing has appreciated my talent, right?'

There were a couple of hesitant nods. I had expected to see

enthusiasm; instead, I could see apprehension build in my family's faces. This did not seem promising. But I continued, believing that every crowd has a cynic or two: 'You know that TV programme of Ed Murray's we all watch every Sunday at eight o' clock? Well, guess what? You might be watching me sing on a show like that, soon!' I blurted it all out in one breath.

The silence that greeted my announcement was, as they say, deafening. It drew out for a long while. Then suddenly, sardonic barbs were shot out at me. 'Keep dreaming!' 'Who's been pumping you up?'

There was utter shock in my father's voice when he finally spoke. I had betrayed the family honour, he said, not only by having found my way to a studio to record my voice but also by daring to dream that I, a Sikh girl, could become a pop star and appear on national television!

I was seven years old again, caught stealing and going to the circus without permission.

Refusing to allow the comments to dampen my spirit, I said, in a firm voice filled with pride, 'I've been taking lessons at the same studio as Cliff Richard. I wanted this to be a surprise for you all. The directors heard my recording today and they were amazed at my talent and the skill with which I carried the high and the low notes. They are especially excited about my Indian background. They really think I can make it on TV someday and have my own album.'

A long silence followed my monologue. And then all of them seemed to find their voices together. I was categorically banned from pursuing any such idea. I was advised not to take what musical talent I had so seriously—it was hardly worth a bean in the long run. Besides, my fantasy would certainly defile the time-honoured doctrine of the 'well brought-up girl from a good family'; I could not be a pop singer under any circumstances. The good homemaker had better abandon such thoughts. Immediately.

The studio never saw my face again.

The crushing pain of this rejection marked a turning point in my development. I finally came to accept that my dreams were totally at odds with my family's plans for me. It wasn't so much my parents' reaction that wounded me—they were conservative people and could not change—rather, it was the reaction of my siblings, who thought it was all very amusing, just another one of my lofty fantasies. I had hoped for their support, but the tracks of tradition were deeply etched in them and singing Western songs on TV was much too alien.

For weeks and months after that fateful dinner, I worked hard to erase the piercing ache I felt. Resigning myself to my fate, I packed my dreams away in a small treasure box that I could nurture in my heart, longing for the day I would bring each one to fruition—once I was married and away from my loving but controlling family. Once in a while, I wondered what might have been had I had the courage to walk away and follow my own star. Through those lonely years, I longed to be back on my favourite rock on the shores in Bombay. Meanwhile, I became an expert at pasting a smile on my face and pretending I was happy, even if I was not. It is probably an integral part of traditional Indian values that daughters are expected to absorb and accept disappointment.

In retrospect, I realize that this pattern, wherein I felt compelled to stay away from the pleasure that I craved in deference to the wishes and values of my family, has been a recurrent theme through the years. This conflict within set the stage for a strange self-denial that I remained unaware of for a long time. It eventually surfaced and was seen and resolved—but unfortunately, not before I had pressed the buttons to self-destruct and created tumultuous hurdles for myself. It took years of suffering, pain and heartache before I finally overcame these obstacles and learnt to gift myself the freedom I needed to be my own self and to act in my interests. My family, too, was deeply tormented in later years when they witnessed my many struggles and the anguish that resulted from my attempts to follow their prescriptions.

■

I managed, despite everything, to squeeze in a four-week diploma course in modelling at the fashionable Lucy Clayton Institute—

naturally, without the knowledge of my family. As part of the course, I had to groom myself with the beauty tools provided to us. My eyebrows were sharply trimmed one day to conform to the stylish look of the time. I arrived home bravely that evening with a major transformation in my appearance, equipped with an exciting portfolio of photographs, defiant of the harsh reaction I expected. It was done. It could not be undone. I had been groomed into a chic glamour girl bursting with confidence.

However, I tempered down my newfound self-image to avoid any confrontations. I could sense, though, that the family liked the new me.

In due course, my sister Mohini got married to a suitable Sikh businessman from north India, and my brother Partap married an equally suitable Sindhi bride who came from India and joined our family in London. Both marriages were arranged, and the grand celebrations stretched for the customary four or five days.

Life continued, with Pushpa and I playing out the role of obedient daughters and accomplished hostesses. Our dream husbands, I knew, would materialize with the help of family members or trusted friends in due course; finding someone on my own was not going to be possible, since dating was not an option for us.

While I adhered to the social protocols of my family and the world of our business, deep down, I always desired an intellectual identity. In time, I developed a select group of college-going friends, whom I met through my best friend at the time, Neela Dhuru.

Neela was a beautiful, soft-spoken, elegant girl. She was as tall as I was, and happened to share my birthday. These similarities aside, though, we came from very different worlds. She had one sister, ten years younger. Her father was a senior pilot with Air India and her mother was a refined and highly principled lady who defined perfection for me, and ran her home with the kind of discipline and grace I admired. Neela and I were drawn to each other's very different ways of life. During visits to my home, she initially felt unnerved by the number of family members and our open-door principles; but in no time at all, not only did she manage to learn and remember the names of my siblings but also came to admire them all.

Neela studied law at London's renowned Bar College, at the Inner Temple, from where Jawaharlal Nehru and M.K. Gandhi had graduated. I would grab every opportunity to go meet her and hang out with her circle of friends. It was an impressionable time in my life, and their company allowed me a wider perspective of the world, beyond the material and religious lexicon of my home. Through my little soirees with Neela, I discovered an esoteric world of art movies, matinee theatre and art galleries. On occasion, a group of us would take a breezy walk in Hyde Park to catch the soapbox speakers who came to air their anti-government opinions to anybody who cared to listen. We would later discuss current issues at a favourite coffee shop in Soho, or go to poetry readings by the Serpentine. Among the people I met was the author Bhaichand Patel, who, like most of the male students, had a crush on Neela. We often reminisce about those days even now, and Bhaichand, in his inimitable style, jests to me: 'I had a crush on you but didn't dare reveal it—I feared your brothers' disapproval.' Well, he was right about that!

With every one of these outings with Neela and her group of friends, my character broke further away from the mould that my family had so carefully set out for me. Some of the girls would dress shabbily and freely express disdain for people who pursued wealth. 'Cash-trash types,' they would scoff. I would then feel guilty because I usually arrived to meet them fashionably dressed, in my black Mercedes or a blue Sunbeam Alpine sports car. I worried about what they would say about me in my absence and began to park my car at the underground station one stop before the college, covering the final leg of my journey by train. It allowed me to feel like one of them, secure in the knowledge that they looked forward to having me join their group. These same girls who dressed so shabbily though, could, amazingly enough, show up at parties dressed chicly in the latest outfits. They accepted me as Neela's loyal friend, though I was aware that I was perceived as someone who was naïve and sheltered.

But they seemed to like my spirit because I had the ability to laugh at myself. This way of life, which allowed such freedom of expression and helped build an independent mind and opinions, appealed greatly to me. It was a fine foil to my other life within my conservative and tradition-bound home.

Home at that time comprised, apart from our rituals and practices, a hectic social life of extravagant dinner parties every time an acquaintance, friend or relative came visiting from India. Entertaining friends and relatives was as natural to us as our daily schedule of meals together, our religious views, our striving for success in business and our concern for family welfare. My penchant for dressing differently for every party sometimes bordered on the obsessive. I sewed my own clothes on the family sewing machine and found ways of wrapping unstitched pieces together at the very last minute. The resulting 'oohs and aahs' sowed in my mind the seeds of becoming a fashion designer.

A whirlwind of parties and social activity, even more hectic than usual, would sweep through our lives whenever our friends, the Kapoor family of Bollywood fame, visited London. The three ultra-handsome Kapoor brothers dominated the Bombay film industry in those years. Raj Kapoor, the eldest, was frequently described as the Cecil B. DeMille of Bollywood and was a super-successful producer, director and actor. The second brother was the flamboyant and roguish Shammi Kapoor, who likened himself to Hollywood's Errol Flynn and was one of India's most popular matinee idols; he had the reputation of a playboy and was sometimes in the centre of drunken brawls among the local jet set. The third brother, Shashi Kapoor, was a sensitive actor who made many crossover art films and was married to Jennifer Kendall, an equally talented actress. We had come to know the Kapoor family rather well due to their frequent visits to London, and had almost become a large extended family. Upon their arrival, our home would become a perpetual centre of excitement.

4

Sindhi Girls

In December 1965, we made a trip from London to Bombay, ostensibly in search of a husband for Pushpa, but also, clearly, for me. Our parents were getting old, and we were the last two daughters at the tail end of an agenda that needed to be settled without delay.

Pushpa and I were cast from two very different moulds. She was the embodiment of the obedient, conservative Sikh daughter who lived by parental guidelines and shied away from any opportunity for adventure. She was fine with marrying into a traditional Sikh family and would undoubtedly shine in the art of homemaking.

My preference list, which I declared to my parents, was quite different from Pushpa's. My ideal man would have been raised in a small family, would have a 'modern lifestyle' and would have earned a degree from a renowned university abroad. I did not want to marry a businessman because I did not like the constant business parlance in our home. I also wanted to marry a non-turbaned man and was fiercely opposed to the tradition of dowry. My residence of choice would be Bombay, or somewhere in the US or Europe—but not London, because I loathed the unpredictable weather there.

I had ample opportunity to air these thoughts whenever the family conversation turned to marriage proposals. These discussions occurred frequently thanks to friends, relatives and acquaintances who liked indulging in one of India's favourite activities—matchmaking. Our parents hoped to achieve their goal of finding suitable husbands and marrying us off within a period of four to five months; Pushpa was twenty-four, I was twenty-two.

As fresh faces arriving from London, our circle of acquaintances in India quickly grew and flourished into regular parties thrown for Pushpa and me. Soon, we each had our separate circles of friends, with only a few overlaps. I hung out with the 'modern' set of Bombay, who were driven by their careers in advertising, or flying for airlines, or banking, or representing international oil companies, if they were not already heirs in the family business. Many were coupled in romances that later led to newsworthy marriages.

The parties often ended with a drive to Santa Cruz at or after midnight because some friend or the other was being dropped off or picked up at the airport. Rarely did anyone get drunk or out of control—an unspoken code of propriety prevailed. There were spontaneous picnics, drives to Madh Island, parties on someone's terrace and, of course, plenty of music and dance. Neither Pushpa nor I fancied anyone in particular. I grew conscious of the fact that our sheltered lifestyle in London had put us in a somewhat prudish slot in the Bombay–Delhi social set, as if we had some kind of invisible 'do not touch' sign etched on us. This occasionally came up in jest, but had no dampening effect on the flow of invitations.

Meanwhile, our parents' highly focused search for grooms continued, well past the intended four-to-five-month period.

One of my closest friends at that time was Farida Khan, Dilip Kumar's sister, who took me under her wing like a younger sister. Through her, I became closer to the young Bollywood crowd comprising people such as Vinod Khanna, Kabir Bedi, Protima Bedi, Persis Khambatta and Simi Garewal. The heroines ruling the silver screen then were Meena Kumari, Asha Parekh, Sharmila Tagore, Waheeda Rehman and Madhubala; among the top heroes were Dilip Kumar, Raj, Shammi and Shashi Kapoor, Sunil Dutt, Rajendra Kumar, Dev Anand and Dharmendra. Rajesh Khanna was yet to grab the nation's heart, Amitabh Bachchan was still in Calcutta, and Hema Malini had not then found her dream role. Nor had the incomparable Rekha, Zeenat Aman or Parveen Babi emerged as stars. Cinema was possibly more of a rage then than it is now; yet, relatively speaking, the industry's dimensions were miniscule—*Media*

Blitz didn't exist, *Stardust* hadn't been born and *Filmfare* dominated the scene.

One lady who impacted me deeply at that time was Sunita Pitamber, whose boutique, Artistic—perhaps the very first of its kind in India—I visited. It was housed in the Taj Hotel and carried the most exquisite handcrafted accessories I had ever seen. She could be very haughty when it suited her, and this attitude served her well, drawing awe and respect from her growing list of customers from all over the world. Her creative flair spoke of a dynamic genius—she had managed to cull out fabulous pieces of costume jewellery, picture frames, evening bags, scarves and more such things from old Indian craft traditions and made them work for a contemporary audience. Her sense of creativity and style triggered a desire in my heart to tread the same path, though it was to remain dormant till much later. Sunita and Parmeshwar Godrej started a unique partnership in the art of interior design and together they scaled heights in establishing a lifestyle that drew envy from faraway capitals of style.

■

Among our closest friends in Bombay were the Raj Kapoor family. Krishna Kapoor, fondly known as Bhabhi-ji, was one of the warmest and most hospitable people we had ever known. Raj Kapoor pretty much dominated the showbiz scene of that era; in large part, it seemed to me, due to his huge personality and his unquenchable passion for 'living it big'. Each event he launched, publicly or privately, was the 'biggest show' of the time, and he threw lavish parties where some of Bombay's most glittering society jewels mingled with a select film industry crowd.

As Raj Kapoor's 'rakhi sisters' from London, Pushpa and I enjoyed a rather privileged position within his family. We spent many memorable nights at their legendary Devnar residence in Chembur, home to a large part of the Kapoor clan, with Bhabhi-ji presiding and dispensing her benevolent hospitality. It continues to be a welcome home for me even today. It was a special honour to be invited to spend an evening with Raj-ji at his private cottage on the sets of the renowned RK Studios, a couple of miles away from his home. This held all of Raj-ji's memorabilia—letters, sentimental keepsakes, trophies, photographs, books, film posters. He would sit on the carpet and invite his guests to join him on the floor. It was not unusual to find oneself in the company of a singer such as Lata Mangeshkar, the wonderful actress Zohra Sehgal, a popular scriptwriter or director, or even a famous Hollywood producer. I often noticed that the essence of Raj Kapoor's true self, with all his creative passion, sparkled like a beacon on such occasions.

There, all of Raj-ji's attendants would be on call, alert to every whim and providing maximum comfort and hospitality to the chosen guests. When Raj-ji was in the 'mood', depending on his state of negotiations with his favourite Scotch whisky, we would be treated to rarefied hours of anecdotes and good humour.

Cottage evenings also meant that Raj-ji might not return home to Devnar that night. Bhabhi-ji had to contend with every range of his monumental moods, which she did with extraordinary grace. Raj-ji referred to her as his 'pillar of strength', and it was clear that it was how he saw her, despite many publicized liaisons with his leading ladies. He once quipped, 'My wife is my wife because she is the mother of my children; my heroine is my heroine because she is the mother of my films.'

Every moment spent in the Kapoor household was a learning experience, filled with humour, candour, forgiveness, love and, of course, drama. I admired the fact that Raj-ji did not allow his passion to diminish, despite life's ups and downs and the occasional failure and negative media attention.

Almost from the outset of our arrival in Bombay, Bhabhi-ji had teased Pushpa and me about our traditional Sikh mindset and often joked about taking us 'fast forward' by clipping our long tresses into modern, more fashionable styles—and, from there, into Bombay's haute society! Deep down I welcomed the idea of such a transition, but at the same time I was filled with guilt and fear of parental disapproval.

My father had once created a scene upon spying a safety razor in the bathroom, which implied that someone had been removing sacred hair. The hair taboo was very strong in my family, and Pushpa, as the responsible older and wiser sister, kept a strict eye on me in that regard. But the daily routine of styling my long hair into imaginative variations had become a tedious task and I secretly dreamt of ridding myself of this encumbrance.

One day, to my great delight, Bhabhi-ji simply drove us down to the Taj Beauty Parlour at the opposite end of town from Chembur, and got her stylist to run sharp shears through our hair. Voila! In barely five minutes, we had been ushered into the liberating world of neck-length hair. I was jubilant at this act of defiance while Pushpa, overcome with guilt, was nearly in tears. Bhabhi-ji's assurances of providing a shield by taking full responsibility did nothing to reduce Pushpa's fears once she saw our tresses scattered on the floor.

Thanks to Bhabhi-ji, we were spared the harsh disapproval of my parents. And for me, this became a milestone in my steps towards freedom from the constricting aspects of my upbringing. I have never again grown my hair past my shoulders; Pushpa, however, immediately began to grow hers back, like the dutiful Sikh daughter she had been brought up to be.

The other secret project that Bhabhi-ji had nurtured since she first got to know me the previous year in London was to introduce me to her roué brother-in-law, Shammi. His wife had died of a sudden illness about ten months earlier, leaving him with two children, and in an inconsolable state. While his film career as an actor was at its peak, he was very lonely in his personal life and was becoming increasingly reckless in his behaviour.

For some reason, Bhabhi-ji had concluded that I had the right combination of traditional and modern values to bring stability back into Shammi's life. However, she was also aware that there were considerable differences in our backgrounds and that potential family objections would be a major barrier. Besides, Raj-ji had already expressed his disapproval of this scheme, as he considered me too innocent and sheltered to be able to cope with his brother's wild ways. But Bhabhi-ji, guided by her instincts, was determined. She was very protective towards Shammi and he had enormous respect for her. She would not be deterred by the opposition.

I had been in India barely a week when a dinner was arranged at the Ritz Hotel for just family and a few close friends. Shammi was there, and we got our first glimpse of each other as we exchanged greetings. I was struck by his good looks and sensed a powerful charisma that made me feel naïve and uncomfortable. In addition, he was twelve years older than me. We left early, and I let Bhabhi-ji know about my reservations the next day and suggested she stop pursuing the idea.

A few days later, Bhabhi-ji deftly managed to arrange a little get-together at Devnar, to which Pushpa and I were invited. Raj-ji was out of town, so Bhabhi-ji seized the opportunity to put Shammi and me together. While I was surprised to meet Shammi there, it soon became clear that he knew why this evening had been planned—his attentive glances and conversation were frequently directed towards me. I did all I could to overcome my shyness, but the first glance at him affected me instantly. I could not believe how good-looking he was in person, having only seen him in a couple of movies and met him once. He emanated a power like I had never experienced or imagined, and his aura dominated the room. His extraordinary blue eyes pierced me whenever he looked my way, and I spent most of that evening avoiding looking in his direction, while desperately trying to behave as normally as possible.

Over the years, I would get over such bouts of shyness.

The only contribution to the conversation I remember making was following one of Shammi's jokes, which had everyone present rollicking, with one of my own. I mustered my courage and cracked a joke—something about a nun in a convent—which meshed with the one Shammi had just told. Mine had a rather dry British kick to it and I was pleased it made everyone laugh. Shammi gave me a very particular smile after everyone else's laughter had died down—it said to me that he liked the impact my joke had made, but that he also liked me for something other than my humour. I was to learn much later that it was at that moment that he had decided he wanted to marry me.

When the evening came to a close, Shammi insisted on driving Pushpa and me to our cousin Gita Vaswani's house where we were staying. It was at the opposite end of town, about an hour away. His house was about halfway there, on Napean Sea Road. Shammi drove a large American convertible, so the three of us sat in the front seat. He politely asked Pushpa to let me sit in the middle, next to him; the reluctance with which she agreed telegraphed her concern.

The drive was wonderful. Shammi pointed out several streets and buildings along the way, sharing humour-sprinkled anecdotes about his many adventures. Ten minutes from our cousin's apartment, he stopped at an all-night fresh juice stall called Bachelors at Chowpatty. The stall owner had recognized Shammi's car even before we pulled up and rushed to help open the door. He welcomed us heartily and bowed deeply to Shammi, his hands folded in respect. Then, with great enthusiasm, he sent his assistants scurrying to prepare a tray of their best juices.

I had arrived in India barely two weeks earlier, after an absence of several years—this unexpected display of affection and courtesy became a treasured vignette of the richness of my country's culture. Now, almost fifty years later, whenever I pass that Chowpatty juice stand, I notice the same man still serving rivers of his famous juices to customers. On every visit to Bombay, I still treat myself at this stall to fresh juice or ice cream with the enthusiasm of a child, wondering how many other romances were born there.

It was past midnight by the time Pushpa and I reached home. I had just enjoyed the most adventurous four hours of my life, and it struck a chord within me that resonated deeply with what I craved. I was over the moon! Pushpa was not amused—she smelt trouble.

Soon enough, Shammi was openly displaying his growing affection for me and, usually with Bhabhi-ji's help, managed to find many occasions where we could either meet in private or 'run into each other' publicly. Raj-ji had already sensed what was happening and reiterated his disapproval to Bhabhi-ji, but she was undeterred. Of course, she was also aware that I could not disobey my parents' express wishes and that they were strictly against the idea of my marriage with Shammi. But her resolve remained firm as steel. Her group of friends had now become an informal committee of enablers; at every gathering, I would overhear little tidbits of gossip trickling out of them about the latest heroine who was chasing Shammi, or some such thing.

One evening, during dinner, Bhabhi-ji suddenly decided to make an overnight trip to the Sai Baba shrine in Shirdi. The decision was triggered by a remark I had made about my parents suggesting that we leave for Delhi soon, as they were very concerned about Shammi's determined pursuit of me. As we all sweetened our palates with the delicious kulfi that came from a local dhaba, Bhabhi-ji announced: 'I know! Sai Baba has never let us down. My prayers in Shirdi have never gone unanswered. These prayers will bring full approval of Mama, Baba [my parents] and Raj-ji too, just wait and see.'

Bhabhi-ji's word was law in the household. Within minutes, she had arranged for a large covered jeep and had it packed with snacks, paranthas and a variety of drinks in a big icebox. Apart from Pushpa and me, Bhabhi-ji invited two of her close friends to join in, along with her fourteen-year-old son Rishi, aka Chintu. We were to leave right away and reach the shrine early in the morning, around aarti time. As we mounted the jeep at midnight, Bhabhi-ji said, looking at me, 'Bina, be sure to make your wish. Sai Baba will never deny you.'

Sai Baba's shrine in Shirdi was housed in a small and simple building surrounded by a large garden. Even at the early hour of 5 a.m., there was a large crowd of devotees, and many more trickled in as we paid our respects. I walked behind the Kapoor clan and followed their rituals. In my prayer, I asked Sai Baba to grant me happiness in my married life and to present me with whoever he thought would bring happiness to everyone in our orbit. I'm not sure, however, if my prayer reached his ears.

■

At the Derby Day at Bombay's fashionable Mahalaxmi Race Course, Raj Kapoor's horse, Sangam (named so after his recent hit film) was the hot favourite for one of the races. The who's who of Bombay society and the film industry were there, doing what they seemed to enjoy the most—to see and be seen. From a distance, I could feel Shammi's eyes follow me everywhere, but I didn't dare acknowledge him in Raj-ji's presence.

I spent most of my time in the VIP section sitting demurely with Bhabhi-ji and her friends, not knowing what to expect or what was expected of me—I had never been exposed to horse racing or gambling before. It was clearly a special occasion. The ladies dazzled in jewels that proclaimed their status, and everyone was dressed according to the latest Indian fashion trends. I noticed numerous darting glances and whispers—this was clearly a place rife with gossip. Sitting in Bhabhi-ji's company was about the best position one could hope for—I was the new face in town and there were a lot of eyes on me.

As the afternoon wore on, it was hard to miss the topic of 'Shammi's new crush' floating around, causing me extreme discomfort. Suddenly, to my horror, I noticed Shammi approaching our box with a purposeful look on his face, his eyes squarely on me. He was not following our usual practice of 'no speaking in public'. His eyes flashed with urgency as he came, carrying a big white sack in his hands. The next moment, in the presence of several high-society ladies, he was right in front of me. To my astonishment, he dropped the sack at my feet, declaring: 'Here, this is yours! I just won the big race, and they have stuffed my winnings into this sack. I won it for you.'

I froze, unable to think of a suitable response. I could feel the blood pulsating in my veins and fervently wished I could become invisible. Overcome with the fear of becoming the topic of gossip, all I could do was shake my head, turn completely red and rush off to the washroom.

Shammi called me that night at Gita's home. I told him that it had been the most embarrassing moment of my life.

'I was disappointed that you left in such a hurry. But I understand,' he said, his voice sincere on the phone. This had become our principal mode of communication. 'I can no longer enjoy my successes alone. I want to share my every joy and pain with you. I really won the race for you. Will you please allow me to buy you a present of your choice, Jiye?' This was the term of endearment that he used instead of my name. But I dismissed his offer immediately.

Shammi did not believe in big weddings and teased me relentlessly about being from the Sindhi business community, for whom weddings were lavish and lasted several days. He told me that he wanted to marry me the same way he had married his first wife. It would be in the middle of the night, at a small temple close to his childhood home. There was a priest who would perform the same sacred ceremony, leading us into our vows. He wanted each of us to have a witness present. Then at sunrise, after the ceremony, he said, we would go to his parents' door first to seek their blessings before proceeding to my family for the same purpose.

Within weeks of our first meeting, Shammi had informed his father—the formidable Prithviraj Kapoor, the godfather of Indian cinema—that he had found his future wife. Prithviraj Kapoor was an extraordinarily handsome man with a towering personality that dwarfed everyone in his presence. My parents met him during a sombre prayer meeting at Shammi's apartment, on the occasion of his wife's first death anniversary. I saw Shammi's children for the first time that day too—they were about five and seven years old, and very well-behaved. It was an uncomfortable time for my family because, although we were deeply honoured to be invited to such a sacred occasion, my father had already expressed his disapproval of the growing alliance between Shammi and me.

'Nobody can stop us from sharing our lives together,' Shammi assured me that night. If I couldn't find the courage to go against my parents' wishes, as Plan B he proposed that we trump the opposition by eloping.

Over and over again, Shammi expressed his love for me and built up beautiful dreams of our life together. He told me that he was not at heart the flamboyant playboy he portrayed on screen; he had been stereotyped, and now that he was stuck with that role, he simply delivered the image that the public loved him for. He was, he insisted, intellectually inclined, sensitive and loved books and classical music, but hardly anyone knew that side of him.

Considering his wild reputation, it was indeed hard to believe that he had such a serious aspect to his character. My conservative parents had judged him harshly, and I dared not question their wisdom. Besides, Raj-ji, whom I respected dearly, was also averse to the idea of us getting married and had told me so on a few occasions. I couldn't imagine how I would be able to oppose him. But despite all of this, I continued to believe that true love would conquer all adversities.

The more opposition that came our way, the more hell-bent Shammi became on pursuing the romance. He showered me with delightful surprises. He knew I liked the song 'The Breeze and I'; so whenever I visited Bombellis, a café I sometimes frequented with my girlfriends, the band would start playing the song, announcing that it was specially for me. I don't know how, but Shammi always seemed to know when I was going there. Soon after the song, a big bouquet of flowers would arrive, and if I stayed long enough, Shammi himself would materialize. Sadly, I would feel the need to leave within minutes of his arrival—I was terrified of gossip and of offending my family. But I would walk out feeling happy, taking his energy with me. One glimpse into his eyes and my heart would light up.

Shammi once found out that I had been gifted a convertible Sunbeam Alpine car in London by my family on my twenty-first birthday. One day, when we had known each other for just three months, out of the blue, a messenger rang the doorbell. When I answered the door, he handed me a car key, asking me to look out from the balcony. 'My master has sent you a gift,' he explained. I looked down from the fourth floor. There, in the car park, was a Sunbeam Alpine! The note that Shammi had sent with the key said that he regretted sending me a beige one instead of the blue Sunbeam I had in London, but this car was to be mine for as long as I was in India. I immediately ran down for a quick spin. Barely ten minutes later, my parents learnt of the incident and insisted I return it. My protest lasted four days before I returned the gift.

Shammi and I never had any serious physical contact, but the rare glimpses, meetings and phone conversations sufficed to inflame our relationship. Expressions of love continued for several months via secret codes and methods. His film career was skyrocketing and he was shooting four or five films simultaneously, travelling all over India and abroad. He would speak to his co-stars about me and occasionally had me speak to some of them on the phone, especially when he was partying.

In his recklessness and daring, Shammi was very different from anyone I had ever met. It was outrageous behaviour, according to my conservative upbringing, but I was completely overwhelmed and delighted.

■

My cousin Gita, an only child, was the same age as me, and more a friend than a relative. Her family lived in a large apartment on the fourth floor of a five-storey building in one of the prized old colonial buildings in Churchgate. Pushpa and I stayed with them whenever we wanted to be in 'downtown' Bombay. Gita was a very talented graphic designer with a master's degree from the Rhode Island College of Art in the US and had a job at Benson's, a busy advertising agency, where many interesting young men and women worked. I had a couple of other friends there too, and we enjoyed some very happy evenings together at Bombay's popular coffee bars, listening to experimental music by garage bands.

Gita was facing similar obstacles as I. At Benson's, she had fallen in love with an equally creative colleague, Frank Simoes. This had led to discontent at home. She was a Hindu from a wealthy family, and a relationship with a struggling Catholic man from Goa, who was living on the wrong side of town, was very far from her parents' plans for her. There were frequent moments of tension between Gita and her father, who was a strict disciplinarian.

The stiff opposition from her family appeared to have spurred a sense of rebellion in Gita, pushing her deeper into the relationship. Frank and she took to meeting in secret places, one of them being the rooftop of her building, after her parents were asleep. Gita was afraid of confiding in Pushpa, so our overnight stays in her home added an extra complication.

There was also plenty of disapproval from Gita's parents and Pushpa over the phone calls I received from Shammi. His unpredictable timings, often late at night, had become a source of irritation, since the phone sat in the hallway outside Gita's bedroom. I had one ear trained to hear the very first sound of the ring and to jump out of my bed as fast as I could before the second ring alerted everyone.

But Shammi's boisterous personality was not to be dampened by other people's disapproval. One night, around 11.30 p.m., he came up to the roof to meet me while Frank was meeting Gita. This turned out to be a workable option and we were able to meet there a few more times, provided everyone else was asleep—we could talk for hours. It was there that I really got to know Shammi and began to appreciate his deeper side, quite contrary to the persona he projected to the public. He told me that he had achieved the highest academic scores in his school and was the only one of the three brothers who had made it to college; though their success in the film industry soared high, Raj-ji and Shashi had barely completed high school.

Wistfully looking at the sky, Shammi said one night, 'I'm stuck with playing the role of the flamboyant, boisterous lover boy hero because that's what my audience wants from me over and over again.' He sighed in resignation. 'I really dislike that person. I am completely the opposite in real life, but, unfortunately, no one gets to see that side of me. I love Western classical music. I read books on philosophy and history. I read biographies. Do you think my audience would believe this about me?'

'It's hard for *me* to believe these things about you!' I blurted out.

'What would it take to convince you?' he asked. He offered to quit cinema and move abroad with me to a country of my choice, if that was what I preferred. In those hours on the rooftop, he would open up his soul and express himself with such sincerity that I was moved to assure him that I would do everything possible to help fulfil his dreams and make them ours.

One evening, when Gita and I were preparing for our rendezvous on the rooftop, Pushpa noticed our excitement and decided to stay awake to see what we were up to. As the moment of the gentlemen's arrival approached, our nervousness heightened. We pretended to be asleep, but Pushpa sensed something amiss and simply refused to go to sleep. Gita or I would usually give the 'thumbs up' signal from our terrace when the men showed up in the compound at the given hour. Shammi would park his flashy car away from our building, then he and Frank would walk through the main gate and up to the roof. That night, they had already waited for more than twenty minutes. We had to somehow let them know what had happened.

While I stayed in the room with Pushpa, Gita quickly wrote a note, rolled it and slipped it into a lipstick case, for lack of any other way of getting a piece of paper down to our targets. Unfortunately, during the toss, the paper slipped out from the case; while the note wafted down to a lower-floor apartment terrace, the men received only an empty lipstick case!

That was it for Shammi's patience. Off went the two to his car, in which he had a little bar. They tanked up on a bottle of whisky and went on a drive into the part of town where Frank lived, near Byculla and Mohammed Ali Road. That area would stay open all night, especially during the Eid festivities, which happened to be going on right then. Of course, hundreds of revellers came crowding around Shammi's car, no doubt thinking some prayer of theirs had been answered. The owners of the food shops that served rich biryani, kebabs and other delicacies opened up their kitchens and their hearts; this, in turn, encouraged Shammi to stand on the seat of his convertible and give them all a lecture on the harsh lessons of falling in love.

I heard of the night's shenanigans the next day from Gita, who was unable to contain her laughter as she repeated what Frank had told her. Shammi had apparently declared to the crowd gathered around him on the street: 'Love is the most wonderful thing. You must all experience it. But no matter what, don't ever fall in love with a Sindhi girl. She will break your heart.' In typical Shammi style, he had dramatized his angst and shared his pain with the people gathered around, pouring all his emotions into the moment.

My parents were growing increasingly uncomfortable with the deepening intimacy between Shammi and me. The thought of losing their daughter to a movie star with a terrible reputation for 'drinking' and 'womanizing' was alarming, to say the least. They began to step up their efforts and introduced me to a series of prospective husbands, all of whom I rejected outright. Pushpa, meanwhile, married a handsome Sikh businessman from Lucknow—a boy worthy of a Sindhi family—in a four-day-long wedding celebration with all the pomp and grandeur she had ever dreamt of.

It had been almost twelve months since we had arrived in India. My family by now had become completely exasperated with my stubbornness and my insistence on continuing the dalliance with Shammi. Finally, they gave me an ultimatum: either I was to accept the hand of the next suitor they presented to me or I would be packed off to London.

I desperately wanted to marry Shammi, but I simply did not have the courage to directly challenge my parents and felt powerless to stand up for myself. There was Shammi's Plan B at hand—elopement—and we had support from Bhabhi-ji. But perhaps most troubling of all was Raj-ji's unambiguous disapproval. I found that it weighed heavy on my heart.

Why was life so full of challenges?

5

Love...and Marriage

WITH PUSHPA MARRIED and happily ensconced in Lucknow, I started to enjoy my long-awaited freedom from watchful eyes, despite the increased pressure at home. As the lone unmarried daughter, I realized I was the last burden for my parents, preventing them from transiting into the carefree retirement that they so deserved. Amidst life's share of upheavals, they had neatly arranged marriages for all their children and they were weary. Apart from this, my mother's failing health needed attention.

Somehow, I convinced myself that the prospect of winning my parents' approval to marry Shammi was less remote now. While I had started to see Plan B as quite an agreeable pathway to the fulfilment of my dreams, my ethical fibre posed its own hurdle. It echoed the wish I had made at Sai Baba's shrine. I wanted to see everyone happy about my choice.

I had to face two more obstacles, given that I could win my parents' approval. There was my eldest brother Joginder in distant Kanpur. He was adamant on not allowing my union with Shammi. He had unwavering views on Shammi's wild and impulsive lifestyle. That was not the kind of husband he had visualized for his kid sister.

The other hurdle was posed by Raj Kapoor. Raj-ji had a conservative streak, despite his flamboyant lifestyle, and the mutual love and respect between his family and ours was deep and long-standing. He was my devoted rakhi brother, and I had always made a bracelet for him on Raksha Bandhan each August, being sure to mail it to him in time for the big day. I did not do that even for my four brothers, though I loved them all. And despite receiving hundreds of rakhis from other 'sisters' across the globe, Raj-ji always seemed to especially cherish mine.

One day, barely a month after Pushpa's wedding, he surprised me with an invitation to lunch at his favourite restaurant in Bombay, the Nanking near the Taj Hotel. I was intrigued by his unexpected phone call, which gave me barely two hours' notice to get ready. The popular restaurant was packed, but Raj Kapoor was not a person to be kept waiting. When we arrived, the owner quickly cleared Raj-ji's favourite table at the farthest corner of the upper level. Several familiar faces greeted him along the way, but he seemed in no mood to be social. I felt a bit unnerved by his seriousness and began to wonder what was to come. Having spent so much time in his family home, I was all too aware of his shifting moods. I had learned from his children that at times like these it was best to do a vanishing act. But now here I was, in a situation where escape was impossible.

We sat down and quickly ordered our meal, consisting mostly of the Nanking's legendary crisp garlic prawns that we both loved. After a couple of mouthfuls, Raj-ji laid down his fork and looked up at me. There was a radical shift in his mood. His furrowed brow signalled an ominous reason for this meeting and I struggled to hide the trepidation I felt. With an intensity in his eyes that I had never seen before, he asked, 'Are you in love with him?'

I froze. I was thunderstruck. I had only seen this intensity in his most compelling film roles. Only, he wasn't acting now. I did all I could to disguise my fear, especially since we had always shared a great compatibility in our conversations.

Feigning calmness, I replied, 'Yes, I am.'

'Do you know who he is and what he is capable of doing to you?' I was silent, stunned by his question.

Raj-ji continued, 'He is my brother and I love him dearly, but his success has gone to his head. He is an impatient and impulsive man, and he will not easily settle into married life. The two of you are complete opposites. He can be ruthless, and neither you nor your family will be able to deal with his wild, unpredictable ways.

You have had a sheltered upbringing, and your parents have very spiritually rooted and compassionate values. You deserve better. And I cannot bear to see your parents suffer the unhappiness of having my brother Shammi as their son.'

He stopped, trusting that he'd made the necessary impact.

I sat crushed, at a total loss for words. I had nothing to say that would counter what the big brother had just made excruciatingly clear. My prawns suddenly looked like cold little stones. They remained untouched. An uneasy silence settled over our table. I hopelessly wished that his words would simply vanish from my memory, as if they had never been spoken.

Raj-ji witnessed the dramatic shift in my mood and tried to bring some cheer back to our corner. He told me that he would host one of his grandest parties when I found the man who was worthy of me. Despite all his cajoling, I could not separate myself from the piercing pain that enveloped my psyche.

He would not let me leave until we had had the classic Nanking dessert of toasted figs with vanilla ice cream. It did not help sweeten my mood in any way. Then came the defining moment: he made me promise that I would give serious consideration to his warning, and that I would keep our lunch meeting a secret. It was as if I had received a court sentence.

I was crumbling under the pressure of my terrible new secret. I felt like I had been turned from princess to dwarf! I also knew that everything Raj-ji had said would be echoed by my family. But I had built faith in Shammi's sincerity when he had told me he was tired of playing to his audience and fans. 'That is not who I really am at all,' he had said. 'I'm desperate to make a cosy family life with you. I regret terribly that I was not a worthy husband to the mother of my children, and I need to vindicate the guilt I live with each day. I feel you are the anchor who can take me there.'

Shammi was travelling, busy with his work, but his phone calls continued. I did everything I could to keep my side of the conversations light-hearted and in the same vein as before. I certainly made no mention of the dreadful lunch meeting with his elder brother. But so deep was Shammi's resolve, and so finely tuned was his sensitivity to my every mood, that he sensed something was amiss. When he questioned if I was wavering, I told him that I was feeling burdened by pressure from my parents and needed to get away and think for a bit.

The timing could not have been better to receive an invitation from the Sobha Singhs, whom I fondly knew as 'Papa-ji and Bai-ji', to visit them in Mashobra, Simla. They were like godparents to me, and even though they were older than my parents I enjoyed being in their company. Sir and Lady Sobha Singh were among the most eminent families of Delhi. On their visits to London, our family had always done everything to ensure their comfort and enjoyment, and they in turn lavished their generous hospitality on us when we were in India. I was also friends with some of their grandchildren, who were a colourful lot. One of them was Rahul Singh, the son of Khushwant Singh. Since Rahul's work kept him in Bombay, Bai-ji and Papa-ji had generously offered his flat in Sujan Singh Park, New Delhi, for Pushpa's wedding.

Mashobra would be a great getaway, a perfect balm for my frayed nerves. It offered a combination of colonial nostalgia, snobbish royals and well-to-do families, mostly from north India. It was far removed from the existentialist drama of Bombay life.

■

When I arrived at the historic Mashobra residence I found that besides the exalted company of Bai-ji and Papa-ji, I was also in company of their granddaughter-in-law, Ruksana Sultana, who was about my age. We got along well, and I sometimes accompanied her to meet her friends for coffee or beer at an elite 'members only' social club called the Gaiety Theatre. Most evenings, around teatime, Bai-ji and Papa-ji took me along to the same club, but then we went into a plush and private salon, where the air was even more rarefied and exclusive. These outings gave me a marvellous peek into the fading world of the royals, before they were stripped of their purses and estates. At the time they were enjoying a new heyday in free India, retreating to their sumptuous summer palaces to escape the sweltering heat of the plains, just as the British had done.

I was soon introduced to all the royal ladies. Dressed in their delicately embroidered saris and fine jewels, the women would gather on one side of the room to exchange gossip while the men sat together at the far end of the salon with gimlets or sherry. By evening's end, several men and women would have crossed over and mingled. The intimacy and content of their conversations offered up a mythical world of delights. It felt like I was participating in a theatrical scene from the *Tales of the Raj*.

A vivacious maharani whom I recall vividly from these gatherings always wore lacy gloves which matched the colour of her blouse. Her stylishly waved hair was partly covered with a chiffon sari that she secured at the shoulder with an elegant jewelled brooch. Crossing over frequently to the men's area, she always held a glass of sherry with her lace-covered fingers while most of the other ladies drank tea from gold-rimmed bone-china cups. One day she sought permission from Bai-ji to introduce me to David, the prince of Faridkot. He had seen me with Ruksana and other young friends at the club the morning before and had asked to be introduced to me.

Bai-ji, always gracious and correct, explained, 'Bina comes from a very conservative background.' This simple statement was enough to suggest that a meeting with David Faridkot, son of a notoriously eccentric maharaja, was out of the question.

A few evenings later, as I sat with Bai-ji and her friends, a Sikh gentleman in his thirties walked in our direction. An instant later I was being introduced to David Faridkot. Bai-ji's face darkened for a moment but then, with her most gracious smile, she added a pointed remark to the introductions. 'Bina is my extra special daughter,' she said.

Within minutes, David had suggested that I allow him to show me around Simla. Bai-ji, speaking to him in Punjabi, promptly let

would not be necessary. I had Ruksana for company
enty of opportunities to sightsee together.

next day, the lace-gloved maharani came visiting and
broug.... re formal proposal—an invitation to the summer palace
of the maharaja for drinks. Both Papa-ji and Bai-ji declined the
invitation, but softened the moment by politely inviting David for tea
the next morning at 11. This was the traditional social hour at their
homes both in Delhi and in Simla, when close friends and extended
family members could drop in for tea and coffee unannounced. During
those sacred ninety minutes between 11.00 and 12.30, a grand silver
tea set would arrive on a trolley with fine porcelain cups and saucers
and a selection of sweet and savoury snacks. Fresh cups of tea would
be served to every guest who arrived to join the exalted 'Bai-ji Club',
where they were welcomed to air their views, along with the latest
gossip.

On the morning of his visit, Prince David actually convinced
Bai-ji and Papa-ji that he could show me certain picturesque parts of
Simla I would otherwise not have a chance to see. As we were about
to leave together, Bai-ji managed to whisper a quick instruction in
my ear. 'Don't let him take you home to meet his father,' she warned.
'That maharaja is an eccentric rascal and I don't want him to see
you.' I loved Bai-ji dearly for her unique mix of worldly wisdom
and childlike innocence. I gave her a wink and a smile as I walked
out the door.

■

So it was that an unexpected new path unfolded before me. David,
though not exactly endowed with looks, was a perfect gentleman and
charmed me with amusing stories and anecdotes. I heard of royal
life in India and student life at Cambridge, where, except for being
allowed to have 'Faridkot' on his car's number plate, he was treated
as a commoner. He talked freely about his father's eccentricities,
including his passion for beautiful women, parties, vintage cars and
his band of musicians that went with him everywhere.

During our evening walks on the Mall, I was struck by how seriously all the 'walkers' took themselves. There were no shops or restaurants, so everyone, be it couples, singles or small groups of well-dressed men and women, simply walked up and down the one-mile stretch because it was their pleasure to do so. Knowing glances darted, and everyone's presence was mapped by the others. David would regale me with tidbits about the attractive men and women of nobility that passed us. We often stopped and greeted some of his friends.

At night, alone in bed, I would reflect on the day's events and recall the conversations and attitudes in this elite world where I had now spent almost three weeks. David had declared his interest in me and wanted me to meet his mother and sisters in his Delhi home. I pictured myself for a moment being part of this insular and snobbish world of nobility, then found a certain emptiness there. Besides, I did not feel attracted to him. Once the reflections had evaporated, I found myself yearning for the chaotic Bombay streets, bursting at the seams with every shade of life in all its noise, smells and street brawls. Its acceptance of poverty alongside unimaginable wealth, the trendy shops and cafés neighbouring the grim slums, all woven together in a colourful melting pot of humanity, really appealed to my senses.

I missed my late-night phone calls, Shammi's tender assurances, the rendezvous on the roof. I also knew the clock was ticking. Shammi didn't want to wait, but I still hadn't mustered the courage to stand up to my parents or to Raj-ji's disapproval. I was relying on the cowardly route of escapism instead of standing up in confrontation. For our marriage to take place, there would be an uneven score—a few happy people, but mostly unhappy ones. I was also aware of all the beautiful actresses, starlets and fans that would want to antagonize Shammi and me and steal our happiness. I couldn't shake the notion that I was being selfish in seeking only my happiness against the long line-up of unhappy people. It haunted me, and I didn't know whom to discuss it with. Shammi's assurances that 'in the end, everyone will share our happiness, don't worry about it now' just didn't weigh as heavily as my parents' disapproval.

After Simla I went to Delhi, where I continued to stay with the Singhs in their grand Lutyens home. David's mother had sent a message to Bai-ji inviting them to dinner, and I was to accompany them. Bai-ji had astutely decided not to lend gravitas to the relationship, because she had noticed that I had no romantic inclination towards David. However, she suggested that I go along and meet his family, which I did. His mother and sister were gracious and warm hostesses and invited me to visit again. But to discourage their pursuit, I shifted my focus.

Despite my reticence, the next day David insisted on taking me for a spin in his vintage Jaguar through new and old parts of Delhi, ending at his own Delhi palace, Faridkot House. After a quick cup of tea, served by a liveried attendant in the elegant drawing room, he walked me towards the large grounds in the rear. He wanted me to see his stable of cars, which numbered fifty-two! Indeed, there were vintage cars of every size, shape and colour as far as the eye could see; some were masterpieces. There, amidst the cars, he suddenly stopped and proposed marriage. He said, 'Now you can have a car for each week of the year, and I will make sure you have a sari to match every car!' Feeling emboldened, he took my hands in his and smiled, 'Let's get married!' It sounded like a joke to me—I was speechless for a minute. Finding no answer to give him, I burst out laughing. Thank God he found the humour to laugh with me.

I realized it was time to pull out of this friendship before any more expectations arose. I did not belong in this world of snobbish elitists, I had understood, after nearly six weeks in the highly approved company of this refined Sikh prince with his easy charm and polite ways. I knew the match would have fulfilled my parents' hope, but it stirred nothing in me, it left me cold. And while my parents thought I might have given up too hastily, it was Bai-ji who came to my rescue. She told them that she did not see the chemistry between David and me, and a marriage between us did not look promising.

Other suitors came and went. One wealthy Sikh industrialist's son in Delhi was so enamoured and unrelenting in his pursuit, he took to sending us sacks of rice and wheat, and gigantic baskets of fruit and vegetables, in an effort to win my mother's approval. But my heart was ensconced in Bombay.

■

My father's elder brother had arranged my first meeting with yet another prospective suitor. This uncle commanded respect in the Sindhi community, and had in fact arranged marriages earlier for two of my brothers, Kartar and Partap. He took his role rather seriously. The meeting, as it turns out, was scheduled exactly twelve months to the day I had first met Shammi.

At the time, Shammi happened to be out of town on a hunting expedition in the jungles. I knew this was a sacred ritual for him because he had spoken passionately about his annual treks. Nothing was allowed to come in the way of this special week at the end of the year with his two best friends. It was an era when hunting big game was still in fashion among India's elite. The three friends took their sport seriously, displaying their trophies with great pride in their homes. For months, Shammi had targeted 2 January as the date when we would elope, seeing it as a fitting end to this cherished annual pilgrimage. Before he left he had told me, with great passion and affection, 'This trip, my prize is assured. Whether I bag wild game or not, I'm getting the best trophy on my return, in any case.' The memory of my secret lunch meeting with Raj-ji burnt holes in my heart every time Shammi talked about his Plan B with such passion. It tore me apart.

My uncle set up the meeting in accordance with the hallowed arranged-marriage tradition. Both sets of parents were to be present. I reluctantly agreed, just to please my family. The prospective groom's name was Andy Ramani. He had come to India from San Francisco to attend his younger brother's wedding. He was the manager for Air India for the west coast of America. Importantly, he was from the Sindhi community, though not a Sikh.

We met at the apartment of his sister, Sheila. She had been a beautiful and admired film star before her marriage to a Parsi businessman, who was somewhat of an aristocrat. She now ran a sophisticated home and was raising two sons. I was introduced to Andy's fashionable mother and austere-looking father, who appeared to be much older than the mother. The apartment was impressively decorated. A lot of effort had been put into making a good impression.

We spent the first thirty minutes in nervous small talk, quickly exhausting each new attempt at furthering the conversation. I simply wanted to leave that drawing room and run far away—somewhere, anywhere. I had already turned down several suitors with similar or better qualifications in the past year. This new one didn't appear particularly attractive or exciting in any way. As far as I was concerned, he was a non-contender. He also did not seem overly enthusiastic about a match. I allowed my boredom to show on my face, especially for the benefit of my uncle.

My bored face, however, was hiding the turmoil I felt inside. With Shammi's magical date of 2 January dancing in my brain, some life-transforming choices were dangerously close. Hanging over my head was a caveat. My parents had threatened to pack me off to London if I continued to refuse any more eligible suitors. Going back was at the bottom of my list. My heart told me that eloping was the only choice, but the fear of repercussions from Raj-ji and family filled me with dread. And now this—my only other choice! While reflecting on my silent torment, I suddenly saw an apparition.

A beautiful lady breezed in from a dimly lit corridor. She was dressed in a soft blue chiffon sari, garlanded with a string of pearls. She spoke in a gentle, impressive voice. She was the epitome of chic elegance, and I'm sure that the shock of encountering this unexpected vision showed on my face, regardless of how cool and bored I may have tried to look.

The lady turned out to be Andy's younger sister, Madhu, who lived in Washington and also worked with Air India. Her presence in the room took me by complete surprise and jolted me into the moment. She seemed to spring life into the dull drawing-room scene that had been played out dozens of times in my life. I began to see the whole family in a fresh, renewed light. In a bizarre way, one could attribute my derailed destiny to Madhu's dazzling entry. The Ramanis suddenly had my full attention, and I began to think it possible that I could be a part of their world. I dismissed the inner voice that told me I was sacrificing my true love to appease my family.

By the time we had thanked them for their hospitality and entered the elevator to go down, I had come back to my senses. I told my parents and uncle, 'No, no. This is not for me. I see nothing in Andy that leads me to want to spend the rest of my life with him.'

My uncle interjected before I could finish my sentence, 'Don't judge only by appearances.'

'But he is shorter than me and ten years older!' I cried out. 'Besides, I can't imagine having a conversation with him.'

'This is not a mature way of looking at the future,' he scolded. Then, with an air of finality, 'I have calculated his date of birth and the numerology tallies very smoothly with yours.'

My father echoed my uncle's words. 'Do not be too quick to judge. Don't be hasty.' His tone was clear. The subject would be dropped—for now. But they knew what was brewing in my head.

Andy's whole family had assembled in Bombay that week to celebrate his younger brother's wedding, coincidentally to another Lalvani girl, unrelated to us. It was not an arranged marriage. Andy's younger brother, Rummy, had been dating his bride-to-be for several years. Now the family saw an opportunity to kill two birds with one stone. They decided to pursue my parents—soft targets—and arranged another meeting. We were invited to one of their wedding parties, where I saw Andy again. We talked for just a moment, in which I recall a witty line from him. But I held on to my resolve. There would be no marriage here.

The following day the Ramanis called again, pleading that I visit them just once more. Despite my protests I had to go, as my determined uncle convinced my mother to agree to the meeting. They promised this would be the last time. Andy had suggested that he and I should talk in private for half an hour, without any pressure from our parents. He was being equally pressured by his family, it seemed, since he had also rejected all the marriage prospects his parents had presented to him on his frequent visits to India.

Against my better judgement, I agreed. In any case, we hadn't been brought up to make our own decisions—on the contrary, it had always been discouraged. So I went. Andy's family again displayed great warmth and offered snacks and drinks, which I refused—a serious breach of manners in India. Then Andy walked me over to an apartment nearby, which belonged to an American friend of the family.

We were alone. Within minutes he got to the point. But first he offered me a drink. 'I don't drink,' I said politely.

He made himself a vodka tonic and then launched into a declaration, which went something like this: 'We both are adults and know why we are here. Our parents wish for us to spend our lives together and think this could be a perfect match. But it's only reasonable that we discuss this for ourselves.' He seemed a bit nervous as we sat on the dimly lit balcony.

'I agree', I muttered in response to his preamble, trying to help him out as he continued what seemed to be a well-rehearsed speech. My eyes were focused on the distant horizon, where the twinkling lights of Bombay's skyline merged between the dark ground below and the starlit sky above. I hoped the speech would end soon and I could say my polite thank-you and be driven home.

In a quick succession of words, he said, 'I know you are from a wealthy family and have known every comfort and luxury. Well, you should know that I am from the opposite side of the fence.'

How vivid it remains! He cleared his throat, as if ordering me to look at him. Then he continued, 'Mine is a very simple life. I am a middle-class working man. I am just a manager at Air India in charge of three states in America, not the whole country.' He paused, as if to weigh his words, and then added, 'My job entails a lot of travel…and not the kind of travel where a wife can accompany me.'

Now he had my attention.

I watched him as he explained, 'My salary is barely enough to support me. It is only $750 per month. I have no savings. I don't own any property, not even a car. It all belongs to Air India. All I own is a TV set and some books. Can you fit yourself into this modest way of life?'

This didn't sound like a successful sales pitch. He must have presumed I would say no and flee. Which had been my intention all along! But as he spoke, with such sincerity in his voice, I felt a bit sorry for him. How can a thirty-three-year-old man live on such a shoestring budget? I thought to myself. I wondered how many times he might have had to utter these very words to prospective brides. Before I knew it, I felt a need to console him. I had to say something, I thought. It was my turn to respond, after all. I didn't want to appear dumb or unfeeling. All through his speech I had said nothing—but his bare-bones honesty had touched me.

In the end, all I could come up with was something silly and inappropriate: 'Are you sure the car is not yours? Don't you get to keep it in the end?'

He laughed out loud, and I liked the sound of it. Something stirred within me. New pictures emerged from my dream factory, and I told myself it was because I valued his honesty. My mind moved into fast-forward mode and I began visualizing our lives together. He was an Air India sales executive and I was the ideal homemaker and hostess, trained at Lady Irwin College to create domestic miracles out of meagre resources. The two of us could team up together and I could become his best asset, charming all his clients to enhance his career. His business acumen would flourish as he climbed to the top of the Air India ladder. This was turning into an exciting challenge—and very much at hand! Besides, it would resolve my impossible conundrum. At last my parents could be happy in their advanced age, unburdened of their last responsibility.

The inner voice, my ally, brought me back to my senses. To my horror, I realized that I was being seduced by the idea of marrying a man who had nothing. And he couldn't be further from the romantic figure I had built up over the years. It also crossed my mind that maybe my parents had simply made a dreadful mistake in promoting this proposal. They couldn't possibly want me to enter into married life with a partner like this. Or was he just saying all this because he wanted me to reject him? And how ironic that his style of proposing marriage was so diametrically opposite to the two most recent ones I had encountered. Now I had heard all varieties of proposals!

My head was reeling. I had no idea what my next move should be. Was I meant to respond from my parents' point of view or my own? And what about Andy's feelings? I felt it would embarrass him if I refused straightaway and made an exit just because he claimed to have nothing. On the other hand…what a daunting challenge it could be! Might I not be the perfect wife for a man who had started with so little in his life? I began to daydream again, seeing myself being credited for my husband's success as he became the CEO of his company.

It was another flight of fancy coming out of a caged soul. How many times had I sat on the seafront and spun such fantasies? I knew, deep down, that naked rebellion and elopement was not an option I had the strength for. If I refused Andy, I would soon be herded back to London to live under the watchful eyes of my parents and older siblings. No matter which way I turned, the choice was between freedom and captivity. I desperately wished some god would descend from the heavens and make the decision for me.

I brought myself back to the balcony in Bombay and mumbled something that sounded positive. I cannot recall exactly what I said. From Andy's response, I immediately realized that I had somehow acquiesced and agreed to marry him. Andy was in utter shock. He could not believe that I had fallen for his sob story! I had reacted purely from a confused and naïve state of mind.

Andy made a gallant move and immediately walked towards the kitchen, pulled out a bottle of champagne from the fridge and popped it open. I appreciated his spontaneity, because he couldn't possibly have predicted my reaction. He held my hand cupped in both his, saying a few endearing words about a 'toast to our lives'. I managed to finish one glass of champagne in the time he finished the rest of the bottle. Everything we may have said thereafter remains a blur. It never registered on me. I was on some auto-command and had taken leave of my senses. But apparently, I had sealed my fate.

Andy drove me home to my mother, who immediately asked, 'Have you been drinking?'

'Congratulations,' he declared, 'your daughter and I are going to be married.'

'But I can smell heavy liquor on your breath—my daughter won't marry a drunkard.' She was adamant, and there was alarm in her voice. My ever alert Mama!

I told her that he had only had champagne in celebration, but it took a little convincing from us both. I found it so ironic that I burst out laughing—here was my perfect opportunity to pull out! But deep down there was anger, accumulated over the years. It was now driving me to speed in the wrong direction with my eyes wide open. Besides, this was the nearest I had ever come to liking my parents' choice of groom, albeit with reservations.

Mama asked me once again after Andy had left, 'Are you sure about this?' There was concern in her voice. 'His parents will be expecting an answer in the morning.'

I said a simple 'Yes'. It freed me from returning to London, and I still had time to figure out a way of wriggling out of this choice with some clever plotting when Shammi returned. In my mind it wasn't final—it was just relieving me from immediate pressure. I simply wanted my eager uncle to unwind and take a back seat.

I would agree to marry Andy and get engaged to him for a few months. Meanwhile he would go back to San Francisco and I would remain in India, ostensibly to gather an appropriate trousseau. At some point I would find a reason to break the engagement and elope with Shammi. It seemed like the perfect ploy that would make everybody happy for now, and certainly dispel the clouds of pressure that haunted me.

Andy and I discussed the idea of a quick engagement and a gap of three months before the marriage. This would supposedly allow my brothers from London to be present. He had already explained that he was not a great one for writing letters, warning me not to expect much communication from San Francisco in those three months. That suited me fine. I clung to the frail hope that this scenario would be my ticket to freedom, with the bonus, in the meantime, of allowing everyone to have it their way.

Andy's parents were overjoyed at the news. But to my horror, they insisted to my parents that the wedding should take place immediately, without delay. Their whole family had congregated from out of town and country for the marriage of Andy's younger brother, after all. It would be foolish not to take advantage of the situation and conclude two marriages on one occasion. My desperate request for a three-month engagement was waved off by my imposing matchmaker uncle. 'There's no difference in engagement and marriage,' he declared. 'When a match between two has been struck, there should be no room for trivial reasons to cause delay.'

It was like a magic spell had been cast on my parents' minds. Their feeble attempts to protest the hurried wedding fell on deaf ears. I was paralysed with shock, hoisted by my own petard! Not one elder relative with wisdom and a strong voice intervened to stand by us and negotiate terms on our behalf. My other brothers were in London and not consulted at all, and Joginder didn't seem to object to the deal. My in-laws had taken complete control of the situation. The yawning gap between Andy and me was simply ignored. We were to be rushed into wedlock within six days of our first meeting.

Suddenly everything was on fast track with hurried shopping sprees, lists of gifts to be distributed to the in-laws and relatives and special guests to be called personally. Everyone was mobilized. I managed to put together a small trousseau with the help of my sister Mohini, who was super-efficient in matters such as this, despite being pregnant with her second child at the time. She arranged for jewellers to bring a vast selection of designs for me to choose from. Saris arrived by the hundreds. None of this activity aroused my enthusiasm for the big day. I uncharacteristically left most of the decisions up to my elders, making a disinterested selection of the rest.

I did manage to choose a saffron and gold tissue silk sari to wear at the morning wedding ceremony and a purple, silver and gold brocade for the small reception in the evening. There were two beautiful sets of jewellery, shoes and evening bags to match each sari. In the end, there were about five suitcases ready to be loaded, which I would only notice when we headed for the airport the next day. My lacklustre mood seemed to emanate from some dead, emotionless place within me. My heart had been given to Shammi. This was just a shell getting married to a stranger from America.

Six days later my name changed from Bina Lalvani to Bina Ramani. An announcement in *The Times of India* invited friends and relatives to the gurdwara in our building for the wedding ceremony. There was a hurried reception party at the only decent spot available on the night before New Year's Eve, the Taj Hotel in the Neptune Suite. That was it. While Shammi was in the jungle with his buddies, engaged in his favourite sport, he lost his love to a stranger from San Francisco—forever.

■

On the morning of the wedding ceremony I was about to enter the temple. Just four steps from the doorway my mother, who was walking me slowly towards my destiny, suddenly stopped. In a strange, slow-motion way she looked into my eyes and uttered the words that would haunt us both for years to come. I could sense the pain with which she whispered every word.

'If you don't want to go ahead with this marriage,' she choked, 'we can turn around right now. I will stand by you and I know everyone will support us.'

Then came the bombshell. 'Andy's aunt informed us this morning that Andy has a live-in girlfriend in San Francisco. He has been living with her for the last three years. This could make your life miserable. You don't have to go through with it.'

Mama must have seen the numbness cloud my face, but she continued, 'The aunt said, "You may as well go throw Bina in the ocean rather than let her marry my sister's son."' She then slowly added, 'This could be vicious gossip, but it might also be true.'

There was defeat in her eyes, which I had never witnessed before. I think she had been too afraid to discuss this with anyone else in the family. She was fighting back a lump in her throat, feeling scared for me and guilt for herself. I couldn't bear to see her in such pain.

I still don't know what power, or what cowardice, made me say what I did. With almost no hesitation, I said firmly, 'No, Mama, now it's too late. I'm going ahead. If this is to be my destiny, I will see it through.'

6

Newly-wed in America

DURING THE ONE-HOUR wedding ceremony, all my senses were numbed. I fought back the tears welling up and choking me, oblivious to the proceedings. I have no recollection of the rest of the day, either, except a few vague memories of the suite at the Taj Hotel, where we had our hurried reception. Standing in front of the mirror, getting ready to step out as a new bride to greet all the well-wishers, I saw a different Bina—a stranger. A mask, impenetrable, stared back. This was not the girl who, just seven days ago, had nurtured dreams of a very different life. That already seemed a lifetime ago—and it was. I don't remember most of the evening, nor the guests who were present. But I do remember seeing a pleased Raj-ji and a very sad Bhabhiji among them. I was in a blank space, without a voice. A zombie with a fake smile pasted on my face.

On New Year's Eve, Andy and I were on a flight bound west, to London. The next day, 1 January 1967, Shammi was to return from his hunting trip. I learned later that on his flight back he had let out an agonized scream when he saw the wedding announcement in the morning paper. The news was devastating to him, and apparently he was inconsolable for several days and went on a self-destructive drinking binge. I, meanwhile, had my own fate awaiting me in the city of dreams, San Francisco.

Through most of the journey to London, Andy and I hardly spoke. It was partly from fatigue, but mostly from the numbness that had enveloped me. What had I done? Where was my voice? Why had I been unable to protest this coercion from my parents and relatives? Why had I not jumped at the chance Mama had given me, not just once but twice? What fear or dark power had held me back? What was in store for me? Was I simply a sucker for punishment? This was not the way I had imagined my destiny. The engagement to Andy was meant to be my ticket to freedom, but it had turned into a cunning trap. I could have resisted that shocking, split-second, perverted decision of six days earlier, but hadn't found the strength. Now I found myself in a situation that in fact would require a lot more strength. Yet, when I tried to introspect and analyse all this, I met an impenetrable cloud. I was sitting next to a stranger and entering his world for the rest of my life. With no answers in sight, I retreated to a dead zone inside me where I could rest my mind. My emotive zone was locked up somehow, protecting me from my anguish, allowing me to function on autopilot, like a robot.

By the time we landed at Heathrow Airport, my physical senses were working again. I could see, hear, smell, taste and my hands could touch. But my actions were being commanded from the brain. My heart was shut. My brothers had all come inside the airport to greet us, expecting to see some dashingly handsome bridegroom who had swept me off my feet in less than a week! When I caught my first glimpse of them I saw the consternation on their faces, their eyes fixed on us in disbelief. It was in that moment that I fully realized my folly. I was their youngest sister, for whom they had great expectations. I was their little star, after whom they had named their business, Binatone. Their fortunes had soared ever since. The knight in shining armour they had come to meet had turned out to be an unimpressive man, with nothing visibly outstanding about him. In my mind, for a brief moment, I fantasized that they would snatch me away from him and take me home. But my face belied all this. Instead, concerned about their feelings, I forced a smile and introduced them to their new brother-in-law.

I could feel the pain and shock in the silence that ensued on the way home. I have no recollection of how the next few days passed, except for a hurried reception dinner arranged at our spacious home for some sixty close friends and family.

Andy had to rush back to San Francisco to prepare for a business dinner for thirty guests. It was an event that he held routinely four times a year, as part of his job with Air India, and was to be on 6 January.

But on my second day in London I developed symptoms of viral fever and became too ill to travel. Andy left alone for San Francisco. I was to follow and be there at least two days before the party. Meanwhile I spent almost all my time in bed, nursing a painful throat infection and high fever, with no opportunity to spend quality time with my family. On 4 January, still not fully recovered from my illness, I was on a flight to San Francisco to take up my new role as Mrs Bina Ramani. This new life was packed into three suitcases, filled mostly with my trousseau and a few of my favourite clothes and shoes. Everything else I owned had been discarded or distributed hastily. I have no clue what happened to it all—my entire past had been erased. All that I cherished was gone. I was no longer me.

I felt no pain. I felt no joy. That long, lonely journey from London to San Francisco is a total blank now. In my numb state, I had neglected to take the prescribed antibiotics. By the time I reached my destination I had a vicious relapse with a throbbing strep throat infection and high fever. On the morning of Andy's party I finally saw a doctor. He gave me a shot of penicillin, not knowing that I was allergic to it.

Andy had said that I was to be ready by 6 p.m., when his guests from the travel industry would begin to arrive straight from work. His assistant, Henry, spent most of the day in the kitchen of our compact, one-bedroom apartment. Andy had taught Henry how to prepare chicken, cauliflower and potatoes, garbanzo beans, raita and jeera rice to perfection. This was accompanied by a bottle of pickles and some pita bread from the local grocery store. The pièce de résistance was always the rasmalai and gulab jamuns that he ordered from a nearby Indian restaurant. For his American guests this exotic menu, sprinkled with the Indian ambience of his apartment, had made his quarterly dinners a much anticipated event.

Except for one couple, Keith and Joan, whom I had met the day before, almost none of Andy's dinner guests knew of his marriage, or that they were going to meet his new bride at his party. I had dressed up, using all the strength I could muster. I wore one of my favourite saris, a magenta chiffon with gold thread weaving intricate floral patterns through it. Andy was late. I had already welcomed a few of his early guests and, with my hand clutching my throat, I explained in a whisper that I was Andy's new bride. Most of the guests thought Andy was playing a practical joke on them. Within an hour of the final guests' arrival, I was convulsing with pain and hot with fever. I thought I would faint. But the entire one-bedroom apartment was by then a party zone. The sliding door that separated the bedroom from the drawing room was open. There was no place for me to escape for a bit of rest. One of his guests noticed my pale, agonized face and brought Andy to me. Before I could say anything I saw the 'party spoiler' irritation in Andy's eyes. His quick solution, before any guest got wind of my situation, was to tuck me out of the way. The only choice was to have me sit in the walk-in closet, where a bunch of stools and our luggage were piled up. I managed to squeeze into a sitting position, grateful and relieved to be away from the crowd so I could deal with my agony. It happened so quickly that no one noticed I had disappeared. Half of the guests had not yet been introduced to me; most still had no idea that Andy had brought a bride home from India. I didn't dare feel sorry for myself. I was not that Bina anymore. I had to fight this out and survive.

.

I must have fainted or fallen asleep, for how long I didn't know. After perhaps an hour the door was opened and the automatic light went on. A male guest, looking for the washroom, had opened the closet door instead and found me slumped half-comatose over a couple of stools. He yelled. Andy came rushing, this time with Joan, his colleague's wife, who, fortunately, was a nurse. Sizing up the situation, she led me out of the closet with minimum fuss, causing the least possible disturbance to the party, and took me to a neighbour's apartment. There I was made to drink large doses of soda bicarbonate to flush out the poisonous effect of penicillin in my system. She called a doctor for instructions, prepared more antidotes and stayed with me till the party was over. I slept the entire next day, heavily sedated to endure the pain.

To my utter shock, Andy left on a business trip for five days the next evening. A friend of his, Felix, who had known about our wedding and had walked into the party with a bunch of beautiful roses the previous night, offered to send his wife to take care of me. He was Romanian, and his wife Dora was an Afro-Latin beauty from the Dominican Republic. In the days that followed, I broke into an allergic rash all over my body, and I couldn't bear to have any clothes touch my skin. It stretched to about twelve days, but the first few days were so hellish that I would sit up and cry half the night, begging God to show his mercy.

The entire episode had a devastating impact on my psyche and on our new marriage. Almost from the moment I had arrived in San Francisco, I had been an embarrassing burden in Andy's life, and a very sick one at that. I missed my family desperately. Other than Dora, I had no one to talk to. I don't know what I would have done without her help. She was a true angel, and her healing ways cemented a friendship so strong that she is the favourite friend of my grandchildren today.

■

Even after I recovered, Andy made little effort to make me feel at home. He came home late almost every night, even though his office was just five blocks away. I stayed alone. I began to try every form of seductive inducement I knew (scant at the time), to persuade him to come home during his lunch break. He laughed at the suggestion. 'I have never had lunch at home on a weekday and it will never happen, so abandon the idea!' was his answer.

In the first few months I didn't have enough confidence to go out of the apartment alone. I listened to music on the radio and browsed through the books on Andy's shelf, which failed to interest me. The TV was an old model and required a few slaps at a particular spot to display clear channels. Besides, this was Andy's domain. I hated it.

I remained celibate for the first three months of our marriage, mostly because I rarely saw Andy. He came home late and exhausted almost every night. Or he went on trips for three to five days at a time. There was no honeymoon, no bonding, no friendship.

I did find numerous passionate love letters and several hints of a woman's presence in the apartment, pointing to a speedy exit to make way for my arrival. I imagined that in the two days I stayed back in London, he had hurriedly packed her off. I never saw any photographs, so I had no idea what she looked like, but I had learnt from a casual mention by one of Andy's colleagues that she was Australian. On some of my nights alone, I would conjure up scenarios of Andy leaving our bed for hers on the nights he was meant to be travelling. Jealousy was a new emotion for me. But Andy was so distant, there was no way of broaching the subject with him. Irrationally, I began to hate everything Australian.

Only much later did I learn to introspect and understand that our union was a recipe for disaster from the beginning. My programmed mind had only one goal: the gossamer world of blue skies, rainbows and lovebirds singing a symphony that we would jointly create. It was the vision that had captivated me on the terrace in Bombay, with Andy's rise to the top of the ladder at Air India while I ran our enchanting home with panache. There would be happy sounds of our children playing, dogs yelping and guests and family visiting from all over the world!

A great deal of imagination and longing had gone into developing that tender image. Many Indian girls of my generation nurtured similar dreams, invigorated by our cinema. Parents and elders reinforced the fantasy by putting away lavish gifts for 'that big day'. Every wish or desire that my elders denied me during my single years was compensated by a standard reply: 'You will get to do all those things after you are married.' Even a request to go to a late-night movie with a girlfriend brought the same response. There was a constant 'build-up' to that amazing future life. Since I was already in love with the image that had been nurtured from my adolescent years, I tried to fit Andy into this scenario. But Andy had no such illusions. He had grown up in an entirely different family environment. They were a rather 'modern' family and quite independent, with no particular traditional foundation. He had not nurtured any image of a doting wife, and probably found me overbearing. He was a pragmatic man, successful and popular in his profession, and almost all his friends and associates came from within that world. He lived like an American. I didn't understand until much later that my naïve fantasy world and my desperation to win his affections were probably driving him further away.

Quite simply, I was a misfit in his world. Only, I refused to realize or accept it. Tenacity and determination were now my only allies, and I was bent on achieving my goal.

■

Gradually I found the courage to venture out. I took short walks, never beyond three or four blocks. Over time, I got to know the wives of two of Andy's American friends and became very fond of them. Occasionally they would drive in from the suburbs and take me around the enchanting city that was now my home. I still hold vivid memories of the first glimpse of Chinatown, the cable car, the Golden Gate Bridge, the marina. These outings, while enjoyable, were like a consolation prize. I would much rather have had Andy show me around his city, which he did only on rare occasions. I craved for his attention.

I missed my family and friends sorely and listened to the one record of Sikh hymns which I'd brought with me over and over again, and cried along with it when I was at my loneliest. But somewhere deep down, I firmly believed that I would succeed in reversing Andy's attitude. That he would come to love me. The idea of breaking the marriage was unthinkable.

I began to fear his outbursts of impatience and anger, something which I had never witnessed or imagined in my twenty-four sheltered years. On the rare nights when we had dinner together, when I had lovingly experimented from a recipe book, there would be long oppressive silences between us. He didn't seem to consider me worthy of any conversation. At least once a day he would find some excuse to berate or belittle me in a tone that I had never known before. He made it clear that I had no right to ask him what had delayed him at work. I wasn't allowed to call him there unless I had an emergency. I ate dinner alone; sometimes I went to bed hungry and heartbroken. On the few occasions when he would come home with friends or colleagues, I was thrilled because this meant a chance for conversation, a hope that he would notice something about me that might touch him. The tiniest gesture of kindness from him would fill me with hope and joy. I would cling to that memory until the next such moment. But I learned never to question him or argue with him, fearing his reaction.

One evening, he surprised me by suggesting that he would teach me some card games. We got into a game of gin rummy after dinner. On another evening we played blackjack. Pretty soon, I became fairly adept at both games and even won the bank a few times. Our little tournaments became a path towards some conversation and fun. The bonus was that I had met him on his own ground, which enabled me to shed some of the fear I had developed. A pack of cards was to be my first ally in winning his attention. We even found reasons to laugh on such occasions, poking fun and taking digs at each other's gambles in the game. It became apparent that we appreciated each other's sense of humour. I hung on to that thread and gradually, humour became the path to a possible relationship.

7

A Walk on the Wild Side

I HAD BECOME MORE adventurous by now, exploring the neighbourhood and venturing a little farther each day, walking through new streets and discovering places of interest. Like a dog on a leash, my hindsight was pinned to my Sutter Street address. I loved everything about San Francisco. I could almost see its smiling heart, even though my own remained achingly empty.

I tended to attract attention because of my ethnic style of dressing—in mini kurtas and churidars or saris—and a red bindi on my forehead. I never saw any other sari-clad woman on the streets. If I had, I would have joyously approached her.

One day I was stopped by a friendly and attractive lady, who was dressed in a colourful bohemian style. She appeared to be in her sixties. After a few pleasantries and enthusiastic comments on my exotic looks, she offered me a job as a model at her art studio. Two hours per sitting, three times a week, $25 per session. Right there on the street, a block from our apartment! She must have expected me to decline, for she gushed on about her lovely place and its serious students of all ages. She explained that it was a historic studio and many successful artists had studied there. Sensing my hesitation, she increased the offer to $30 per sitting.

It was all too much too soon. I lived up to her expectations and declined. She was crestfallen, but in an optimistic manner she pressed her card into my hand and asked me to think about it for a few days. She extracted a promise from me that even if I decided not to accept her proposal, I would call her.

The next day, feeling newly appreciated and relishing the thought of meeting some more of San Francisco's arty lot, I wandered a bit further. I was drawn to a sign outside a small building which read 'BAGELS—Boys and Girls Everyone Loves'. Below it was another sign: 'Looking for volunteers'. Impulsively, I decided to investigate what it was about. My timid knock on the door was answered by an attractive woman in her thirties. Speaking slowly, as if every word she uttered had a delicious taste to it, she greeted me warmly. 'Hi, I'm Judy. Come on in.'

'Oh! I was just passing by, and noticed the sign on your door,' I said.

Judy noticed my hesitation. 'Come.' She led me by the hand. 'Do you live here, or are you a tourist?'

Her warmth and enthusiasm put me at ease. 'I live nearby, but I'm new here. What kind of volunteers are you looking for?' I enquired.

'Two of my volunteers have gone on leave and I am desperately short-staffed. No experience is required, as long as you are comfortable being with challenged children.' She quickly added, 'I know my children would just love you.' Without further ceremony, I was simply inducted into the job, at a wonderful work and play space for mentally challenged kids between the ages of four and eighteen.

Judy required help with her beautiful children, and apparently I looked like the perfect fit. Fortunately, she asked for no resume or work experience, for I had none. But my colourful sari was definitely a big plus. I was led from the corridor into a large, noisy room decorated with brightly coloured cut-outs of animals, alphabets and streamers. There were about twenty kids in there, who immediately stopped what they were doing and stared at me in silence. Then one fourteen-year-old boy, his head bobbing from side to side, walked up, grabbed my hand in both of his and kissed it. He turned around and laughed aloud, trying to get the other kids to join him in his merriment. Within minutes of being there, I knew I had found a calling. I felt completely at home with all the children, who seemed to see me as someone different, like themselves, someone they could trust. They opened up their hearts to me—their curiosity about me was touching in its innocence. It took all my willpower to fight back tears and smile, pouring out my love that so desperately needed an outlet.

As a bonus, I now had something wonderful to discuss with my husband that could make him proud of me.

Andy seemed surprised when I shared my good news. He could not fathom why I would want to work with mentally challenged children, and that too for no pay. But we didn't dwell on it for long that evening. His favourite TV programme, *Bonanza*, was on. It was a sacrosanct time, definitely not for conversation.

■

I couldn't wait to get to BAGELS every morning. The children loved my Indian attire and complained when I switched to Western-style clothes. They preferred to have their stories read by an exotic-looking person, and to play games and make conversation with her. In turn, their innocence helped me appreciate the grand canvas of God's agenda. I was humbled by the frailties and strengths of these special children. Here, I found a brief respite from my troubled married life. Still, the diversion could not change the painful reality of the loveless marriage that awaited me at home, every day.

I had called the artist and explained that I had found another job for now. I promised her that I would call should I ever change my mind about her modelling offer. Which I did, about five months later, when BAGELS was closed for vacation. I had actually decided that it might be good to sign up for classes and learn to paint, and went to the studio with that intention. But the minute I entered she assumed I was accepting her modelling assignment, and introduced me to some of her students as such. She dismissed out of hand the notion of my enrolling as a student and proceeded with my tour.

I was led to a large room where there was a portrait session in progress. With her finger on her lips, she whispered, 'Look, this is our portrait studio; it's the best in the city.' In the centre, on a raised platform, an elderly African-American man sat on a comfortable chair in a reflective pose. Three deep horizontal lines of wisdom across his forehead and a thick head of silvery pepper hair added character to his attractive face. He sat very still, like a statue, while about fifteen students of various ages worked on canvases propped on large easels. All were deeply engrossed in creating their personal vision of this model.

A week later I found myself occupying that same chair, with the same students and their canvases surrounding me. I wore my favourite floral printed chiffon sari for each of the next five sessions, taking utmost care to sit in the exact same pose and ensure the folds of my sari were draped as in the previous session. The students would proudly show off their portraits of me, each capturing different angles, under the pretext of guiding me as I arranged myself.

All in all, it was the most tedious and unsatisfying job I have ever done! My body would freeze in its position and then my brain would go numb. Sometimes I would imagine a loud scream coming out of my throat, just to reassure my numb brain that I was still alive. That I was not a statue and this would soon come to an end. I couldn't wait to be done with the agreed six sittings. These were my first earnings, but I concluded that the $180 was not worth the torture. For a long time afterwards I avoided walking down the street of the art studio, though I did run into the owner on occasion. I used up an imaginative stash of excuses not to accept her invitation again.

One positive outcome of the ordeal, however, was that it opened up further opportunities for conversation with Andy. Humour had become my main device, and my suffering as an artist's model gave us something new to joke about. By then, the marriage had been consummated and our intimacy was gradually growing. Still, I did not feel fully accepted and embraced by him. I still walked on eggshells and feared his unexpected explosions. But the periods of painful silence had become fewer.

■

A couple of weeks before BAGELS was due to reopen, the director of the India Tourist Office met Andy and me at a friend's home and mentioned that he needed to fill a vacancy for a public relations position at the office. Andy encouraged me to take the job. It was only a few blocks away from our apartment and about three blocks from Andy's office.

I was thrilled to bits. Now I could walk to work with Andy in the mornings, though our schedules were very different and he still kept long hours. My new job gave me an opportunity to learn about the travel industry, particularly about India's rich and colourful history. Within three months, I was spotted by the *San Francisco Examiner* and featured on the first page of the newspaper, along with half the second page, under a big headline reading, 'A New Year, A New Face'. It featured photographs presenting me as an Indian icon who had taken up residence in San Francisco and as offering a dose of Indian culture to that city. It certainly drew plenty of focus to India as a travel destination.

I wasn't at all prepared for this kind of attention. Nevertheless, it was a coup of sorts and put me on the fast track to learn more about India's historic past and my own heritage. I was filled with a new sense of pride and started to look beyond the limitations of my emotional hunger at home. I had become the 'face' of India in a city where one rarely saw anyone from my country, except on the Berkeley or Stanford campuses.

Among the several calls I received was an amusing one from Mary Stanyan, the writer from the *Examiner* who had done the story. She phoned a few days after it appeared to tell me that the paper had received many comments and questions about the article. The response had been tremendous and they were very pleased. 'But here's an unusual one for you,' she said. 'The warden at San Quentin (an all-male prison) has requested poster-sized pictures of you as their "pin-up of the month". If you have no objection, may we send them a set of four photos?' Before I could muster a response, she quickly added, 'Please consider this a compliment.' I burst into laughter and she laughed with me. We just decided to go ahead. It would be the first time the prisoners would have a female pin-up, fully clothed from almost head to toe, in a sari! The pictures were sent, three in my sari and one close-up of my face. I was delighted to provide a morale boost to the occupants of San Quentin prison.

∎

My new job at the India Tourist Office had taken me away from BAGELS. It was time to visit the children and explain my absence from their lives. I brought them cupcakes and we had a farewell that was sad, yet happy at the same time. I promised to drop in on them periodically, and I kept my word. They had found a permanent place in my heart.

By 1967, San Francisco had become a magnet for the flower children and the centre of the free love movement among the American 'Baby Boomer' generation intent on transforming the world. 'The Summer of Love' had caught the imaginations of people from all walks of life, breaking down barriers of race, age, religion, nationality and profession. The new wave grew like a tsunami and the city attracted thousands of free-spirited young people from all over America and the world. They came to protest the Vietnam War with messages of love and peace, and free drugs and sex. Among their symbols of protest was their appearance, which included a strong Indian influence in their style of dress. The guru kurta and 'beggar beads' were a noticeable trend. Inspired by the highly publicized trip that the Beatles had made to India seeking nirvana with their guru, Maharishi Mahesh Yogi, many embraced transcendental meditation. Strains of sitar, sarod, flute and tabla were heard everywhere.

The most popular address for the enthusiasts of this phenomenon was at the crossroads of two streets, Haight and Ashbury. To hang out at Haight–Ashbury was either frowned upon by the elite society of San Francisco—not to mention President Johnson's America, who saw it as a curse—or it was considered the coolest spot in the world.

One day, when Andy's sister Madhu was visiting from Washington DC, the two of us decided to go on a voyeuristic tour to see what all the fuss was about. Most of the locals appeared 'stoned' on a cocktail of drugs. The dark interiors of cafés and boutiques were festooned with psychedelic lights of every colour. From nearly every storefront and apartment window above them, Janis Joplin's gut-wrenching laments mingled with the wry commentaries and calls to action of Joan Baez or Bob Dylan. The Doors and Jimi Hendrix vied with the strings of the sitar and the beats of the tabla to draw listeners into the record shops on every block. It was a perpetual festival day and night, as if humanity in this square mile had been possessed by some transformative force.

As Madhu and I traced our way through the myriad happenings on the streets, our saris garnered constant attention. Passers-by would stop and beam, or give us a hug, hand out a flower or perform a namaste. They saw us as the embodiment of the dream they were pursuing. A couple of times we were even asked whether we were real or fake Indians. The East and the West had finally met. It was a 'happening' in the true sense of the word. Needless to say, I found myself quite drawn to that district long after Madhu was gone. Though had the people there known me, they would have fitted me into the 'square' slot!

When Madhu and I related our experiences to Andy and some other friends, they were horrified that we had dared risk such a trip. The media had painted a rather lurid and dark picture about this 'hippie phenomenon', linking it with free sex, drugs, lack of hygiene and violence. There were the participants and then there was the rest of the world, which judged them harshly, as if they were strange beasts from another planet. I saw it as a unique and fascinating phenomenon and was always ready to visit if a guest showed interest. In a strange way, the combination of my failed marriage and the discovery of America's new enthusiasm for Eastern culture made a deep impression on my yet-naïve mind, and contributed to the shaping of my character. I still cherish the memory of those idealistic times.

8

Hot Chocolate

Dr Sanky Mukerji and his feisty American wife, Betty, lived more than an hour away from the city, in the Napa Valley wine country. They were close friends of Andy, and I was very fond of them and their two young daughters, Elizabeth and Victoria. One evening, during one of Andy's trips out of town, Sanky and Betty dropped by the apartment for a drink, as they often did. This time they insisted on taking me out to a dinner party in their friend's restaurant, where a legendary artist from Chicago was to be honoured, following the opening of his highly publicized exhibition.

The restaurant was just a few blocks away, and we were finishing a light dinner when there was a commotion at the entrance. Multiple cameras flashed as Adil Chowdhry*, the eagerly anticipated guest, arrived. As I watched all the fuss at the doorway with amusement, the VIP group headed in our direction. The star artist was staring directly at me, almost as if he were leading the host and hostess—who had long awaited his arrival at the door—straight to our table. I looked away, not wanting to be caught ogling. But before I knew it, he was being introduced to the Mukerjis and to me as the wife of the Air India manager. He took my hand, his eyes piercing into mine, and started to tell me about his most recent experience on Air India, which he had rather enjoyed. But he was cut short as the hosts urged him to move along to meet other guests across the room.

Something electric happened in that instant when he held my hand. My heart missed a beat. I instinctively felt that I was in the

---

*I have given this artist a pseudonym to respect the privacy of his family.

wrong place. I began to feel insecure without my husband. I needed to leave, because I feared catching his glance again. I found an excuse to depart, but the Mukerjis wouldn't hear of it. So we lingered at the bar for a while, as the star settled around a table with his closest friends, some thirty feet away. Unabashedly, he continued to stare in our direction, over the heads of scores of guests who sat in between. I became very uncomfortable and swivelled my bar stool towards the bar, presenting my back to the rest of the room. The Mukerjis, noticing my discomfort, finally agreed to take me home, but not before getting Adil Chowdhry's autograph. I waited at the bar stool while they went over to his table. Moments later, Betty rushed back and pulled me by the elbow, whispering, 'He wants to talk to you.'

I walked in the artist's direction, oddly feeling like I was betraying my husband with each step. With a warm smile on his face, he asked, 'Were you at the opening this evening?'

'No. I will go in two days, after my husband returns from his tour,' I explained.

Adil turned to the Mukerjis and suggested, 'Why don't you all come tomorrow afternoon? We will have another private reception there for a group of VIPs. You won't need an invitation, I will be there. In fact, we are showing a retrospective film at 5 p.m.'

As we thanked him and turned around to leave, he gave me a last deep, piercing look, which the Mukerjis did not miss. In the car ride back home, Betty was like a gushing teenager. 'I don't believe it. An invitation from the master artist himself!' They were so overcome by this event that they decided to come up to my apartment at that late hour to have a nightcap, to rejoice in and stretch the moment. But I was weighed down with an inexplicable inner war between fear and anticipation. The fear came from a feeling that I had been targeted. The anticipation came from my starved emotions that had hungered for a flicker of attention from the object of my dreams for over a year now, my husband Andy. Adding to my confusion was Betty, double cognac in hand, exclaiming how thrilling this whole thing was.

Suddenly, she whirled around, looked at me and said, 'We only got invited because of you, Bina. I bet he won't even remember us tomorrow.' Her candour only increased my discomfort.

Sanky was quite amused by all this, but seemed to agree with her. At some point in their euphoria they decided, 'What the hell, let's call him now and ask him to join us for a nightcap. That is, if it is okay with you, Bina.' They looked at me imploringly.

I thought this was going too far, but despite my protestations Betty picked up the phone, called the restaurant and asked for Mr Chowdhry. While she waited she jabbered away nervously, rehearsing how she would invite him. When she heard his voice, she panicked. She handed the phone to me and ordered, 'Bina, say something!'

'Oh my God' were the first words that came out of my mouth. Then somehow I mustered enough courage to say, 'My friends, the Mukerjis, and I wondered if you might like to join us for a drink. We just wanted to express our appreciation.'

The long silence from the other end made me cringe. He must have thought we were some gushing fans who couldn't contain themselves. A long moment later, he said, 'Let's see, I'm with my friends.'

'Please bring them along,' I offered.

'Give me your address and phone number,' he said. I did, and we hung up.

I was upset with Betty for putting me through this ordeal. Everything about it was uncharacteristic of me. 'I am feeling so humiliated,' I said. 'I don't think he even noted the address and phone number I gave him.'

Realizing how mortified I was, the Mukerjis' enthusiasm finally began to dampen. They hastened to finish their drinks and prepare for their long drive home. Just then, the doorbell rang. Barely twelve minutes after the phone call. We froze and stared at each other in disbelief. He was on his way up with a couple of his friends, to the third floor, where I lived!

For the next two hours, Adil regaled us with fabulous anecdotes from his most recent world tour. He had a mesmerizing gift for storytelling, and all of us were transported to the wonderful places he described. I learned that he spoke seven international languages fluently and had a photographic memory for numbers and addresses. When I offered him a drink, I was rather surprised and impressed to find that he was a teetotaler. He decided to walk into the kitchen to see what he might find, and settled for hot chocolate when he saw that there was only orange juice and milk in the fridge. He had a manner that put one at ease, with no airs about him, especially considering his success and recognition.

Time flew by. After 2 a.m. the Mukerjis, with their long drive ahead, managed to bring the enchanting evening to an end. They offered to drop Adil at his hotel. A couple of times during the evening I had brought up Andy's name, stating my regret that he was missing such a great evening in his home. But I no longer felt uncomfortable in this stranger's company.

Twenty minutes after their departure, by which time I had cleaned up, changed and gone to bed, my phone rang. It was Adil.

'I just called to tell you how much I enjoyed the evening, and to thank you for the delicious hot chocolate.' I was too surprised to muster a response.

He continued, 'I'm amazed how close my hotel is to your apartment. I'm used to staying up late, especially on launch nights, so I will be going out for a walk. I wouldn't mind some more of the hot chocolate and a chat, if you're up to it.'

As my surprise turned to apprehension I quickly found words. 'Remember when you had your third cup of chocolate, we ran out of milk? So no more, I'm afraid.' I didn't want to sound rude so I added, 'Besides, San Francisco has a high drug-related crime rate. You should not be stepping out of your hotel at this hour.'

He then asked about Andy, 'Is he Indian or American?'

'Indian,' I replied.

'He must be very special to have a wife like you,' he flirted.

'Yes. He is a very special man. I'm also very lucky to have a husband like him. You will understand when you meet him,' I assured him. 'We look forward to your exhibition tomorrow. Good night. And don't step out at night!' I closed the conversation.

The Mukerjis came to pick me up for the exhibition the next day, still riding high on the success of the night before.

'Andy is very foolish for not taking you on his trips,' Sanky said. 'Given half a chance, you could get stolen away by this dashing artist.'

I laughed it off, saying, 'Andy never has to fear any such thing.'

At the gallery I realized that I was in the company of a man who had world-class stature in his profession. I had never met a person with such recognition before. I was in the domain of the elite. The place was packed to the nines with admirers, eminent collectors, art dealers and some of San Francisco's important social set, whom Adil engaged with his easy charm. As we got ready to leave, he invited us to join him for dinner the following night, and to include Andy. That was music to our ears. All the way home, we celebrated our good fortune. The Mukerjis jested that it was, in fact, the delicious hot chocolate that had won his friendly overtures.

The following night, after Andy's visit to the exhibition with a business colleague, we all met up for dinner. It was a fascinating evening, with conversation ranging from world cuisine to art to politics. Throughout dinner, I was receiving more than average attention from our host, but Andy seemed not to notice or care.

Later, on the drive home, the Mukerjis jested with Andy, 'Don't take your wife for granted. You have competition from other sources.' They continued, 'She might get swept off her feet with that kind of focus from another man.'

To my astonishment, Andy retorted, 'Thank God she's getting someone's attention. Maybe now she will get off my back.'

■

My niece Mira, the daughter of my eldest sister Kiki, was only three years younger than me. She had married just months after me and now lived in Los Angeles (LA) with her husband, Jotu Advani. Since

LA was just an hour's flight away and our travel was free, Andy and I went there a few times. The men enjoyed each other's company and, on those weekends, I would get to see Andy's softer side. Those were some of the happiest days of my marriage. Mira and Jotu's cosy affection for each other would start to rub off on us a bit. Weekends at the Mukerji estate in Napa were also rather happy. In their company, there was always much wining, dining, laughing and taking hilarious digs at each other. Sanky's daughters—Elizabeth, the budding artist and Victoria, the aspiring cellist—engaged as equals in our company. I enjoyed watching the interplay of Betty's wicked sense of humour and Andy's repartee. Such occasions led to cementing our path of communication. They became my favourite family.

On the other hand, there were a couple of Andy's bachelor friends who clearly contributed to our unhappy times. They were his drinking buddies and had a jargon of their own, spiked with peals of laughter that I never understood. Their presence always seemed to widen the divide between Andy and me. Felix, the Romanian Jew with fierce blue eyes that revealed angry memories of the Holocaust, was married to Dora, whom I had cherished since the days she had looked after me in my first week in San Francisco. They were about fifteen years older than me. Felix was a borderline alcoholic with a rather direct and caustic sense of humour, which he often used to abuse his wife. Dora took it in her stride, ignoring his jibes most of the time. But once in a while she would give him a good lashing with her fiery Latin tongue. I witnessed many ear-shattering fireworks in their company, much to my shock. The crude language would sometimes cause me to leave the room. In time, they became more sensitive to my discomfort, while I, in turn, began to adjust to this dark side of their relationship. We ended up adapting to each other's cultures, a compromise from my side.

Given the choice, I would have preferred to avoid Felix, but I had no choice in the matter because Andy loved his macho friend's musings and racy sense of humour. He had even begun to emulate Felix, sometimes taking on his persona. Soon enough, our relationship at home began to resemble theirs. Andy took to abusing me verbally, much in the way that Felix abused Dora. Except that I didn't have the Latin heat to fight back. These verbal abuses, usually without any apparent provocation, took permanent root in our relationship. I probably reinforced it by not retaliating or standing up in my own defence. I had begun, in other words, to facilitate this abhorrent behaviour—taking on the role of the verbally-battered wife.

Alas, verbal abuse became common in our household and continued throughout our thirteen years of married life. Andy thought nothing of throwing a couple of demeaning barbs at me in the company of friends and acquaintances. In response, I made a practice of dismissing it as if it were a joke. This exchange seemed to satisfy his macho side. I had become Andy's Dora. Some friends commented about their discomfort in our company and asked why I tolerated this behaviour. I had no answer.

This relentless assault made me relate to blues music. In fact, I had begun to appreciate the blues so much that I had gathered a collection of those singers whose pain touched me the most. Placing myself in the company of blues composers and singers, if only as a listener, gave me a sense of belonging, a perverse sense of comfort.

Meanwhile, we were frequently invited to LA by Mira and Jotu for various events. During one of these trips we met the dynamic conductor Zubin Mehta and his parents. We became good family friends very quickly. Zubin won our hearts almost instantly with his magnetic personality and zany sense of humour, not to mention his amazing talent!

We became his 'Little India', as he hardly had any Indian friends at the time, and received many a coveted invitation to attend his brilliant concerts and, occasionally, some of his rehearsals. His mother Tehmi, who had also been starved of Indian company, embraced our presence and our close connection with India, and decided to turn this it into an opportunity to enhance the image of India in LA.

One day, after a sumptuous Parsi lunch at their home, she suggested to me, 'It is always such a delight to see you and Mira in beautiful Indian dresses. Why don't we put together an Indian fashion show and raise a little money for starving orphans in India?' It was hugely presumptuous, and though it took us by total surprise, Mira and I exchanged glances and struck an instant chord with this idea that Mrs Mehta had just thrown out.

'Why not?' in short, was our chorused reply. A sudden burst of excitement filled the air as both Mira and I started our brainstorming to identify pretty young Indian ladies in our tiny worlds in San Francisco and Los Angeles. Mira herself was highly accomplished, beautiful and loaded with traditional Indian flair—having actually graduated from Lady Irwin College, unlike me. Not to mention that she was a classmate of Ritu Kumar, who was to become one of India's most renowned designers for traditional wear. This was back in 1968, when our fashion attire was restricted to a limited way of wearing saris and the churidar kameez. Mira and I had once experimented with wearing mini kurtas showing the leggy churidars, which raised many an eyebrow in the Indian community in London. These days both of us mostly wore saris, as newly married girls, and drew attention that often irritated us.

We quickly got down to brass tacks and let Mrs Mehta be our guiding light. She suggested that we do our—and perhaps California's—first Indian charity fashion event at the newly opened Dorothy Chandler Pavilion, which later expanded and became the venue for the Academy Awards. We were to occupy a small section of it. Zubin had recently inaugurated it with a concert, and he ruled the culture scene in LA. Mira and I needed to pull together a captivating fashion show worthy of this address.

Mrs Mehta had already been a patron and provider to a charity project for orphans in India. We pooled all our respective resources for this project. My experience at the India Tourist Office, combined with the support that Andy's Air India office could provide, gave us a vigorous start. The idea of bringing India's rich cultural heritage to LA, at a time when the country was seen as an impoverished nation with an empty begging bowl in hand, was a huge and exciting challenge. We exhausted every avenue available to us, including our personal wardrobes that spilled over with colourful saris, numerous untouched finery from our trousseaus, and borrowed costumes and jewellery. Mira managed to find enough beautiful new brides and career ladies of Asian origin for us to display about forty outfits. We even managed to sneak in a couple of Mexican and Philippina beauties to model for us!

Our event created a buzz that lasted for days and appeared widely in the print media. We made our impact on the elite society of Los Angeles, and raised a handsome contribution for Mrs Mehta's charity. Andy supported the effort, and I carved my first footprint on the path of fundraising, which was to become a passion for me in later years—especially in the world of women's and children's aid, later extending to AIDS awareness and rape issues.

The snowballing publicity from our maiden effort at fundraising with an Indian theme had caught the imagination of some of the important citizens of LA. To our utter surprise, we were invited to present another such event shortly thereafter! Of course, getting the maestro Zubin Mehta's support made a huge difference and opened every door for us. One small step at a time, my life was forging new paths to a distant future.

■

Meanwhile, in San Francisco, I was receiving attention from Adil. He would call me occasionally and update me on his most recent adventures. His sense of humour and his talent for human observation was a refreshing diversion from my dry life. I was riveted by his anecdotes, which could sometimes go on for over an hour. On one such occasion, about three months after we first met, he told me that he was coming to San Francisco for a day and would like to have lunch with me. I told him I would ask Andy to book a nice restaurant for the three of us. He advised me not to do anything until he had reached San Francisco and worked out his schedule.

After arriving in San Francisco, he called at about noon. His meeting was in the vicinity, and he would drop by for a few minutes, around 2 p.m. I nervously waited for him in the lobby of my building, as I did not want him to come up to the apartment when I was alone. As soon as he alighted from his taxi, I stepped out hurriedly on to the street. 'Let's walk to Andy's office,' I suggested. 'There are many restaurants near there and it is only a few blocks away.'

He protested, 'I don't have time for lunch, unfortunately, but I have something important to show you and it is private.' Apprehension gripped me at the thought of walking into the apartment alone with a man other than my husband.

'It's an interesting piece of paper and I need to show it to you. Don't look so worried.' I put my reluctance aside, and with some trepidation rode up the three floors in the elevator with him, trembling like a guilty child, feeling like a sinner, but trying my best not to let it show.

I insisted on seeing what he had to show me as soon as we were in the corridor. But he was in a hurry to get into the apartment, pressing me to pull out the keys and unlock the door. The moment we stepped inside, he threw his arms around me in a tight embrace and urged me towards the sofa. In total shock, I pushed him away, protesting loudly. I tried opening the door to show him out, but he pushed it shut. Finally, I broke into helpless sobs. He suddenly stopped and threw his head upwards, slowly turning it from side to side as if he was feeling shame and regret. Then he turned to look at me and in a soft and compelling manner, he said, 'Sorry. I'm so sorry...please forgive me, I lost my mind.' As I pulled away, he added, 'You know, I have been struggling to get you out of my mind. You have made such an impact on me. I would never want to hurt you...'

He walked me to the sofa and sat me down. He pulled out an envelope from his pocket and explained, 'This is my itinerary for the next six months.' He spoke very gently, one careful word at a time, trying to calm my fear. 'I am going away to Europe on a lengthy tour across the continent.' He looked deep into my eyes, which were welling with tears.

'I am aware of your unhappy marriage,' he continued. 'One thing which has attracted me so much to you is the way you respond with innocent joy at the mention of Andy, even though you are trapped in a completely empty relationship.' He poured this out in one long breath. Then he added, 'Anyone who sees you two together knows it.' At one point in this conversation, I consciously moved his hands away from me and let him know that he did not have the liberty to touch me. He respected my gesture and kept his hands away.

Then, with a serious look, he continued in a whisper, looking deep into my eyes, as if wanting the full sound of each word to enter my psyche and nothing else. 'That night when I entered the restaurant, the first person I saw was you. Even as our eyes met the first time, from that distance, something happened to me. There and then, I knew I had to know you better. I wanted you immediately. Something guided me straight in your direction.

'Thank God for the Mukerjis!' he continued. 'Had they not called me, perhaps we would not be together right now. I was somehow expecting that call, and I rushed immediately to reach your home. Our destiny was etched the instant I came through the door in the restaurant and saw your silhouette on the bar stool in that smoky room.'

I felt almost paralysed. His declaration sent shivers through me. Was God playing tricks with me and arousing my deeply buried, unfinished symphony with Shammi Kapoor? Adil's words echoed in my heart. I had been living out a hopeless dream, trying to fulfil a programme instilled in me from my childhood. Was God giving me a second chance? I was swept by a tidal wave that raced like a roller coaster from my heart to my head—up and down. There arose a strange urge inside me to fall into a deep sleep and never wake up. Nothing had prepared me for this!

Adil was trying to extract a promise from me. 'Please consider my offer. I want to marry you. I will wait until you leave Andy. I will not touch you till then.' He wanted my assurance immediately. My heart, my head and my moral duty waged a war inside me. My mind was exploding. Like a yo-yo, I was sinking and soaring with extreme emotions. He witnessed my torment and reached out to comfort me. His gentle touch opened a floodgate of tears that I had stored over the past year. At last, I could simply let the torrent flow.

There was a feeling of God's presence in the long moments of silence that followed. Neither he nor I spoke. We just did what was natural. We looked deep into each other's eyes and entered one another's soul.

This awareness of each other's presence empowered us into a state of acceptance and dignity. It seemed that my prayers of the past fourteen months had just been answered. With this realization, another gigantic burst of tears took over, with hysterical strains of laughter mixed in. These were tears of joy. Then, moments later, I sank again into a fear of failure and the realization that I was going to have to acknowledge a broken marriage. That was unthinkable.

The invisible wall I had built to contain my misery was crumbling. My new messenger of love watched me as my mind and heart spun through these emotions. By now, he was weeping with me. He then held me close, in silence, like a mother cradling her child, and transmitted a miraculous energy to me in that embrace. We were engulfed in an innocent, sacred space.

When I opened my eyes, it seemed that a new world had replaced the one that had just crumbled. I felt Shammi's presence, as if he were validating the new course of my life. God seemed to reside within me now. More than two hours had passed. I was not capable of advancing to a sexual relationship outside of marriage. Yet, we had become true lovers.

■

We suddenly realized we were very hungry. I was now about to learn about Adil's cooking skills. He walked me to the kitchen and quickly assessed the possibility of a meal with a peek into the fridge and the small pantry. He saw a container of milk and said jovially, 'Oh, I can have hot chocolate today!' We laughed like children. I watched him with admiration as he put together a delicious meal of spicy chicken and vegetables, while I cooked the rice. The child in me was dancing with joy. I was a new person inside the same skin when I went to the garage with him and rode with him to the airport.

'I am going to call you every single day, no matter where I am,' he promised. He was off to New York, then on to Europe the next day, and would return to New York six months later.

True to his promise, he called me every weekday for long hours and enthralled me with his tales of glorious places, eminent people, the paintings he had sold and the accolades he was receiving on his tour. Surprisingly, I managed to maintain equilibrium at home with Andy, knowing that I would have to find the appropriate moment to break the news to him. The strange thing was that my role of adoring wife to Andy continued as it had been. I still loved him and yearned for his crumbs of emotional gratification. I was pleased whenever he gave me a smile or acknowledged my presence in some way. No matter what, I had to win this battle of affection and love with Andy. The goal had been set.

I now believed that it was perfectly possible to love several people simultaneously and keep the relationships neatly apart without hurting anyone, if it was sensibly and sensitively handled. Shammi occupied a very tender place in my heart. I knew that I loved Adil dearly, beyond anything I had known. Then there was Andy, the reluctant husband who simply did not want to fit into the fantasy image that I had been in love with all my life.

No one had ever proved that this was unachievable. Isn't it like loving three different desserts equally, or having three best friends, or three favourite songs? There is no disloyalty in that.

There are so many aspects to loving, and the human being's capacity to adjust is infinite. The purity and potency of that reality has been lost to religious and man-made dogmas.

9

Moving Out

PROVIDENCE WAS AGAIN at work. Strangely coincident with Adil's proposal and invitation to leave my marriage, Andy was transferred to New York. We packed up our lives in beautiful San Francisco and moved to the Big Apple.

Compared to the San Franciscans, the New Yorkers could often be harsh. People were tuned to a different pace. Time was money. Everybody seemed to be in a hurry to get it and, perhaps, angry that they weren't getting it fast enough. The word 'friend' had an altogether different meaning here.

No one seemed to have the time or patience to stop and talk. God forbid (a very New Yorker expression) if you lost your way and needed directions. One of the first rude shocks I received in the city was when I got lost and asked a passer-by, 'Excuse me, do you know which way is Hudson Street?' He snapped back, 'No I don't, do you?' He hurried on before I could conjure up a smart retort. I would later develop a stock of them.

A typical New York story is one where some elderly lady, using a walker with difficulty, is trying to board a city bus. The disinterested driver looks down at her and opines, 'Lady, you don't need a bus. You need an ambulance.'

Cold. Those times have mercifully changed!

I felt like a tiny insect during my first few months in Manhattan, dwarfed by the towering buildings, flustered by the noise, the traffic, the flow of uncaring humanity. Most of the time I wanted to curl up and shut myself off from the overwhelming power and heartlessness of it all. I had to make a choice between giving in to my fears or learning to find my place in this new environment. Once I opted for the obvious choice, it became easier to adjust to the steel and concrete powerhouse that is New York City. Of course, I had the added incentive of a friendship waiting to lead me to the altar. That in itself was perhaps motivation enough.

Andy and I rented a large one-bedroom apartment on the upper west side of Manhattan. It was considered a 'mixed' neighbourhood, some twenty-five blocks away from Harlem, and was all we could afford on Andy's salary. From there, Andy could commute on the subway to his office in an elite area of midtown. I, meanwhile, spent my time getting to know the neighbourhood. From 96th Street, where we lived, it was an easy walk into New York's Central Park in one direction, and Broadway and Riverside parks in the other. But whichever way I went on my exploratory strolls, I saw sadness and depression. There seemed a pent-up anger in the community, which was largely a mix of Black Americans, Latinos, some Philippinos and now Indians. The few white Americans I saw were generally senior citizens—retired professors and nurses, pensioners, the man running the local laundromat. On my walks I found no tales of adventure to bring home, unlike in San Francisco, where there was a pleasant surprise around every corner.

At home I found that Andy was beginning to show little expressions of tenderness that I had not seen before. Our communication, when we spoke, was marginally better. We spent the weekends setting up the apartment, delighting in the experience of hunting for furniture that would belong to us, not to his company. On Saturdays we would go to auctions, the only affordable option within our budget. We discovered, to my joy, that we had similar tastes. Our apartment was soon charmingly furnished and decorated with a cosy, inviting and eclectic flavour. All pulled together on a shoestring budget! A few Indian pieces of art and artifacts added an ethnic character to our home.

It was several months before I felt comfortable enough to travel on the subway alone, to venture beyond the immediate neighbourhood and explore the larger city. I had by now made some Indian friends, among them Andy's colleagues from work.

Meanwhile, the phone calls from Europe continued. Adil managed to fill my heart with a brightly coloured canvas of adventures from his travels. My excitement spiralled as the day of his return to New York drew near. He was already making plans for what we would do. He wanted to invite Andy and me to several events to which he was committed, warning me that he would always have a date with him. He wanted to create a delicate balance, and I welcomed it. I observed that I was already balancing 'duty and temptation' with devious skill.

Within a few days of his arrival, we were attending events and parties at venues which Andy and I would otherwise not have been able to afford, nor have been invited to. We were being exposed to the privileged world of the rich and famous. For the first time I had an opportunity to wear the beautiful saris and jewels from my trousseau that had remained locked in suitcases for nearly two years.

On the other hand, there was a Cinderella-like quality to these grand events. Each time after we had wined and dined and mingled with New York's jet set, we had to return home to a part of town where cabs were reluctant to go because they couldn't easily get a return passenger. Other guests arrived and departed in their chauffeur-driven limousines. The contrast of these glittering nights versus our humble uptown digs often left a bittersweet taste to it all.

Some days I would venture out for lunch with Adil to a trendy restaurant. His favourite was the Ginger Man near Lincoln Center, where inevitably we would be joined by some famous artist, actor, musician or writer. One regular was Marc Chagall, the renowned artist, who had at the time been commissioned to paint murals for the grand entrance of the Metropolitan Opera House at Lincoln Center. He would join our table and get into animated conversations, often sharing his views about other great artists with his charming accent, which I guessed to be a combination of Russian peppered with French. I never grasped much of what he said, but was thrilled to meet this frail, wiry man, with large expressive eyes in hollow cradles, then in his eighties. His long, gesticulating hands with knotted fingers always had a residue of paint.

■

We had been in New York for three months when I was offered a temporary job. It was during Diwali season, sometime in October, that I met a vivacious, tough and impressive lady called Mani Mann. She ran America's best Indian merchandise shop, Sona, 'The Golden One', which was owned by the Indian government's handicraft and handloom ministry. The location, décor and size of the store showed that it was a highly prized operation. It was just off Fifth Avenue, four blocks from Andy's office. Mani had a lot of flair and a certain haughty way about her that appealed to me. I was drawn to her, even though I was a bit overawed by her no-nonsense attitude.

I was visiting the store one afternoon with my friend Bharati Chadda to see a mutual friend, Maya Sawhney, who worked there as a sales assistant. Within minutes of our being introduced, Mani offered me a job for the upcoming festival season. It was going to pay a total of $400, she said almost apologetically, but it sounded like a lottery win to me. After a phone call to Andy, who saw no reason to object, I accepted. Everything about the job appealed to me, and in no time at all I was learning about Indian textiles, arts and crafts, along with the knack of dealing with a wealthy and discerning clientele.

Sona was a gathering place for like-minded people, whether they were clients, acquaintances or close friends. I befriended a charming young student from Bangalore, Arjun Sajnani, who worked as a part-time waiter in a trendy restaurant nearby. Every once in a while he would drop by and feed us spicy anecdotes from his workplace. One day he breezed in to share some good tidings: 'I found a $100 bill on the chair after a client had left the restaurant. I gave the money to the boss and guess what? He gifted it to me!' That was a lot of money in 1968! Excitedly pulling out the bill from his pocket and waving it at us, he offered to buy us all a drink and then froze mid-sentence. Jacqueline Kennedy had walked into the store.

We girls sprang into action. She was friendly, soft-spoken and told us she had a hair appointment with her favourite stylist, Kenneth, who was nearby. But first, she wanted to visit one of her favourite stores—ours! She spent almost two hours browsing, trying on saris with help from me and another sales assistant, and examining odds and ends of furniture. She bought miles of silk fabric to furnish her apartment. It was a landmark day for Mani and her girls.

We didn't even notice that Arjun had been hanging around all the while she was shopping. When she was ready to leave, her hands full of packages, he gallantly offered to carry her bags and walk her to Kenneth's. Some ten minutes later he danced back in through the door. 'She kissed me on the cheek to thank me for carrying her bags and said I was an exemplary gentleman!' he exclaimed, nearly faint with excitement. The joy over the $100 bill had faded into nothingness.

The next day, the world learnt from screaming headlines that Jackie Kennedy had married Aristotle 'Ari' Onassis, the Greek playboy shipping magnate. She had chosen to have a big shopping spree the day before—in her favourite Indian shop, with us!

Added to such adventures was the unpredictable delight of friends popping in. Zubin would sometimes drop in with a friend or two on a little shopping spree and engage us all in his zany jokes that would have us laughing long after his departure. Then there was the renowned violinist, Alexander Schneider, who admired our boss Mani and often made surprise visits to the store. Ismail Merchant was almost a regular; his very dear friend, Purnima Aggarwal (now Jain) worked at the store. On the odd days he was in town, Adil would arrive, loaded with sandwiches and milkshakes for all the girls, and regale us with his inexhaustible store of amusing tales. The four-week job ended all too soon, but I remained part of the Sona gal pals and popped in anytime I needed to fuel up on a dose of happiness.

At home, I was getting increasing attention from Andy and we would actually have meaningful conversations. It didn't matter that many such conversations ended in silence because of my lack of exposure to his world, which he attributed as ignorance on my part. His lack of patience matched my lack of knowledge, I thought, justifying his barbs to buy my peace. But I had allowed this submissive pattern from the first week of our marriage. Now it was set in stone. I made a practice of notching up the times I could slip my arm around him without being rebuffed, which proved he was getting fonder of me and acknowledging my role as his wife.

•

I had managed to slot the two men in my life into separate compartments of love. I did not believe there was a conflict, or even a trespass of a moral code. I believed, in fact, that a quirk of fate had brought me the gift of love that had been snatched away from me in that fateful week in Bombay. I wasn't allowing myself to predict how this would end. I felt God would simply deliver me to my destiny. All I hoped for was that no one would get hurt and that somehow, my role as the dutiful wife would simply transfer to my beloved at the correct time. My prayer at Sai Baba's shrine had its own timing, I knew. I simply needed patience.

I explored the love legends of Krishna and the gopis depicted in song, dance, art, theatre, folklore and religion. 'Where did that come from?' I asked myself. I was intrigued. Was it just a myth, or did it reflect a basic truth about human nature? I drew a parallel between my life and Krishna's love life. It seemed analogous. I did not feel any overwhelming guilt because both my paths were pure in love, balanced equally on a backbone of integrity.

Lord Krishna, one of the ten incarnations of Vishnu the Preserver, revered by millions of Hindus all over the world, was always with his beloved Radha. Their love, their ras lila, is represented in every form of art and entertainment in India. He supposedly had three wives, while Radha had her husband. Little has been written about these spouses. Radha was also seven years older than Krishna. Their games of love depict pain, joy, play, anger, frivolity, anguish, attachment, detachment and every other emotion, culminating in a godlike embrace of surrender and ecstasy. It is an inexplicable, divine legend of love. Authors, poets and intellectuals have analysed it over the centuries, but the interpretation of Radha and Krishna's love for each other transcends all reasoning.

'So,' I asked myself, 'why can't the god and goddess of love be my role models?' Each one of the thousands of Hindu gods and goddesses has been a role model for their devotees. Hinduism addresses human failure and human victory in the same degree. It is really about a test of endurance in every human's life. And after every form of attachment throughout one's material and physical lives, the ultimate aim is to achieve detachment. I was too inexperienced to fully understand or appreciate this truth in my twenties. I had to stumble along my personal journey and allow my senses to be awakened with every experience.

By November, Adil had become restless and wanted a commitment from me. He wanted me to talk to Andy and make arrangements to move out of his life. This was a difficult task, even though I knew it was inevitable. I had become used to the convenience and ease of the duality.

'I am sure Andy is aware of our love,' Adil said, 'and will not come in our way. Andy has never been committed to this marriage—all your friends know that.' He reminded me gently, 'Besides, he has been a facilitator in our relationship right from the beginning, hasn't he?'

At that point we were still not sexually intimate. I had been adamant that he not expect that of me as long as I was still Andy's wife, and he had respected this. Of the several girlfriends he would bring along to parties and events, I became very close to two. I still remain friends with them to this day. They were both aware of our secret and supported our romance. One of them confided in me, 'I feel privileged to be part of the "inner" circle.'

By the end of the month, during one of Andy's tirades, I found the opportunity and the courage to tell him I would not tolerate his abuses any longer. I packed a couple of bags and left for London. He made no attempt to stop me.

It was much easier than I had expected.

10

The Dilemma

MY FAMILY IN London was overjoyed to see me. They knew how unhappy I had been, and they wholeheartedly supported my decision to leave Andy.

They learned about the new developments in my life and the love that I had found. They respected my wishes and firmly believed that their prayers had been answered. That month of December 1968 was the happiest of my life. My beloved Adil had flown back to Chicago to fulfil his work commitment, which was to finish on 26 December. He promised to be in London by the end of the month, after which we would get engaged.

I made arrangements to file for divorce with a very good lawyer that my brother knew. It appeared like an easy case, as I was seeking nothing from Andy and I had 'aggravated incompatibility' as grounds for the divorce. My happiness was so infectious, it seemed to beam out everywhere I went. Even the unpredictable British weather seemed to cooperate—London had more sunny days that December than ever previously recorded. The world seemed to be in sync with me. I could now dance to the rhythm of my own heartbeat.

Daily phone calls came from Chicago, sometimes three or four in a day, just to say the three magical words that would send my heart fluttering. Through those phone calls, Adil got to speak to some of my family members. He had already been embraced as the long-lost son-in-law. On the morning of the twenty-sixth when we spoke, he declared, 'I am the happiest man alive! By the end of the day, I will be on that flight to London to be with you.' I was enraptured by the longing and joy in his voice.

Just moments after our call ended, the phone rang again. I was shocked to hear Andy's voice at the other end. He was weeping and incoherent, but it was unmistakably Andy. 'I have just realized what a mean and awful husband I have been to you these last two years.' I was dumbstruck. 'It has taken a lot of courage to make this call, but I'm not going to give up until you say you forgive me.'

'What?' I managed in a choked voice. 'What are you saying?' I made him repeat himself twice over, just to make sure I had heard him right. I couldn't believe he was saying the words I had craved to hear from him for so long. But why now?

'No, it's too late, Andy,' I replied. (In the two years we had been married I had never called Andy by his name, out of old-fashioned respect). 'Our marriage died a long time ago.' The words felt weak as I uttered them. It was like a bad dream where I had been overpowered and lost my voice. 'I am in love with someone else,' I managed to say.

'Please come back,' he pleaded. 'Give me one last chance. You will see, I am a changed man. I'll do anything for you, I beg you to come back.' I was stunned. This had to be the cruellest joke that fate, and perhaps Andy, had ever played on me. But as he repeated his words, over and over, the reality of it began to set in. What should I say? How should I respond? For so many months I had yearned to hear the words he was repeating over and over again. 'I love you! I love you! Like Romeo loved Juliet. I'll never stop loving you,' he cried. To me, it was as if a great general had just fallen. I almost wanted to prop him back up to his position of power. I couldn't bear it! How desperately, over the past year, I had craved for just crumbs of this declaration!

It was exactly two years since the day we had met. Ironically the same date on which, three years earlier, I had met Shammi. It was incredible, eerie, as if some great power was toying with my life.

'But it's too late now,' I mumbled repeatedly to his pleadings. My body had turned cold, yet I was breaking out in a sweat. The frozen words tumbled out again. 'You know there's another man in my life, who treasures me and respects and loves me for who I am.'

'But you have to give me another chance,' he pleaded.

It just didn't make any sense. This couldn't be the same hard-hearted man who had punished me and starved me of all love and affection. My heart began to go out to him as I heard him pleading, so unprepared and utterly confused was I.

'I can't take your insults and abuse any more. I'm not coming back,' I said weakly, yet with finality, and hung up.

Three minutes later he called again, seeming more in control of himself. He said, 'Okay, I'm flying out to London to fetch you personally. You will see the changed man I have become.' Before I could answer, he continued, 'You owe me just one chance.'

At that point my sister Rani, who was visiting from New York, walked into the room and saw my condition. Alarmed at my sudden change of mood, she stood before me, trying to make sense of what was going on.

'I will think it all over and call you back,' I told Andy and hung up.

I looked up at Rani, tears streaming down my face, and blurted out what had just happened. We both sat there in shocked silence, staring into space. Rani lived in New York and had witnessed some of Andy's rude and abusive behaviour towards me. Her husband Atma had, however, managed to establish a thread of friendship with Andy through discussing philosophy and history. Both Rani and Atma had offered support and a shoulder for my tears on a few occasions, and Rani's presence in London at this time was a good omen for me. I could count on her insight and guidance.

We continued to sit in frozen silence, unable to fathom what to do next. For the next hour we picked at shreds to piece together a plan. I was in panic mode. My sister took charge and discussed all the pros and cons of the two options staring me in the face, but with no real solution. Then I had a brainwave. Foolish as it was, it seemed to make sense at the time. 'Let's consult a good astrologer.' I didn't want any of the family to know about my dilemma, not wanting to be influenced by them in any way. Rani reluctantly agreed.

I opened the London telephone directory, urgently scanning all the listings for astrologers in the northwest district of London, where we lived. It was as simple as that. It was also stupid. We would select geographically and then just trust fate that we had picked an authentic soothsayer, not a charlatan. One who would reliably guide my destiny. My sister must have sensed my torment, and in her wisdom she decided not to question my flawed judgement.

There were almost three pages of astrologers with Indian names. With the mad path I had chosen to take, I felt safer going to an Indian. Running against time and not wanting to risk losing my sister's collaboration, I simply picked one that was within our neighbourhood and made an appointment. My naïve mind overruled all rationality. Apparently, Andy still held some dark power over me.

I navigated our way in one of the family cars, into the neighbourhood I knew so well. My heart was pounding erratically and my mind was reeling. We drove in silence but I played out hundreds of conversations in my head.

We found our way to the astrologer's apartment on the first floor of a small house. It smelled of stale spices and sandalwood incense. Leaving our shoes at the door, we entered the house and were invited to sit on heavy cushions on the floor, across from him. A table covered with a saffron-coloured cloth stood in the corner, displaying several small deities in brass and silver. Another small table held burning incense sticks and a small bowl of water with a float of red and pink rose petals. A diwan lined one side of the room, and pictures of various Hindu gods and goddesses, all garlanded in plastic flowers, covered the other walls. When I saw the astrologer's face, with two red vermilion spots on his forehead, hair growing from his ears and eyes that seemed to radiate a deep knowledge, I decided I had made the right choice. I was a starved child who had just found a buttered hot toast dripping with honey. He was a priest attached to a local Hindu temple who could read horoscopes and make predictions.

To put us at ease, he smiled warmly and told us about himself and his practice. 'I was orphaned in childhood but had the good fortune of growing up in an ashram in Rishikesh, brought up by learned sadhus. I learned the science of astrology at the age of ten from my guru,' he said in a soft voice. His strong Indian accent had a charming British clip to it. His story fit right into my hopes and expectations, reinforcing the choice I had made.

Clearing my throat several times, I broke my silence. 'You see, I have come to you with a strange problem,' I said. A thought passed through my mind that if he really were a mind reader, why was it necessary to explain my problem? He could have saved me the awkwardness of my question. The thought passed.

'Aha, but everyone who comes here has strange problems. It is my duty to bring equilibrium into their lives.'

'But in my case, you see, I have gotten attached to two men. One is my husband, with whom I had an arranged marriage and for whom I feel a combination of duty, love and fear. We have been married for two years, but he has never shown me any affection or love. I tried very hard to win it, but it always seemed impossible. The other is a wonderful man who came into my life about ten months ago, showering me with the love for which I had been so hungry. He wants to marry me, and I feel the same way too. But I am filled with guilt and also unable to face the fact that my marriage has failed. Why doesn't my husband return my love? And will the promise of the other man's love be true and last throughout my life?' All these words just gushed out. I desperately hoped that he could see my dilemma better than I was explaining it.

The astrologer had looked intently into my face when I started my story. After a while, he had turned his face towards the ceiling, his eyes were closed, and he nodded at every word I spoke, as if savouring the taste of each one. He looked at my sister. She remained silent. She was always the quiet, noncommittal one in the family. He then stared back at me, as if in a trance. I hoped he could read the solution to my happiness in my face.

Suddenly he returned to the 'now' and asked if I had brought the janam patris, the horoscopes of the two men in question.

'No, I don't have their horoscopes, but I can give you their dates of birth. I'm sorry I don't know the times of birth, but I hope that won't prevent you from finding the answers.'

Hot flushes raced through my body as I gave him the birthdates, and within ten minutes he had drawn up the charts of the three protagonists of the drama—Adil, Andy and me. His opening line was, 'These two men have a karmic connection from your past life.'

'So what does that mean in my present life? I don't remember any of my past lives. I don't even know who I was!' I was bewildered by his response.

'It doesn't work like that,' he explained with a smile. 'Old karmic debts live on for many lifetimes.'

He then went on to describe the two men, 'The one you're married to is now a known devil. It won't get worse. I can see that you have had a very difficult struggle with him, but you already know all his faults. The trouble is, you are very timid, and scared of him. But you will surely encounter this problem with the other one too!'

My mind was whirling like a top and my surroundings seemed to be spinning too. 'You must stop living in fear, sister. Become assertive and stand up for your rights, and they will respect you more. But,' he continued, 'your husband has no patience and has a very hot temper due to a negative communication with his mother. He did not receive her love when he was young. He does love you, but is afraid to show it. If you work hard to find a harmonious path with him, you can do wonders for his future career and find happiness together.' He was echoing what I had tried my best to do these past two years but failed.

'What about the other chart?' I was anxious and very disappointed with what he had just said. It revealed no great secret. I felt I knew all this already.

'Oh, now this one, he's just like Lord Krishna.' He broke into a big smile, raising his eyebrows in glee, and looked straight at me, shaking his head slightly. 'He has hundreds of gopis, so many ladies around him. They follow him like a herd, everywhere he goes. What a magnetic chart! This one is going to be rich and famous, receive honours in his work. He is very artistic, with unusual gifts. But,' he shook his head very lightly, 'he will not be loyal to you, or anyone, for long.'

'Oh! But surely once he's married to me and finds fulfilment with me, he will learn to be loyal, won't he?' I exclaimed, trying to redefine what I had just heard.

He smiled again and slowly shook his head. 'No, his Venus and Jupiter are in an enhanced embrace position. He creates beauty and will be drawn to beauty all his life.' Then he added, for good measure, 'Though he does love you very much, and always will, you will have to share him with others occasionally. You're in a difficult situation,' he concluded. 'You will have to make up your mind and decide which of the two pains you can handle better.' He paused, then added, 'You see, every human's life has a dose of pain attached. That's when real growth comes.'

'What?' I was aghast. 'I have already experienced so much pain, and that's the reason I have come to you, Babaji! I can't decide. That is why I am here in the first place! Besides, how can I share my husband with other women? What kind of marriage would that be?' I was trying to reason with myself more than with him. I was now feeling more confused than ever and already regretted the folly of coming to see him.

My sister, unable to bear my despair, wrapped her arm around my shoulder. She rephrased the same questions and asked him again, hoping to salvage some sliver of hope from his interpretations. But he just repainted the same canvas with a different hue.

He tried to console me, saying, 'You have a wonderful chart, my sister, which gives you leadership qualities. Your own career will bring you wealth and fame. You will do great things in your life by your own efforts and leave a legacy with your name.' Such meaningless words, I felt. Nothing to remove the dark cloud that now engulfed me because I was forced to take a decision in an even more divided state of mind. I got into my car, thinking, 'What leadership? What legacy? Such empty words! All I want is love, and I have such an abundance of it to give—but who am I going to give it to?'

I could see no way forward. Time was running out. I had to have an answer. I sank into despair and my sister, sitting beside me, remained silent for most of the drive home. She was concerned for me but unable to offer any suggestions. The course of my life would have to be charted before the end of the day.

I tried my best to avoid acknowledging my brother Gulu's concern when he saw my crestfallen face as I entered the house. He was my favourite brother and best friend, and hadn't a clue about what had transpired in the last few hours.

He and I had the same zest for life, unlike my other siblings. He was closest to my age among my brothers, and by the time I was about eighteen years old we had formed similar tastes and had some common friends. Together, our energies created many a memorable London social event in the trendy 1960s. Gulu, with his larger-than-life magnetic personality, had a gift for throwing the best parties and ensuring that everyone present was having a good time. He enjoyed spreading his wealth among people he liked, and he liked a lot of people. My intended had a very similar personality. Both men attracted beautiful women like bees to honey. Yes, in fact, they both were heavily endowed with the 'Krishna' factor. But the resemblance ended there. One was a master in pursuit of the arts, the other in pursuit of serious commerce. Gulu's ambition had been to become a self-made millionaire before he turned twenty-three, and he had fulfilled it. He had even bought himself a gold Rolls Royce.

I kept no secrets from Gulu and knew I had to share my dilemma with him. He saw my tormented face and prepared for the bad news by going to the window and staring out of it, but his ear was tuned to my words. I slouched on his sofa, red-faced and tongue-tied.

'What's the matter?' he finally asked, anxiety in his eyes. When I didn't respond, he sat on the couch across from me, looking into my face with grave concern.

'Gulu, I have a huge problem.' My voice trembled as I fought back the tears. 'Andy called. Imagine, after six weeks, he remembered me.'

Gulu's eyes popped in shock. Andy's ill-treatment of me had riled all my brothers so much that the mere mention of his name was enough to raise their hackles. But even as I was choosing every word with care to express my predicament, the phone rang.

It was Adil from Chicago. 'I have just wrapped up my work. My flight is in a few hours. We are going to be together in less than twenty-four hours!' He was bursting with excitement.

At my silence, he repeated himself, 'Darling, did you hear me? I just wrapped up my last show of the season and within a few hours I will be on a flight to London, for that long-awaited day. The happiest day of my life!'

I could find no voice. He repeated his words and asked me to speak louder. 'I can't hear you,' he said.

I broke my silence and whispered words which Gulu, sitting next to me, had to strain to hear. 'I have no words to explain what has happened!' I said, in a broken voice. Shaking and trembling all over, I continued, 'Something weird has happened today.'

'What, honey? Are you okay?'

I was sliding into a vortex of doom. The words finally tumbled out, almost incoherently. 'I can't go through with this!' I burst into uncontrollable tears.

'What?' he exclaimed. 'What did you just say?'

I heard a dreadful fear in his question. Gulu was equally stricken at hearing my broken, wounded words, as I sobbed them out again. I heard a simple click on the other end. My heart shattered into a thousand pieces.

11

Diamond Earrings

I PACKED MY SUITCASE and flew back to New York amidst tears and protests from all the members of my family. It was a dark day in their lives and mine, but I had brought it upon myself. What had possessed me to be so self-destructive for the second time in my life? What perverted power led me to be influenced by the astrologer? I have never understood, despite endless introspection. Obviously, Andy's pleas caused flimsy hope to triumph over good sense. But deep down I lacked the moral courage to face yet another major decision, instead choosing to cling to the easier status quo.

The first few days after my return to New York were marked by long, awkward silences, which would be broken by Andy. He was trying to live up to his promise of being a good and loving husband. He would return early from his office in a cheerful mood, while I numbly performed my duties at home. He lent a helping hand in the kitchen and at times even succeeded at making me laugh. But the sting in my heart was unbearable. Equally heavy was the burden of having torn myself away from my family in such a state of desperation, causing them so much distress.

Andy never asked me about my 'other' and I offered no information. The subject made its way into the secret treasure box secured deep in my heart. I sometimes wondered where all that locked-up romantic passion would fly if it escaped from its tender chamber. My mind played games during my brooding moods—was it all pickling in there? Or would it get mouldy? In lighter moments I figured it was leaking out of its box and nurturing my senses, giving me an inner strength, feeding my instinct for survival and, above all, keeping me sane.

Just four days after I returned, Andy planned a romantic dinner for our second anniversary. That morning I got a call from Atma, my sister Rani's husband, who worked for a diamond merchant. With greetings and good wishes, he blurted out what was to have been Andy's surprise for me. 'You are a lucky girl. Andy has bought you a very special gift—a pair of fine diamond earrings. He insisted on buying you the best, premium quality diamonds.' I had never received a present or a compliment from Andy until then, but I just felt numb. How ironic, I thought to myself. I have traded my true love for a reward of diamond earrings. Later, I couldn't bring myself to wear them, not for a long time. In fact I still have an aversion to diamond earrings, and possessing or wearing diamonds does not hold the charm for me that it once did.

With this symbolic box of diamond earrings, Andy became amorous like never before. But my feelings had faded. As hungry as I had once been for this display of love, now when it came, I had no appetite for it. I felt dead. I had lost respect for myself, become a nonentity who had no attachment of any kind with anyone.

■

Two months later, calls from Bombay invited us to attend the wedding of Raj Kapoor's first child. His daughter Ritu was getting married to a prominent industrialist based in Delhi. Rajan Nanda was the eldest son of H.P. Nanda, who owned India's largest tractor company. H.P. Nanda's sister, Vimla Singh, was our neighbour in New York. We had just got to know her and her second husband, Jindi Singh, a few days before the Kapoor–Nanda wedding announcement.

The Singhs were a delightful couple, and Vimla-ji in particular had an infectiously happy way about her. She and Jindi-ji had a five-year-old boy, and there were five older children and a couple of grandchildren in India from Vimla's previous marriage. As I got to know her I heard many a saga about the terrible hardships and challenges she had faced and survived. She had brought her challenges upon herself, much like I had. With her inimitable style and characteristic twinkle, she once said to me, 'Good judgement comes from experience. And most experience'—she took a deep breath, then resumed with a chuckle—'well, that comes from bad judgement.'

Vimla-ji was just the tonic I needed to start feeling good. Having her and her husband just a few blocks away was the best thing that had happened in my life since I returned from London, and our visits helped heal my stinging emotional wounds. Now, the prospect of going to India for this wedding was something to look forward to. The anticipation of a legendary 'Kapoor style' extravaganza was an ideal prescription for my melancholia.

I had learnt by now that Shammi had proposed marriage to a lady from the royalty, whom he had met soon after my wedding to Andy. As it turned out, they finally took their vows in the very temple Shammi had described to me. The ceremony occurred in the early hours of the same morning that Andy and I arrived from New York for the much-anticipated Kapoor–Nanda wedding.

Bhabhi-ji told me later that Shammi had been mulling over the date for his marriage for a while, but when he learnt that I was coming to Bombay for the wedding, he decided to take the plunge. Marrying Neela Devi turned out to be the right choice for him. Not only did she help ground his high-flying lifestyle, she also led him into the spiritual path of her guru. She partnered him with dignity and grace, gently steering him away from his reckless lifestyle into a more family-oriented one. When I saw him many years later and we had the opportunity to renew our friendship, he beamed when he told me that Neela had been a wonderful wife and mother to his children and he was very happy. Somehow, that news nurtured the tender box of love in my heart. I respected Neela for fulfilling his life. She had once been a great fan of his. (Much later, she and Shammi invited my second husband Georges and me to their gracious home, and the men got on exceedingly well.)

The Kapoor–Nanda wedding was a spectacular seven-day affair, unlike anything I had ever imagined or seen. Shammi and I exchanged only a few words, mostly avoiding any contact. Nevertheless, a trace of the flame from two years ago still glowed and somehow affirmed the fact that love may dim but it never dies. My relationship with Andy continued to improve, and we were actually enjoying each other's company equally for the first time. We had the opportunity to meet many friends and family whom he had never met, due to our speedy wedding two years earlier.

On our way back to New York we stopped over in Delhi to be with Andy's parents for a few days, where the frenzy of parties continued. One night, after a fine dinner party at the Oberoi Hotel, as we slept Andy suddenly woke me up in a panic. He was clutching his throat and seemed to be choking. His left arm, all the way to his shoulder and jaw, was in severe pain. As we rushed to the hospital, we realized that he had suffered a massive heart attack. He was taken into intensive care immediately, where he remained for some days. We were told he was lucky to have survived. It was almost three months before he was well enough to travel.

It was during that time that I discovered I was pregnant. I think the joy of this news gave him the will to fight back to good health and helped him recover sooner than the doctors had predicted. He quit smoking and we started on a new regimen of healthier habits. We returned to New York with renewed hope and faith, eagerly looking forward to parenthood. Andy was sure I was carrying a baby boy, and he would fondly stroke my growing stomach as he talked to 'Kabir', his unborn son.

About six weeks before the due date I was taken seriously ill with a bad infection of herpes zoster virus in my left eye. It was an acute attack in which I nearly lost my eye, spent three weeks in the hospital in excruciating pain and was left with permanent scars across my forehead. I then moved from the eye hospital into the maternity hospital with just a few days at home to recover from the debilitating herpes attack. I was appalled to see the ugly scars that had spread all across the left side of my forehead. My left eye had lost a patch of its eyelashes. The effects of the attack, I was told, would be permanent.

The scars were so deeply etched that it might take twenty to thirty years for them to fade. My vanity took a beating, but I learned an important lesson about the fragility of life. We take so much for granted, I realized. It was becoming amply clear that my life's most important lessons were to be packaged with big doses of pain.

Instead of our son Kabir, we were blessed with a baby girl. She came three weeks early but, much to my relief, was perfectly healthy and not affected in any way from my bout with the virus. We had never considered a name for a girl, so sure had we been of having a son. Quite unprepared with a name for the hospital records, we simply named our baby after the first person who came to visit me in the hospital. Her name was Malini, the niece of Vimla-ji, my delightful neighbour who had now become a protective big sister to me. Fortunately, my daughter Malini has approved of her name.

Andy was beside himself with happiness over his newborn girl. Soon there was a second pregnancy—all too soon. He embraced the second growing belly, once again getting acquainted with the imaginary Kabir, the son he so desperately wanted. But when, exactly twelve months after Malini's birth, our second daughter Gitanjali came along, Andy's absence from the hospital was telling. Kabir had once again failed to appear. Andy's dream of having a son remained a dream.

He loved both the children but was particularly attached to the first one. Once Gitu came into our lives, Andy began to take charge of Malini and suggested that I should take charge of the younger girl, declaring, 'Gitu is yours and Malini is mine.' He didn't believe that parents could love their kids in equal measure.

This became a bone of contention between us, as I could not go along with the new set of rules he had suddenly designed. Unable to digest the defeat of not fathering a son, he simply introduced a new parenting philosophy into our lives. I learned that my marital life was to be as quirky as the British weather I had left behind.

12

Jesus Christ!

ABOUT THE TIME the girls were old enough for nursery school, our revered friends, the Kapoors in India, were facing a financial crisis. Raj-ji had had just launched the most ambitious production of his career, *Mera Naam Joker* (1972). He had spared no cost and, in fact, had borrowed huge sums of money as his project had stretched and gone on to become a grand trilogy. The Indian film audience was unable to appreciate his creative experiment and the film bombed. It drove him to depression and, to add to his woes, his father Prithviraj Kapoor (Papa-ji) was diagnosed with cancer, for which he was to be flown to New York for treatment at Sloan Kettering.

At this point Raj-ji had already created a new script for a fresh format in Indian cinema. There had been rave reviews about his son Rishi's debut role in *Mera Naam Joker*. Encouraged by this, and captivated by the bubbly personality of a pretty young actress called Dimple Kapadia, he built a charming love story about teenage love hitherto never shown in Hindi cinema. This challenging project had helped distract him from some of the emotional wounds brought on by his recent failure.

Andy and I happily welcomed Raj-ji's request to stay with us during the period that Papa-ji would be in the hospital. I knew that while Raj-ji appreciated luxury, he was a man of simple needs. In his own room in Bombay he slept on a mattress on the floor. That's what he wanted at our apartment. We quickly adapted our little dining area into a cosy makeshift bedroom for our VIP guest. He hung up a picture of Jesus Christ, and placed two small silver statues of Lord Ganesh and Sai Baba on the small corner table.

During the four or five weeks he stayed with us, Raj-ji adapted his pattern to ours. We could not afford taxis—our mode of transport was subways and buses. Besides, we lived on the wrong side of town if you wanted to get to any important or entertaining part of the city. Raj-ji chose bus transport over the subway, and in the first few days I would accompany him while the girls were in school. We would take the crosstown bus from 96th and Central Park West to 3rd Avenue. From there we changed to the downtown bus, which would take us almost to the doorstep of the hospital. Papa-ji awaited Raj-ji's visits and a daily routine was in place. Often on the bus, an Indian or Pakistani or Russian passenger would recognize Raj-ji and jump to greet him. You could see the shock on their faces when it registered that the great Raj Kapoor was travelling just like one of them. Years later, he would tell me that these memories were among his most cherished.

In the evenings, while I cooked up a meal, he and Andy enjoyed long 'happy hours', often finishing a bottle of scotch between them. His Black Label brand slipped downward to the Red Label we were able to offer. He would sometimes take on the role of maestro in the kitchen and cook up a rich storm of delicious dinner—lamb, mushrooms and even a great biryani. He loved playing with the girls and they enjoyed playing pranks on him as their way of returning his love.

One night, after a particularly long happy-hour session, I was awakened by a loud monologue coming out of Raj-ji's sleeping area. When I focused my ear to the sound, it was real—he was indeed yelling at someone! I listened for a while, and as it continued I tried to wake Andy. He was in deep slumber, so I decided to go and take a peek myself. It was an adorable sight—Raj-ji was sitting on his mattress, directly facing the picture of Jesus and throwing curses. He would point his finger occasionally at the two other statues, but mostly he spoke to Jesus—almost as if he were an equal, right there in real life! He demanded to know why he had been let down so badly, yelling repeatedly, 'What have I done to you, haan? What have I done to harm you? Why are you putting me through all this hell? Why do you promise salvation and deliver the opposite?' I was equally aghast and amused—I had seen nothing like this before! He did not notice me, and I didn't dare interrupt his dialogue with the Son of God.

The next day I asked him, 'Raj-ji, I heard you having a fight with someone last night, who was that?'

'That was Jesus Christ!' he said with a combination of passion and anger. 'I treat him like a human being, and we have our conversations. I told him he had no right to put me through this hell. It has stretched far too long, beyond every limit!' His blue eyes flashed. Even though it made me chuckle, I got a wise insight into harvesting God's grace.

He frequently discussed the ideas and anecdotes from real life that he wanted to incorporate in his new script. *Bobby* (1973), the new movie in the making, was on a very tight budget. Goa was a large part of the theme. Witnessing my shoestring-budget lifestyle, he suggested I shop for dresses, shirts, shorts and the like for the movie, keeping its low budget in mind. I happily complied. My favourite store, Alexander's, had been my main source for my children's wardrobe and I often found wonderful discounted designs for myself and Andy there too.

We managed to pull together quite a collection for young Dimple and Rishi Kapoor in their roles. The entire wardrobe cost under $500! The movie went on to soar great heights of success and carved out a niche for a new genre of teenage romance on the screen. The RK banner broke records in India's film history. After being given such a tongue-lashing, Jesus had responded to his friend, Raj Kapoor, very generously!

13

Rosy

I OFTEN WISHED THAT I could work and supplement Andy's income, so we could have a better life. But I was already overburdened with caring for two toddlers and running a home. We were unable to afford babysitters, so I ended up staying home a lot. I wished we could get an Indian nanny for the girls. But Andy disagreed on this. He believed that we didn't need the privilege of having a live-in nanny-housekeeper in America. He had somewhat of an egalitarian attitude about this. I, on the other hand, was not able to see it his way, because I had to shoulder most of the burden, and servants had been an intrinsic part of my everyday life in India. The discussion came up again on our visit to Bombay when we went for my favourite brother Gulu's wedding in 1972.

I had recently lost both my parents to cancer, within six months of each other. Rosy had been their loyal and trusted maid, who had continued to take care of them till their last days. During our stay in Bombay my family offered me the chance to take Rosy as our nanny to New York. This proposal came to me as a gift from heaven, something I had longed for.

Andy flew into a rage at the suggestion. I was unable to make him see the logic of this relief for me, neither through gentle pleadings nor heated arguments. Finally he gave me an ultimatum: I had to choose between husband or nanny. With only the briefest hesitation, I picked the latter. He left the hotel in a huff, carrying three-year-old Malini with him, leaving me with Gitu and Rosy.

By his rules, Malini was his property; I had no say in the matter. My pleas about not separating the children fell on deaf ears. That was that! My heart felt like it had been cut in half. The rest of that dismal day, I showered an abundance of love on Gitu and took her and Rosy for a little shopping spree to tide over the nagging depression that was setting in. The toughest part was keeping up the façade in line with the festivities. Once the celebrations were over and guests thinned out, I broke the shocking news to my family. They were neither surprised nor concerned about Andy's departure. They were by now used to the ups and downs in our life.

I guessed that Andy would have gone to Delhi so Malini could spend time with her grandparents. I also thought his parents might try and mediate a truce between us and call me. Instead, Andy had flown off to New York. This was the most cruel and shocking example of his mood swings that I had experienced in the past years.

Like a manic-depressive, I alternated between cycles of sadness followed by strange delight in that I could have Gitu all to myself without negative interference from her father. I decided to view this development in a positive light. Gitu was going to miss her sister terribly, but I was going to do everything possible to fill her little life with happy days and unhindered love. I was less concerned for Malini, as she had her father's undivided love, and I knew that my sister Rani's family in New York would be her shelter.

While I was confident that the children's lives would somehow be sorted out by the intervention of the elders in our families, I myself was in a heightened state of loneliness. I cried a lot, although always making sure that Gitu and my family were not aware of it. What was I going to do? Where was I going to stay? I was at a frightening crossroads. Both my parents had died. My dearest brother, my closest ally and support, Gulu, had just married the girl of his dreams, the gorgeous Vimla Watumull from Hawaii, and was on the threshold of a new life of his own. I had, in fact, promoted the union. I could not burden him with my troubles.

My older brothers naturally presumed that I would move to London under their care and supervision. For them, it was a foregone conclusion. They were willing to fulfil an earlier promise to buy me a home of my own and help me start a small business of my choice, but with their approval. While this offer was an assured safety net, I feared that taking it up would cripple my emotional and creative spirit. I concluded that it was a secure but unappealing opportunity.

New York was no longer an option, and India offered no particular promise. And yet, India was pulling at my heart. The rest of my family, who had assembled at the Taj for the seven days of wedding festivities, were now dispersing. I knew that after the next few days, I had nowhere to go. I had no base for Gitu and myself. The prospects were as bleak as my mood.

I needed healing, a vision of a path for putting together the puzzle of my shattered life. I was grateful for the reassuring presence of my remaining family, but I had no idea what I would do when they all left in the next forty-eight hours. On the last night, I excused myself from the family farewell dinner soon after it had begun. I raced to my room and watched Gitu in deep, blissful sleep, with Rosy nearby, also asleep on the couch. I kissed Gitu gently and felt a divine presence in our room. Acknowledging it, I made a wish for us. But still feeling very much alone, I walked over to my hotel window. It overlooked the same Arabian Sea I had contemplated in my childhood, from my rock. As the cool spring breeze wafted in, I gazed past the historic Gateway of India. I could see traces of the dark horizon in the distance and images of dark boats here and there, with twinkling lights. Doing my best to swallow the large lump in my throat, I looked up at the shimmering star-filled sky. I searched for some refuge, for some omen. In fact, I was searching for God in any form. I thirsted for answers to a thousand questions but I didn't even know how to articulate one of them.

Still, I sensed some hope as I watched each wave come rolling in gently, swaying the boats docked at the shore. It reminded me of the secret hours I had spent as a child in dialogue with those waves. I just knew at that moment that there—in that vast ocean which was beguiling me once again, teasing me with its seductive waves— there lay the mystery of my destiny. I needed to believe in it, to seek answers. But all I held was a blank canvas, with no paint or brush or clear subject. The previous day's painful episode with Andy kept intruding like a cunning devil, trying to disturb this private dialogue with the ocean.

I walked back to Gitu's bed and thanked God for giving her to me. At that moment I made a commitment to her that together, she and I would conquer all of life's adversities and sail through triumphantly. 'I know we have God on our side,' I promised her. We were now a tiny family, but I nurtured the conviction that a great new destiny awaited us.

Seduced by the sea outside, I walked over to the window again, convinced that an answer still lay in the dark mysterious horizon. I closed my eyes, this time allowing fountains of tears to flow to release my tension, to let go of my anguish. Thus comforted, I suddenly began to receive insights from some divine force. I couldn't tell if the wisdom came from within me, or from the ocean, or from some outer force. But suddenly, time stood still.

In the following half hour or more—it was impossible to know how long I had remained in this suspended state—I could see, with clarity, a mental and visual breakthrough. It was a decoding of little gems of wisdom, bringing the answers I was seeking.

I understood in that moment that we had all come into this world for some greater purpose. I was born into a business family, which respected the values of integrity, spirituality and generosity. But their focus was the material path. There were others who focused on an artistic path and yet others who chose the path of war or sports or spirituality, the path of altruism or of service to humanity, through politics or medicine. Still others sought to alleviate their suffering through creating harmony with nature, and some sought a direct communion with God. I saw myriad paths. In fact, there were as many paths as one's imagination would allow.

This finally led me to my own question. So what was my path or purpose in this life? I hadn't been able to figure that out yet. I realized, for the first time, that I had never given enough thought to my own needs or interests, who I was or why I was here in the first place. Nor did I have any particular skill to pursue a career or profession.

I was born as someone's daughter and sister, to be someone's wife and a mother to a couple of children. My moral conditioning had shaped the existing 'me'. And I had agreed to live my life in accordance to these social expectations, to the best of my ability. I had taken my role and purpose so seriously that I had sacrificed two great passion-filled romances, along with my dreams of being an athlete and a singer. I had allowed myself to be cut off from all of them—and now I had failed even as a wife and mother. So who was I? Were some of us born to fail? I wanted desperately to know the answer.

A wonderful realization came to me then. If I had failed, I would not have Gitu here with me. She would have to be my purpose. I had to live for her. My life felt like it had crashed into a thousand pieces, but there remained a solid purpose and responsibility. I had finally taken a momentous decision, on my own. My focus suddenly rushed into the 'now'. My 'now' was Gitu's life, and I was going to find the courage from within myself. There was nothing else in sight but to embrace my mission.

14

Fate Steps In

TRAIPSING THROUGH A multitude of thoughts and insights, I finally fell into a trance-like state of sleep. A lot of mental load-shedding had taken place. I felt light and had found an agenda that required me to draw upon my own internal resources. My immediate priority, though, was to buy time to stay on in Bombay for a few more days and take stock of what course my life should follow. I needed courage to tell my family I was not joining them in London, even though I had no Plan B in sight. I was scared, but I had to be brave for Gitu.

We had a cheerful breakfast in our room together, and while I found many funny responses to give Gitu about her missing sister, underlying it all was my big question—where would we be tomorrow? With no one I could talk to or share my woes with, I followed my intuition and scanned the whole spectrum of my past and present social circle in Bombay. I came up with no names that I could call upon.

We entered the elevator to go downstairs towards the pool. There, I ran into my answer! It was Camellia Panjabi, smiling at me. I had known and admired her as a senior who had been the head girl in my school, Queen Mary High, years earlier. I had got to know her better in London whenever she would come for a visit from Cambridge University, where she was studying economics, and later in Bombay, before I got married. She was now the head of marketing at the Taj and commanded great respect. She was happy to run into me and invited me to join her for lunch at the Harbour Bar, while Gitu and Rosy went to the poolside. I just knew that she held the answer and the direction to the next step in my life.

My hunch was right. She brimmed with ideas, mostly quantifying my qualities as a person with great creative flair, and suggesting how I could best put it to use to become economically stable. The best part was, she thought I would flourish in Bombay. This was music to my ears. I admired her wisdom and even as I started to feel some of my confidence return, a flash of despondency replaced it. I couldn't think of any skill I could put to use! That very moment we were interrupted by Camellia's boss, Ajit Kerkar, who was passing by.

After we were introduced, he asked if he could join us. There was something about his piercing eyes that held my attention. 'So,' he said with a smile, 'that was quite a wedding between the Lalvanis and the Watumulls! Our hotel staff was given instructions to put out their best hospitality and to ensure there would be no cause for complaint!' He exuded a humble confidence.

'Oh yes', I smiled, 'we are all very happy. The Taj exceeded our expectations. Everything was perfect and the staff has been very gracious and thoroughly efficient. Sadly, we are all departing by tomorrow.'

'Where do you live? In London?' he asked suddenly.

'No. In New York,' I replied, a little surprised at his interest.

Then something incredible happened. Like a bolt out of the blue, Ajit, after a quick glance at Camellia, turned to me and without preamble, his sharp eyes looking straight into mine, said something that changed my life forever. 'Bina…may I call you Bina? How would you like to work for us in New York, where we are opening an office soon?'

Stunned by what I had just heard, I looked at Camellia, as if she would confirm that I wasn't imagining it. I found my voice, even though it came as a quiver. 'Mr Kerkar, thank you, but as I was just explaining to Camellia, I no longer have a place in New York because my husband and I have parted ways.' Then I added, '…only yesterday.' The familiar lump returned to my throat. I was so scared that if I couldn't control it, I would burst into tears and be embarrassed for life.

He looked at me for a while and then, in a firm but consoling voice, responded, 'I wasn't offering you the job because of your New York residence. Anyhow, we will organize that for you, don't worry.'

'But', I stuttered, unable to believe my ears, 'the trouble is, I don't know how to tell you this, but I have no job skills. In fact, I've never really worked before.' I felt like an ant.

Then came some golden words. 'Look, I saw you at your brother's wedding. We didn't meet, but I observed your social skills. You have a positive, winsome way with people, and that's a rare and valuable skill.' He was being gentle yet impactful.

Still unable to grasp the reality of what was unfolding, I looked quizzically at Camellia again before facing this heaven-sent messiah. Then I said a bit apologetically, 'Mr Kerkar, I am really grateful, but I know nothing about the hotel business and I don't think I will be able to do justice to the role.'

He cut me short: 'Bina.' And then, putting power into every word he uttered, 'I have faith in you, and if you have faith in yourself, the job is yours!' This time I saw that Camellia was as shocked as I was. And then, to my absolute shame and embarrassment, I burst into tears. Waves of disbelief and profound joy swept through me. Unable to talk, I just nodded, trying to stretch my mouth into a smile. Through the cloud of emotions and the rain of tears on my face, we acknowledged the commitment.

With my face buried in a napkin, waiting for the feelings to pass, I heard him say, 'Well done, Bina! Don't cry. Celebrate this good news and your new life.' Then, as if to seal the deal, he said, 'Call me Ajit. That's what my executive team calls me. You are the director of sales and marketing for the Taj Group in the Americas!' It was clear to me that the previous night's dialogue with the ocean and waves was bringing me a bounty of benefits, faster than I could handle.

Suddenly, the reality of my situation struck me. 'The trouble is, I have no place to stay, Mr Kerkar. I was supposed to leave for London tomorrow. Besides,' I added, 'I have my little daughter Gitu with me. So I come with a bit of a load, you see.'

During the next half hour, we discussed logistics. I was expected to stay on in Bombay for three months and be trained and gain an understanding of sales, marketing and public relations in the hotel industry.

'There is a lot to learn,' he explained. 'We are expanding rapidly. We have just taken over the management of palaces in Jaipur and Udaipur, the Rambagh and the Lake Palace, and we have signed a contract with the American chain of Intercontinental Hotels. Their office in New York will be our American headquarters and you will be in charge.' This was an entirely new vocabulary for me, but I resolved that I would never let him down.

For the next three months I moved into Camellia's new apartment, within walking distance of the Taj. Gitu and Rosy were warmly welcomed. Camellia lived with her mother. Her sister Namita was in England most of the time that I was there. We became a family, and Gitu was the favourite of everyone in the building and at the hotel, where I brought her on certain days as a treat. I was sent on a familiarization trip to the two palaces in Jaipur and Udaipur, where I was extended the full royal welcome. Camellia and I attended a conference of the travel industry too, giving me an opportunity to visit Kashmir and meet up with travel industry stalwarts.

There was indeed a lot to learn. I understood years later how lucky I had been to be taken on as protégée by mentors such as Ajit Kerkar and Camellia Panjabi. Camellia was about the best person to learn marketing skills from, and being exposed to Ajit's dynamic and personable style of leadership was an incredible gift. I worked out of Camellia's office, and one morning a tall, thin, shy young man walked in to ask if I could offer him and his brother a membership at the newly opened club called 1900. It was Amitabh Bachchan! Some eight years later, after his meteoric rise to the top, I was to meet him again and take him and his brother Bunty on a memorable evening out in New York to the legendary Studio 54, where they were both suitably enthralled.

During the last month of my stay in Bombay, Andy suddenly surprised me with a visit. Friendly and hinting at a reconciliation, he said, 'Malini misses you and her sister. We may as well be family again!'

He was agreeable about Rosy, having no doubt learned something about the hardships of running a house and caring for children while working. His mother had arrived in New York to take care of Malini and him, but her trip was time-bound.

Even as he acquiesced to accepting Rosy, he lay down another rule. 'You will not go to office for the full day,' he ordered. 'You can only go to work if it's a part-time job!'

I knew better than to argue with him about this triviality. 'I will ask the boss. If I am to take home a full salary, I'm sure I will be expected to spend the whole day at work, right?' I answered, feeling more confident about standing up for myself.

The boss, however, was very accommodating. He advised me to avoid any kind of argument. I knew that the nine-to-five job would not necessarily apply to my position because of the time zones between India and the US. Ajit predicted correctly that in a short time Andy would come around to the time demands, and it was best to go along with his wishes in the early months.

Life was turning sweet again! The best was yet to come.

15

A Woman's Psyche

My excitement at the anticipation of meeting Malini again was hard to contain as I landed in New York with Gitu and Rosy in tow. Visions of seeing the two sisters together after three months apart played anxiously in my mind throughout the journey. Gitu was by now speaking fluent Hindi and Malini spoke none. What would be their opening line to each other, I wondered. For that matter, would Malini be more enthralled to see me, or her sister? And how about Andy's attitude in that whole equation—would his ideas about loving one more than the other have changed?

These thoughts dogged me till I finally reached home and ran straight to Malini's bed, only to find her in deep slumber. She looked so pure and innocent. I stood quietly beside the bed and watched her, allowing tears to well up in my eyes. As I stood there, filling all my hungry senses with the sight of her in real life, she suddenly opened her big beautiful eyes, blinked a few times as if she already knew I was watching her, stretched out her arms and jumped into the waiting cradle of my body. I rocked her in a long embrace, with sobs that choked my words. 'Mummy, Mummy, you're back from India,' she cried with joy. 'Where is Gitu?' She jumped out of my arms and ran into the drawing room, where Gitu was pulling out toys from our bags to give to Malini.

Gitu became suddenly shy when she saw Malini, and clung to Rosy. The next few moments we silently witnessed their halting steps towards reunion with both choking emotion and amusement. Their accents were markedly different and gave us plenty of laughing fits over the next few days. Each new day together felt like the unwrapping of a fantastic new present. Watching the intensifying attachment and love between the two sisters worked wonders in reviving the dead relationship between Andy and me. Malini's extroverted personality put Rosy in a comfort zone very quickly, despite their language barrier. Rosy adjusted smoothly into our household and became, in fact, the best gift we could have hoped for. Even Andy was suitably impressed and appreciated her presence in our home. She became family in no time at all.

Within a week I got to visit my office, which was located on the fourth floor of the iconic Pan American building in the heart of Manhattan at Park Avenue and 45th Street. It was barely seven blocks away from Andy's office at Air India on Park and 52nd Street. Fate was setting up interesting logistics. We enrolled the girls in a nursery school housed in our building complex and went to work on the same subway together each day at 8.30 a.m. I would come home by 2 p.m., while Andy had a full day at the office, as always. Gradually, just as Ajit had said, my job not only demanded more work hours, but also called for occasional travel to other destinations. That, predictably and even understandably, did not go down well with Andy.

Being positioned among the top executives at the headquarters of Intercontinental Hotels and with close proximity to the top brass of Pan American Airlines, which owned the hotel chain, I was rapidly exposed to the travel industry on a worldwide scale. My virgin mind went on an exploration binge to quench the thirst for academic learning that had so long evaded me. I couldn't believe my good fortune at being given this gift via the fascinating travel industry, that too with a salary that almost matched Andy's.

I had two diametrically opposite roles. At home, I was still the housewife who had trouble standing up to the mood swings of her unpredictable husband, while outside of that closed-door life, I felt I had the world at my fingertips. My job offered exciting challenges five days a week. I was experiencing the meaning of power, which I had never known before. The organization I represented was among the world's best, and the elite clientele I dealt with had a savoir faire that filled my days with stimulation and excitement.

The job gave me the opportunity to learn about India's lesser-known treasures from the cultural tourism perspective. I discovered a lot about our rich heritage and colourful traditions, thereby enriching my own existence as an Indian in America. I got to meet and mingle with very interesting people with esoteric tastes and lifestyles.

My deeply absorbing job snatched away time from my girls at home, and I realized that a delicate balance had to be maintained. I soon learnt that I could replace quantity of time with richer and more intensive quality time with them. My rationed hours with Malini and Gitu were now value-added. They loved hearing the enchanting stories about India, its colourful culture and mythology, that I was now able to share. While being immersed in the influence of American culture, they were able to get a little dose of vibrant Indian identity from me. I sensed a healthier growth in our relationship. And they were enjoying their new friendships in school.

Gaining equal status at home was, of course, still an elusive dream. In Andy's opinion, my opting for work at the expense of spending time at home as a mother was a misplaced priority. Among our closest Indian friends, those women with young children like ours were 'stay-at-home moms'. But I loved my job, and it certainly helped our financial status. There was a serviceable balance between the discord at home and my success at work, so I simply slipped into that pattern of compromise and justified it as the best choice. The hypocrisy of it all was lost on me!

The word 'divorce' came up on occasion when Andy and I were engaged in a heated argument—then the compromise pattern worked to make each argument a passing cloud. In public, we were seen as a 'happily married couple'. I often wondered how Andy perceived our marriage. Did he see it as a compromise? For that matter, how many marriages in the world were built on such compromises? Surely it had to be more than 50 per cent? Otherwise how could couples continue to live together under the same roof the world over? Didn't that make us 'normal'? My marriage at least deserved a 'consolation prize'—or did it? These thoughts crowded my brain.

I became preoccupied with trying to study other couples, trying to look beneath their public images to get a glimpse of what was going on in their minds and within the walls of their homes. I wanted to believe that every second couple I met also had skeletons in their closet, like we did. Most of all, I wanted to believe that it was normal for every other wife to suffer her husband's mood swings the way I did. My mind chattered incessantly, seeking X-ray vision into every marriage to see if it was as dysfunctional as mine. Did these women possibly have a 'gift' outside of their marriages, like I had for a while? It was only fair. I perceived my job as my very personal gift. It had saved my sanity, not to mention my self-esteem, and helped me overcome my depression. Why shouldn't other suffering wives deserve similar good fortune?

I felt I had exhausted every avenue to make my husband happy. Maybe I was not destined to have a happy marriage. Maybe Sai Baba had some other kind of fulfilment in store for me. I had prayed so earnestly! Or maybe my prayers had never reached his heart. Or had Shammi's curse worked? He had once said, in a rage of passion, 'If you marry *anyone* else other than me, you will never be happy!' Those words rang in my mind many a time. I had betrayed him so cruelly, I probably deserved every bit of the mental and emotional turmoil I had experienced since my marriage.

On the odd occasion when Andy and I would have a terrible, violent row, I would muster up the courage to pack some bags and fly off home to London—sometimes with the kids, other times without, depending on their school schedule.

My brothers and their wives would welcome me with protective, loving arms and provide every comfort to soothe my rattled nerves. I enjoyed the pampering and the spoiling now, unlike in the years before my marriage, when I had found it smothering and suffocating, and wanted to flee from it. On these occasions I tried to come to terms with who I really was. Somewhere deep within me, I was aware that this strife-filled life with Andy in New York was, in fact, helping me grow as an individual and shape my character, which could never have happened in the tender atmosphere of my family home.

The longest I ever stayed away during these separations was about six weeks. Andy would implore and make his usual efforts to convince me, through phone calls, that he would never be violent again, persuading me to give the marriage one more try. My family had become all too familiar with this pattern and had come to dread it. With every such move, like the 'boy who cried wolf', I had lost credibility and caused a lot of pain to those who longed to see me put an end to this neurotic existence. But I had lost respect for myself in this sordid compromise of a marriage.

At the same time, I knew that I was not the only one in such a marriage. I witnessed a parallel situation with Andy's sister Madhu, who came to visit us sometimes from Washington. Madhu was married—long before I had met Andy—to a man the family had disapproved of for several reasons, not least because of his dependence on alcohol. The mention of Bish's name evoked the same reaction in Andy's family as did Andy's name did in mine. Madhu had divorced him, much to her family's relief, and subsequently made a good life for herself in Washington. However, around the time that I married Andy, she had come in contact with Bish again, and he had wooed her with his considerable charm, to the extent that she was seriously considering remarrying him. There were tears, trauma, anger, appeals and every effort made by Andy and his parents to dissuade her from taking this dreadful step, but she defied them all and remarried him. The second time around they had a happier union and produced two sons in succession. But poor Madhu was not destined to see much bliss. One of her sons was tragically snatched away at the age of twelve by leukemia, and her marriage ended in divorce again. A third marriage to a doctor also did not run a smooth course, but Madhu being Madhu, a fighter and survivor like me, created a new and successful life for herself in the remote island of Guam with her surviving son.

Only much later in my life did I understand the complicated thought processes of women who allow themselves to be emotionally and physically battered once they have lost their self-esteem. I hungered for deeper knowledge on the subject and encountered case studies by volunteering my time at shelters for battered women in Delhi and New York. I was quite amazed to learn that more than 60 per cent of such wives came from more affluent homes than those they had married into. They allowed their sense of self to be undermined by husbands who felt inferior deep down, who feared they would never be able to 'measure up' to their wives' standards. Most of the time, these women brought themselves down to accommodate the husband's insecurities, thereby giving them a perverted power, which resulted in abuse.

The imbalance in such marriages was unmistakable, generally resulting from the imbalance in the woman's own family pattern where, as the girl child, she was brought up as unequal and therefore ill-equipped to determine her own destiny. The key word in the character of such a wife is 'submissiveness'. It is a pattern that transcends cultures, religions and countries. This was very much the slot that I had fitted myself into. Pulling out of it was to be a painfully slow and costly process.

16

Godman

ON A VERY chilly evening in December 1975, Malini and Gitu, now six and five years old, were both down with pneumonia. My maid Rosy, who had been with us for three years now, had suddenly, without warning, left us for a man she met in New York. I was beside myself being nurse to my little girls, trying to hold a challenging job and taking care of all the household chores. I was home early in that afternoon when I got a call from Andy's office informing me that he was bringing home a 'very special swami' for dinner. 'I cannot cook a meal today,' I pleaded. But Andy was insistent: 'He wants very simple food, without onion and without garlic.' To me that seemed an even tougher task—I had never cooked without onion and garlic! Besides, I was in no mood to entertain a Hindu holy man on this crisis-burdened day. I was still distraught beyond words by Rosy's sudden disappearance.

The holy man was none other than Chandraswami, who was in the country as Indira Gandhi's spiritual ambassador, come to cement relations between India and the US. It was, politically, a very sensitive time in India. Emergency had been declared, and Sanjay Gandhi was all-powerful. Swami Chandraswami was a special friend of his, and was in the New York at his behest. A request had been made to Air India to roll out the red carpet for him. He was Andy's honoured guest and I, as the dutiful wife, had no choice but to comply.

I mustered up the energy to plunge myself into the preparations, cursing under my breath. The good news was that the swami had sent his apologies that he was jet-lagged and would not stay too long. The bad news was that he was bringing three disciples with him.

As I prepared the dinner and mentally rehearsed what I knew of the Hindu religion for the evening ahead, I was reminded of being forced to swallow bitter medicine in my childhood.

Just as I was tucking the girls in for the evening, I heard the doorbell ring. I opened the door and in walked a tall young man with a thin beard, wearing a saffron lungi and a kurta. His expression was one of childlike curiosity, together with a studied authority. He was accompanied by Chander and Inder, two brothers in their twenties who were his 'bodyguards and interpreters', plus a third man, an older sadhu. Andy was already chatting and laughing with them in a familiar manner as they entered the foyer of our apartment. This was not at all the religious group that I had been expecting. I was relieved, no longer daunted by the evening ahead.

As the evening progressed, I learned about the swami's 'clairvoyant' powers. My heart raced as I asked him the only question that was paramount in my mind that evening.

'Could you please see where my Rosy has run away to? My children and I are very miserable without her,' I pleaded. The swami looked totally puzzled. He had come prepared to discuss plans for meetings with high-powered American dignitaries, politicians and leaders in the Indian business community. I think the innocence of the question charmed him and appealed to the childlike instinct in him. We broke the invisible ice in that instant and established a connection. Soon he was in the girls' room, giving them blessings and getting them to recite a 'mantra' after him.

He assured them that their fever would be gone the next day and they would be able to go back to school within two days. His prophesy came true, and the children established a special bond with him. After that, they spoke to him daily on the phone, and he made them repeat the mantra over and over again until they had memorized it. I was to discover that he was known for his winsome way with young people and kids; not that he did badly with older people. Although my problem remained unresolved—he could not or would not tell me where Rosy could be found—he had succeeded in charming the young and naïve Ramani household.

In no time at all, 'Swamiji' became a regular member of our household. I learned to whip up all kinds of veggies without onion and garlic in a jiffy. Rosy became history. Not only did he impress us with his soothsaying powers, he made a habit of picking up the phone and making long-distance calls, courtesy Air India, to the two most powerful people in India, to issue them advice on a daily basis. Meanwhile, his US courtiers grew in numbers. They came from all walks of life—politicians, businessmen, rock stars and the rest.

To us, his mission was never really clear. He dressed in the garb of a holy man, but his conversation on religious matters was limited and his interest in politics and commerce was infinite. Occasionally, he was called upon to bless strained business or marital relationships. He always complied happily, in return for favours or help in adding to his growing band of devotees.

Over the next few years, though we saw less of him, his bond with us remained as strong as ever. He treated me like an elder sister. He was concerned for our welfare and showered blessings upon us so that Andy and I could bond in our turbulent marriage and rise to the top in our careers. He loved my children and they returned his love. I had even stitched some lungi-kurtas for him in my spare time, which he wore with pride. We helped him settle into a new apartment, not far from our workplace. Every evening Andy and I would finish our work and meet at 'Swamiji's place' and then walk home together from there. Our marriage seemed to improve somewhat, but our careers moved along at the expected pace, with no miraculous leaps. The leaps, if anywhere, were happening in Chandraswami's career.

He began to travel extensively, first in the United States and then to the Middle East. This was a golden time for the Arab world's oil fortunes. We would hear from him once in a while as he shared his rise in fame, fortune and power. The little apartment that we had found for him in New York was now too humble for him and was used more often by the numerous assistants who regularly came from India. The elevator of the building had to only pass the fifth floor, where his apartment was, to be filled with an odious smell of stale oil and strong Indian spices. Entering the small, grimy flat was another matter altogether.

His private room was treated with somewhat greater care. A big mattress covered half the room, covered with white sheets that begged to be laundered. Foreign visitors would sit on the four cane chairs that took up the rest of the room. The brothers Inder and Chander, plus a few other young men, would serve masala tea and dry Indian snacks to the chosen few. At night, once the swami was asleep, the others—at least seven of them—would sleep on the floor in the living room. They all shared one bathroom.

While several young Indian business executives remained sceptical of his powers, Chandraswami's American devotees were like putty in his hands. The swami had a line-up of them, ranging from Adnan Kashyogi, the emir of UAE to the actress Elizabeth Taylor!

I, too, was blown away by his 'powers' for a while, but soon understood the reality of his abilities. I even learned later from Mrs Gandhi, when I met her, that she did not know Chandraswami at all. It took us a long time to accept the truth, as he had endeared himself to our family. In time, much to our dismay, we learned about the pain he had inflicted on some of his innocent devotees.

17

Stepping Stones

For the next four to five years, life moved on in a slow but steady upward spiral. Both our careers flourished. We were able to move from our cramped apartment to the pleasant suburb of Hartsdale, north of the city. A healthy routine of suburban life nourished the harvest of our family happiness in large measure.

During our happy interludes, Andy and I would talk about our respective careers, our children's lives, and even manage to fit in a few short holidays, thanks to our free travel and hotel benefits. The common jest among our friends was: 'Andy puts them in seats, and Bina puts them in sheets.' With the rich ingredients of our uneven journey together as source material, I would sometimes indulge my whims and clown with Andy and the kids to create make-believe scenarios. They often made us laugh till we cried. Andy's innate sense of humour would come to the fore in those moments, rare gems that found a permanent place in my heart's memory bank.

We were earning similar salaries, and Andy had worked out a formula whereby 80 per cent of my salary would go into the family kitty, which he managed. Those were the conditions under which he allowed me to work. I got to keep 20 per cent of the total as my personal money. The rest went to pay our bills or was invested in the stock market, strictly according to Andy's choice. On a couple of occasions when I asked about 'our' portfolio, his response was, 'Indian wives are meant to trust their husbands implicitly and shouldn't be questioning their intelligence.'

Andy's career reached a high point when he launched an ingenious campaign, in coordination with his headquarters in Bombay, whereby

Air India would introduce a jaw-dropping round-trip fare, New York–India–New York, for a mere $450. The sagging sales at Air India suddenly shot up, and while this campaign was created primarily to attract non-resident Indians in the US to go on home visits, it reached across into the tourism sector to include swelling numbers of American travellers. Inevitably, this caused consternation in other airlines that flew to India, who could not afford to drop their rates to a competitive range. More broadly, this move by Andy brought a surge in tourism figures for India's miniscule tourist ministry. Hotel rooms were usually sold out, as there wasn't much competition in India at that time.

Barely five years into the job, I was looking for more challenge in my own work. The Taj Group had expanded into other Indian cities and opened India's first two five-star resort hotels: Goa's Fort Aguada on the west coast, and Madras's Fisherman's Cove on the east coast. The Indian Ocean was about to get its first taste of tourists. A hard-earned worldliness after so much struggle had ignited my creative side and I was tired of apologizing to clients who couldn't be accommodated because we were usually fully booked. A thirst needed to be quenched.

During these years I had carved out a cosy niche for myself in New York society, representing the legendary palace hotels of India to sophisticated clients in America. I now had a network of friends who gave me a sense of success, power and an identity of my own—much more than just an Eastern mystique.

Occasionally, my job entailed receiving royals visiting New York from Jaipur, Jodhpur and Udaipur. Andy had his own winsome brand of communicating with them, and we watched with amusement as the elite cognoscenti of the city tripped over themselves to be among the first to meet and entertain them. 'The Maharani of Jaipur' as they chose to call her, Rajmata Gayatri Devi was a particular favourite—she had a stature and grace that sent all the society columnists into a tizzy. One summer, when she and Shanta Rama Rao were spending long weekends working on her autobiography (*A Princess Remembers*), she told me how cathartic it had been to relive her memories. She found Shanta to be very disciplined and tough. 'Shanta is relentless,' she sighed. 'She makes me talk into her cassette player for long hours, without a break. She asks really tough questions and expects answers immediately.' She then said, 'All memories are not happy ones and I wish I didn't have to dwell on them again.' I can still recall the fascinating image of these two icons together, sharing their weekends, creating a future bestseller.

One late night, I got a frantic call from her. I couldn't believe my ears when I heard what had happened. She had been returning to her apartment from a party in her honour, accompanied by her hostess in a stretch limousine, and just as she was about to step out, she was accosted by some armed men. One of them held a gun to the chauffeur's head.

'Give us all your jewellery and money quietly and we won't harm you,' they ordered. The rajmata, being the royal warrior that she was, just sat there unmoved. The other woman hurriedly took off her diamond bracelet, earrings and rings, and offered them to the thieves, pleading for her life and begging them not to harm her. Gayatri Devi wore only a pearl necklace, a steel bracelet and a ring. Clutching her necklace, she challenged them: 'This is my late husband's heirloom. You will not touch it. In fact, it shall never leave my neck.' She even said daringly, 'Kill me if you want.' They stared back at her menacingly and, as she was about to repeat her dare, they put their weapons back into their pockets, retreated and disappeared into the dark night.

■

The Taj Group now had five fine hotels in India. I helped inaugurate the two that opened in Madras and Goa by putting together an all-American VIP list of the most important travel agents, tour operators and travel journalists I knew. There was even a Hollywood star, Michael York, whose wife was a journalist and who travelled with us to India. These were magical trips; our hotels offered the guests a superb taste of Indian hospitality in majestic style and with royal flourish, as only the Taj Group could do.

That particular trip to Madras and Goa remains vivid in my memory thanks to a grandeur I had never before experienced, one that scaled my vision to another level. Quite strangely, on a personal level, the grandeur confronted me with a reminder of where I had come from. It opened up many memories of my struggles and broken dreams, and some inner intuition reminded me of the importance of balance. I consciously tried to treat the seduction of it all as momentary and fleeting, keeping myself grounded so as to not be swept away by the glitz and glamour, of which there was plenty.

I never allowed myself to forget that day of great despair when Andy had left, taking Malini with him, and my life had taken a 180-degree turn. Only hours later on that same day, a fabulous new world had opened up that I couldn't have dreamed of, thanks to Ajit Kerkar, who taught me the meaning of faith.

This was a rare, important crossroads in my life. I had become a member of the 'Hospitality at its Best' family that needed no explanation or introduction. It was now natural to mingle with the upper echelons of New York society and, in equal measure, with the 'best' of India. I had access to magnificent palaces, luxury fairy-tale heritage properties and the wonderful families that owned them. I got immense joy from representing these splendours of India to the western hemisphere. But after seven beguiling years in this job that I loved, I ached for new creative challenges.

To channel all my extra energy, I convinced the boss that New York desperately needed a fine-dining experience in Indian cuisine, since none existed at that time. Hitherto, there had only been small dhaba-like restaurants, serving limited Indian food, mostly run by Bengalis who had jumped ship. The Gaylord had just opened, stirring up the taste buds of adventurous New Yorkers for good Indian food. It was time for the Taj Group to launch a classy restaurant in Manhattan.

This new restaurant initiative of mine would require a new direction in the group's corporate plan. Visionary that he was, Ajit threw the challenge back at me and asked me to send him a project report. I explored the streets of New York and prepared a detailed brief about possible locations, restaurant styles and the eating and entertaining habits of New Yorkers. Within a couple of months I had found a fantastic location, very much in keeping with the Taj image, in the classy Rockefeller Center, where the legendary Forum of the Twelve Caesars restaurant once stood.

New York was going through its historic 1976 financial crisis, so we got lucky and struck an excellent deal—but not before David Rockefeller himself had to be convinced by none other than J.R.D Tata, CEO of the Tata Group which owned the Taj hotels, that our restaurant would match up to the standards of the Rockefeller Center's other legendary restaurants.

Until now, in New York, Indian food had been considered synonymous with spicy and greasy curry and rice. The Rockefellers were loath to see such an image polluting their property. In fact, a top executive whom I had met earlier simply dismissed the idea outright: 'Every Indian restaurant in New York City tapes its menu to the window,' he said. 'And the spicy odour is like an assault on every passer-by when the door opens. Sorry, but Rockefeller Plaza will not have any of that.' I was taken aback, searching for appropriate words to counter his opinion. But, in fact, this dialogue had prepared me for the many challenges I would meet along the way.

I learned to evaluate, assess and predict locations, business trends and people's habits—and in a city that was the world's restaurant haven. The very act of analysing and assessing the big picture was in itself a new experience, and then having to put it on paper and sell it to the group was a dimension that no college degree could have taught me. I thanked God for my good fortune and the many gifts of this process where I learned so much. It would serve me very well throughout my later life.

The restaurant deal was struck. The Taj brought into action their strongest team of experts in Bombay, ranging from a renowned chef to operations and management staff, not to mention Elizabeth Kerkar, one of the most talented interior designers in the business. I had the enviable role of marketing and public relations. The restaurant would be named Raga.

To make a really serious impact on the hard-to-penetrate social scene in New York, I knew we had to launch Raga with utmost panache. The prospect of promoting a product of India, hoping to make a dent on the elite of the city that never sleeps, was daunting. First, we needed a gilded guest list for the opening. Our trump card would normally have been India's royalty, at that time considered among the world's most glamorous. The presence of the Jaipur royals alone would have worked as a magnet to draw out the reluctant glitterati of New York. But that was not an option because Emergency had been declared in India; the celebrated Rajmata Gayatri Devi and the Maharaja and Maharani (Bubbles) Bhawani Singh and Padmini Devi, were all grounded.

By a wonderful stroke of luck, I met one of New York's most renowned party maestros, an event planner named George Paul Rossel. His parties were legendary. He had the ability to transform the most mundane space into a wonderland. He was a close friend of the owners of the legendary Studio 54, Ian Shrager and Steve Rubell. It had just opened and had not yet quite caught the public imagination, but it would eventually be dubbed 'The Most Famous Club in the World'. George Paul suggested that I link up with Studio 54 for our opening night party. I liked the idea, but felt that we needed a famous American personality who would have some link with India.

This was during President Carter's presidency. Like everyone in America, I had read about the president's mother Lillian Carter, who was reputed to be more popular with Americans than he was, and a darling of the American media. Miz Lillian (as she was known) had enjoyed an interesting life. At sixty-eight she had trained for the Peace Corps, and had been posted in India at the Godrej Colony for a year. As a result of this adventure, she was reputed to love India and all things Indian. One of my favourite (of many) anecdotes concerning her was when her son, Jimmy, had announced to her that he had decided to run for president. Her response had been: 'President of what?' On another occasion, she had been quoted as saying, 'When I look at all my children, I sometimes say to myself, "Lillian, you should have stayed a virgin."' She was the salt of the earth.

She would be the best possible guest we could hope for, but it seemed improbable that she would accept such an invitation. I nevertheless decided to take a shot and wrote a letter addressed to her at the White House, to invite her to be our special guest for the launch of Raga. I was utterly shocked—and euphoric!—when I got her prompt reply, accepting the invitation.

From there on, the going was good. I invited Coretta King, the widow of Martin Luther King. I had heard her make references to Mahatma Gandhi's ideology. She also accepted. Next, the Indian ambassador, Nani Palkiwala, agreed to grace our launch.

Finally, to add extra masala to the eminent guest list, I invited Andy Warhol, whom I had met a couple of times with my friend Asha Puthli, who was a pal of his, at his famous studio, where we had spend animated evenings. He readily accepted. I shot off invites to all of New York's high society that had been associated with the Jaipur royals. They were aware of the shocking arrests of Rajmata Gayatri Devi and Maharaja Bhawani Singh, and decided to show their solidarity by attending the opening night of Raga.

This line-up of star personalities virtually assured us a glittering success. But the cherry on the cake came when Miz Lillian decided she wanted to attend the opening wearing a sari, along with chappals and a bindi on her forehead. The challenge of dressing Miz Lillian fell upon my own wardrobe. I proposed a new turquoise sari set from my trousseau that had never been worn.

At the launch party, the enigmatic Andy Warhol was drawn to Miz Lillian, in her resplendent costume, like a bee to honey. He thus became her 'arm candy' for the duration of the evening, as his ubiquitous tape recorder popped frequently out of his pocket to capture enthusiastic and pithy quotes from her. The paparazzi had the time of their lives snapping shots of these two American icons—

one from the underground art world, the other a president's mother.

After a fabulous Indian meal and lively partying at Raga, the party moved on to Studio 54 as planned. As soon as Miz Lillian stepped inside the club in her sari, entertainment history was written. She immediately proceeded to the dance floor and waved to everyone to join her. Her bodyguard remained close by, and even managed to shake a leg. So electric was the atmosphere that everyone, including several media persons, broke into rhythm, and the enchanting evening that had started with the launch of Raga restaurant went on to become a major media event.

Studio 54 remains immortal in the memories of the thousands who subsequently embraced it and virtually made it their home. It had a major impact on popular imagination all over the world. To many who were present that magical evening, it would be the memory of a lifetime.

The Rockefellers, no doubt, took notice. Raga not only became one of the favourite business lunch venues for their executives, it paved the way for introducing American taste buds to a more spicy palate. Many memorable parties were subsequently hosted there over the years as Raga went on to become a mainstream New York watering hole.

For me, it was time to take a bow and move on to other entrepreneurial challenges.

■

My brothers wanted me to participate in the family business supplying microwave ovens from the US to the UK, as the latest modern appliance to hit the British kitchen. We named it the 'Binatone Empress'. I rented a triplex apartment to serve as my business quarters. While the success of this venture helped our financial status at home, I was restless. I missed my contact with India.

By the end of my second year, I landed an opportunity to enter the world of commodity trading with India. While I knew nothing about trading commodities as such, I had an efficient office from where my telex machine and Kathy Reagan, my brilliant secretary, could reach the world. We rapidly immersed ourselves in the world of commodities and, even though it was not an arena in which I ever achieved great expertise, I found it exhilarating and lucrative. My triplex apartment-cum-office in the heart of Manhattan was drawing eminent businesspeople from all over the world. India was opening doors and windows in my life, and many interesting visitors left their imprint at the office.

Chandraswami had often bragged about his contacts, and had offered to help me in any way he could. When I heard that the state of Kentucky had very large reserves of coal, I recalled that Swamiji had spoken of his friendship with the governor of Kentucky. I decided to put him to the test and asked him to introduce me to the man.

'Zaroor, Bina,' he beamed. 'Ab dekho yeh karamat.' (Certainly, Bina. Now watch this miracle.) He picked up the phone, asked an assistant to dial the governor's personal number and punched the speaker button.

'Governor's mansion, may I know who is calling?' said the official voice over the speakerphone.

'The governor's es-piritual brother, from New York,' answered Swamiji, in his thick Indian accent.

'Yes sir, but the governor is hosting a reception. May we connect you through in about forty-five minutes, sir?' she asked, politely.

'Okay, I'm waiting. Tell him,' he said, and hung up. Within five minutes the phone rang and the governor was on the phone, apologizing.

'Swamiji, my brother. What can I do for you today?' Quickly adding, 'I'm hosting a reception. If it is urgent, please tell me now.'

'Yes, yes, it is important,' the swami exaggerated. 'I have Indira Gandhi's spiritual sister here with me, Bina Ramani, and I want her to visit you in Kentucky.' He continued in the same breath, 'You have to find the best coal from your state. She wants to ship large quantities to India.' A short pause, and he continued, 'Okay, I will wait for your call after your reception is over.'

By the end of that hour, while Swamiji updated me on all the conquests he had made in the US, including trips to President Carter's White House, the governor had called back and extended an invitation for me to visit Kentucky and be his guest at the governor's mansion just two days later.

I arrived in Lexington, Kentucky, on a crisp Tuesday morning in April. A sleek black limo took me through massive ornate gates into a rambling estate which resembled Tara, the legendary mansion of Scarlett O'Hara in *Gone with the Wind*.

I was warmly welcomed by the governor's wife and led to a lavish, well-appointed guest room where I was to stay for three days until I found the ideal mine owner willing to supply large quantities of coal to India. I knew that India was not a priority nation for US trade. But at the governor's cocktail party in my honour on the following day, I was introduced to the owners of the top three coal mines, one of which was called Crescent Coal. The mine owner, Donald Johnson, showed interest in doing business with India. The other two probably hadn't even seen India on the world map.

Mr Johnson turned out not only to be one of the biggest coal mine owners, he was also a racehorse breeder. The next day, he arranged for me to tour his vast mining estate from his chopper, and after that we landed at his rambling breeding estate called Crescent Farm. It stretched to the horizon on three sides, so vast it was. After a three-course formal lunch served by his efficient staff, I got a short tour of some of his stables. Just as we turned the corner to examine the second round of stables, we were informed that one of his horses had given birth to a filly, amidst much hoopla and rejoicing.

Before I was seen off in his chauffeur-driven limo to the governor's mansion, he asked me if I would give them permission to christen their newborn filly after me, Bina. I was delighted! I learned three years later that his Bina had been entered at the Kentucky Derby, though she did not manage to win any of the legendary trophies.

As for the coal purchase by India, despite its superior quality and the attractive price that Crescent Coal offered, India opted to

Participating in the high jump at the National Games, 1956, in Patiala

*(Left) At the age of nineteen; (right) At twenty-one, after completing a course
in modelling from the Lucy Clayton Institute*

A photo of mine which was sent
as a pin-up for the prisoners of
San Quentin prison

Putting my best foot
forward for the camera

With my ex-husband Andy Ramani (centre) and
our families during our engagement

Exploring the streets of San Francisco in 1967

With my best friend Leela Ellis aka Mary Leela Rao

With my dear friend and guardian angel Dora

Showing my designs to Indira Gandhi at her home

My niece Ramona (right) with Mrs Lillian Carter during the launch of Raga restaurant

With Maharaja Bhawani Singh of Jaipur

With Bhabhi-ji (Mrs Raj Kapoor) at the launch of my first boutique in Delhi

At a family party with: (L-R) my brother Kartar, former boss Ajit Kerkar, sister Kiki and friend Asha Puthli

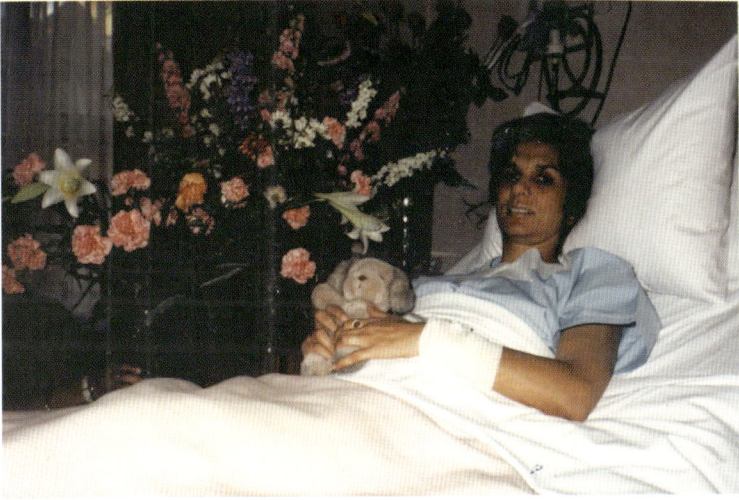

Staying strong: Post my cancer surgery at Princess Grace Hospital, London

Brothers and sisters: With my siblings and their spouses in 1992. (L-R)
Gulu and Semiramis, Suriender Bawa and Mohini, Kartar, Rani, Kamla
and Joginder, Kiki, Pushpa, Partap and Padma

One of the US senators' wives
modelling my design for the Palna
orphanage charity show

At my boutique, The Asian Opera,
with my partner Belle McIntyre

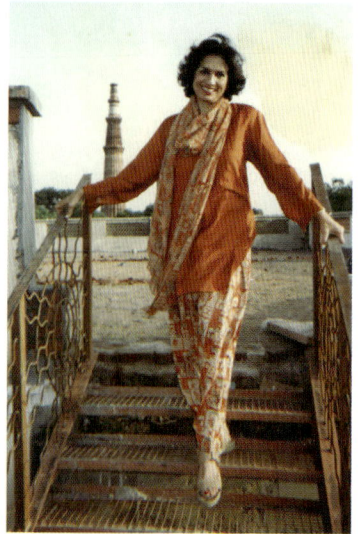

A journey of ten years: (Left) Outside Once Upon a Time with my designs;
(Right) On my roof at the Qutab Colonnade

My Umang charity group. (L-R) Top row: Sally Holkar, Nafisa Ali,
Vasundhara Raje and Browyn Latif. Bottom row: Shirin Paul; Me;
Christine Wizner, then American ambassador's wife; Vinu Baig;
Anne-Marie Petit, then French ambassador's wife; and Sunita Kohli

With Richard Gere (centre, holding child)
at Sahara, an NGO for AIDS patients

With the former choudhary of Hauz Khas Village, Raghuvir Singh

My favourite Manbhari (left) with author Dominique Lapierre (right)

The Qutab Colonnade from the outside

The Tamarind Court Café

My parents, S. Tirath Singh and Devi Kaur Lalvani

With Shashi (left) and Shammi Kapoor (centre) in 2005

My pillars of strength: Gitu (above) and Malini (below)

At Georges's Golf Links home with friends: (L-R) Kitten Muskar, Rajmata Gayatri Devi, Naveen Pattanaik, Oliver Musker and Browyn Latif

Impromptu soirees: (L-R) with Sonal Mansingh, Zubin Mehta, Georges and Kiran Gujral

A new beginning: at my wedding with Georges

My daughter Gitu (right) with her husband David and two sons, Kaspian and Kai

With my beloved grandsons

At peace: With Georges in Goa

buy its coal supplies from Australia, compromising on quality in favour of the shorter travel distance and lower cargo costs. Besides, the agent representing the Australian product was a close friend of Indira Gandhi, and freely bragged about it.

18

The Last Straw

LIFE AT HOME seemed to be improving. A house I had inherited in London from my family had just been sold and I was able to use that windfall, in addition to money from the sale of our smaller house in New York's Hartsdale, towards a down payment on a beautiful property in a classy suburb of New York called Dobbs Ferry. It was about a century old, built on two acres of land just adjoining a beautiful golf course. The Ramani family now had a grand house with about fourteen rooms and the girls, aged seven and eight, went to a fine school nearby.

It was whispered in the neighbourhood that Michael Wilding had bought this Tudor-style mansion for his bride, the actress Elizabeth Taylor. But he had died in an air crash before they could ever live in it. Since that tragedy, the mansion had changed hands three times before we found it, some fifteen years later. We couldn't believe our luck at the throwaway price they were asking for it. This was attributed to three factors: first, New York was in a deep recession and real estate prices had plummeted; second, and possibly the main reason, the owners had hit hard times, had divorced and declared bankruptcy; and third, it seemed that there were no other takers even at this low price because of the stigma that had attached itself to 'the unlucky house'.

Andy and I decided to turn a deaf ear to the chorus of whispers from some of the brokers, waving it off as 'sour grapes'. In fact, the two years following our move were the best ones of our life together. Family life had never been better. The children were enrolled in an excellent school nearby, we had wonderful neighbours, and our friends came visiting from faraway places. We had a great Indian nanny-cum-cook, a precious pug named Danny Boy, and weekend parties were the norm. My prayers were full of thanksgiving. Life was coming up a fragrant bouquet of roses.

But, much like the rose that fades and sheds its fragrance, our marital joy soon started to diminish. The demanding hours of my flourishing commodity trading business fell out of sync with Andy's steady nine-to-five job, as did my erratic income versus his steady, predictable paycheck. At some point I delayed in handing over my monthly earnings. While I was in charge of the supply end, I had to rely largely on my agent in India to submit bids at an opportune time to the appropriate ministries in order to win contracts. Sadly, for almost four months, no bid had been successful. Yet, the monthly costs of the business had to be covered.

By the third month of my refusal to hand over money to him, Andy's patience had run out. He had been nagging me with the same demand every evening when I reached home from my office. One day I received a call from my banker informing me that my husband had called him, wanting to know the activity of my account over the past three months. My banker had rightfully declined to turn over the information and now was calling to explain and apologize for any misunderstanding that might have occurred.

I was shocked and infuriated. This act by Andy was not only a breach of trust, it was a deep insult to my integrity. It was the last straw. Finally I found the courage to take a decision that should have been taken years before. I had already come to realize that I owed it to myself and to my children to establish some degree of financial independence, and had managed to tuck away a small nest egg from the '20 per cent share' of my income Andy had allowed me. For the first time in our marriage I stood up to him and challenged him, and it ended in an explosive fight.

Fearing that if it continued the fight would get out of control, I left the house and drove to the home of my cousins, Lovina and Sunder Thadani, some ten miles away. I checked on the girls before I left; they were sleeping peacefully in their rooms. This time, I knew the marriage was over. There was a finality in the air, quite different from the four or five previous separations. This was finally *it*—and I was deeply shaken at the realization. By now, the children were ten and eleven years old.

In the morning, Sunder and Lovina rushed me to the Family Court of Westchester, where Andy was summoned. I was granted interim custody of the girls. Even though I avoided looking in Andy's direction I could sense his deep animosity towards me. My lawyer advised me to keep the girls in a place separate from me, because he felt Andy might take some bold action, given his mood in the court. We decided that the family of Gitu's best friend from school, Candy, could take the girls in for a short while until things were sorted out. I made the arrangements, and as soon as the girls returned from school that afternoon I took them to Candy's home and settled them in. Candy's mother assured me they would be safe until I had found a more secure and practical solution for them. I had her phone number and was to stay in constant touch.

Meanwhile, my friend Beverly Perry had heard my news and gathered a close group of friends at her apartment on Fifth Avenue. We celebrated my newfound courage and pooled our resources to figure out how best to carve out my new life so that the kids could continue at their school, uninterrupted. I knew it would not be easy to placate Andy, and I couldn't bear the thought of any confrontation with him.

I spoke to the girls a couple of times on the phone and they were playing happily. At one point in the early evening, suddenly I couldn't get through to them—inexplicably, the phone seemed to have gone out of commission. A premonition told me that this spelled bad news. My friends and I called the telephone company, who were normally prompt at rectifying problems and explaining the cause of faulty lines. But they could offer no explanation.

Three hours later, by which time I was a nervous wreck and getting ready to make the one-hour drive to the house where the girls were staying, I received a call from Andy's nephew, Zal. 'Auntie

Bina,' he matter-of-factly informed me, 'Uncle Andy has taken Malini and Gitu on a plane somewhere out of the country. He had me drive them all to the airport, but he would not say where they were going.' In response to my panic and desperate probing, he offered, 'I think I heard him say Holland. Maybe that's where they are headed.' I was thrown into such a shock that I collapsed on Beverly's carpet in a faint. Our gathering of close friends had turned into a nightmare.

From that moment, I was sucked into a vortex of hopelessness and despair. I made emergency calls to my family in London, to the American embassy in Holland and even to the Indian ambassador in Washington. I told each of them that my daughters had been taken from me and that I needed help to find them. No one had any answers. My family offered consolation and invited me to come to London.

All at once, I realized that I was really all alone in this world to face this disaster. No one could provide me with any solutions. In the eyes of the law, this was a 'civil matter' and had to be handled by attorneys and special courts. No crime had been committed.

I had to be master of my own destiny now. I had to fight for my rights on whatever shaky ground I stood. The consolations and sympathy that were offered made me cringe. That was the last thing I needed when it was as if both my arms had been cut off—so helpless did I feel. What I needed was some fuse to ignite the fire of rage in me, so I could be ready to fight single-handedly for my rights. It was to be another turning point in my life, emerging from a combination of intense pain and shock. But it unlocked my Sikh warrior's path, and awakened a fierce determination in me.

∎

The next days and weeks went by in a blur. My imagination had conjured up all sorts of possible places the kids could have been taken to. My appetite and my sleep were stolen by the dark force that surrounded me. Then, about five weeks later, I received a call from my sister Mohini in Kapurthala. She informed me that Malini and Gitu were in Kasauli at Sanawar School, where her daughter Jotika was also a senior student.

I left for India immediately. In Delhi, Mohini and her husband were waiting to take me on the seven-hour drive from Delhi to Sanawar. The journey took us through picturesque hill terrain with numerous blind curves, going ever uphill. From the moment our car reached the big colonial gates of Sanawar, the 150-year-old school from where Rudyard Kipling had graduated, my heart began to pound. I just wanted to get out of the car and run until I had my arms around my girls. My sister and brother-in-law had to physically restrain me. 'We are only at the gates,' they said. 'We have a long way to go uphill.'

After what seemed like aeons, we passed several large buildings and finally reached the playground. Boys and girls of all ages in blue uniforms were playing, or just sitting around chatting, oblivious to the world outside. My eyes hungrily searched for my girls in the sea of children. I spotted Malini first, playing with a couple of friends. She had lost weight, was tanned and, thankfully, appeared happy. She wasn't exactly overjoyed to see me at first. She was surprised and a little hesitant to display her affection openly. After the initial hesitation, though, the floodgates opened and she excitedly started to tell me everything at once. Words tumbled out of her mouth almost incoherently, jumping from one thing to another, as we hugged each other tight. Then we walked over to where Gitu was in the distance, sitting among other uniformed students. She had grown very thin and was a little taller than I remembered, even though only a little more than a month had passed.

Gitu spotted me and came running to embrace me, proudly showing the fabric she was embroidering. Her delight washed over me and I had to fight hard to free the lump that choked my throat. I didn't want the children to see my pain.

After their initial excitement and happiness, the girls oddly seemed a little wary of me. Within minutes of my arrival, teachers and students had begun to gather around us, and the other children were pointing at me and staring in a way that began to feel strange. Only later would I discover that Andy had warned the school that if I ever turned up I had to be watched closely, because I might try and run away with the children.

The girls looked at me. 'Mummy, you are not insane, are you?' they asked innocently. I held them in a tight embrace, assuring them that I was fine, the same as I had always been. I was in tears by then and held them for the longest time. Yet, I was aware that since the moment I had arrived all eyes had been on me, and it continued. It was unnerving, and I began to wonder if I was indeed insane, thanks to all these events.

It was difficult to pull myself together for my next task, which was to meet with the headmaster, Mr Das. Had I known what he was going to tell me, I cannot imagine how much more difficult it would have been.

Andy had brought the girls to Sanawar with the help of his sister Sheila. Sheila knew the headmaster well, and had arranged for instant admission to the school—a school where admission was generally booked a generation ahead! The two of them had concocted an elaborate story about me, which I was about to hear for the first time.

As soon as he arrived in India with the girls, Andy had gone to the High Court in Bombay and obtained an ex parte court order against me. He claimed that I was mad, and that was why he had pulled the children away from me in New York. He had arrived in Sanawar with the Bombay court papers that gave him interim custody and restricted my access to the girls until a trial could be convened.

I could not believe what I was hearing! And, in my distraught state, I felt totally intimidated by this man, legendary for his toughness as a headmaster, who suddenly had so much power over my life and my access to the girls. In my shock and incomprehension, I muttered a few incoherent words in response. I sensed immediately that I was only confirming everything he had heard.

I knew at that moment that I had a tortuous battle ahead of me. I was going to have to face custody hearings in the courts in New

York and Bombay. On top of all this I was broke, and I had lost my footing, along with my confidence. But I had to save my children from Andy's unpredictable temper, and my sanity through regaining my custodial rights. At that point it was the only thing worth living for.

The battle stretched over nearly five years, and my sister Mohini was my saviour through most of this period. My new focus in life revolved around ways and means to visit Sanawar, to find a new and steady source of income, and to win each round of the long and complicated series of the custody battles in court.

I lived in New York and visited Delhi a few times a year. It took many more trips to entirely convince the school that I was indeed a sane woman, just like all the other mothers who came to visit their children. Andy never once visited the school after the day he had admitted the girls, so my regular visits as a parent also helped them feel more 'normal' among their peers.

Andy did, however, make it his mission to do everything within his power to prevent my access to the kids and obstruct my trips to India. In the meantime, he left his job at Air India and started a travel agency in New York.

I moved out of the home we had shared as a family and converted my triplex office into an apartment. Andy continued living in the Dobbs Ferry mansion for another four years with his nephew. The house finally sold for a small gain in value, of which I got my 50 per cent share.

19

Lucky Beads

To ENABLE MY frequent visits from New York to Sanawar, I needed a layover place in Delhi. I was fortunate to be hosted by the only two sets of friends I knew there, each warm and very hospitable. The two families gave me a home away from home—Ritu and Rajan Nanda, who had built a luxurious mansion in Delhi's fashionable neighbourhood of Friends Colony, and Maya and Nanu Virmani, who lived in their grand old ancestral house with sprawling lawns in historical old Delhi.

I was soon to discover that Maya's home not only provided a convenient exit north for my Sanawar journeys, but was only a few kilometres away from the legendary and exciting bazaars of the 400-year-old Chandni Chowk. I was drawn to the area like a bee to flowers and spent most of my spare hours exploring the winding, crowded lanes, discovering the ancient treasures of just about every Indian art and craft—bookbinding, perfumery, silver and gold jewellery and ornamental decorations of every kind. Like Alice, I had fallen into Wonderland! Sitting amongst the artisans and craftsmen gave me immense pleasure and inspiration.

I was discovering, for the first time, the richness of India's artistic tradition. However, while exquisite, the designs of the jewellery and embroidery that I saw tended to be somewhat repetitious. I yearned to breathe new life into the traditional ornamentation, and to introduce an occidental influence into them and expand the repertoire of these craftsmen. Fearing that I might offend their sensibilities, I nevertheless offered the idea to them. To my joy, they welcomed it wholeheartedly and agreed to take on some commissions.

My creative juices flowed; I was pushing boundaries with all kinds of experimentation. This newfound synergy with my collaborators turned out to be a glimpse of the path that awaited me in India. I wouldn't fully realize this until much later, but my future was being fashioned. Meanwhile, this creative outlet served as a healing balm for my turbulent mind.

My passion first resulted in colourful beaded necklaces, using imaginative patterns in gorgeous hues. I often wore these exotic pieces, choosing from among them even before I selected my clothes for the day. Then the traditional hair accessory, the parandhi, found new life as tassels dangling from my shawls and evening bags. The potential of reinventing old ideas for new purposes seemed unlimited. I became my own model and, somewhat to my surprise, these necklaces, along with my other experiments, began to be noticed.

Over our morning tea one day in 1982, Maya and I decided to experiment and invest in a small accessory business partnership. We recognized that we complemented each other well. Maya was a gifted organizer and could handle the administration, while I could do the designing. We each invested ₹20,000 and built our first collection together.

Our first opportunity came knocking when, in April 1983, my brother Gulu and his glamorous wife Vimla arrived in Delhi to attend a Young Presidents' Organization (YPO) meeting. Members of this organization were a select group of very successful businessmen. They usually picked exotic locales for their conferences with an eye on shopping potential for their wives. Gulu suggested that we exhibit our accessories to coincide with the conference being held at the Oberoi Hotel in Delhi.

We set about the task with great enthusiasm. Our collection consisted mostly of shawls, jewellery and evening bags fashioned from a unique combination of materials. We booked a small office space that happened to be available for three days, and sent invitation cards to all the YPO guests. Even as we were completing our display, some clients began to walk in. Incredibly, within six hours of opening that first day, we were sold out! A business plan hatched over our morning tea had earned us a 300 per cent profit—and the customers were begging for more.

Within three months we held our second exhibition in Bombay, again at the Oberoi Hotel, where a dear friend, Parmeshwar Godrej, owned a boutique called 'Dancing Silks'. Quite spontaneously, she offered the use of her chic boutique for no charge. We arrived better prepared this time, with a larger inventory. But even though Bombay did not prove as successful as Delhi, Parmeshwar generously invited us to use her boutique on a permanent basis. As much as I wanted to return to the city of my childhood, I realized it would be too far and too expensive for me to reach my girls up north on a regular basis. I often regretted that missed opportunity over the years, because the upbeat pulse of Bombay always resonated for me.

Maya and I soon parted ways as partners, because my frequent trips to New York for child custody court hearings came in the way of running a regular business. But we remained friends and still often reminisce about our brief and happy partnership. Meanwhile, the 'East–West' design concept continued to flower from my own efforts. I was receiving and filling orders for custom-designed necklaces for a couple of New York's high-end stores. While my fortunes were not rising as quickly as I would have liked, I enjoyed this agreeable new path between Delhi and New York with routine stopovers in London to visit family. It more than covered the cost of the children's education at Sanawar.

On one of my trips, I came to believe that God had personally intervened in my affairs. A London visit happened to coincide with the first of the several large 'Festival of India' celebrations that had been started by the Indian government in 1983. The festival, which was an ambitious representation of every aspect of India's rich cultural heritage, was a pet project of Rajiv Gandhi, and this debut event was being personally supervised by his mother Indira Gandhi. She inaugurated the month-long London festival showcasing art, music, dance, films, theatre, fashion and textiles with the aim that India would dazzle the British audience like never before. A who's who of India and the Indian community in London mingled with British royalty in the exclusive four-day inaugural festivities, which later opened for the public in all the major department stores, parks and streets of London before moving on to other major cities in England.

An inaugural night at the Royal Festival Hall was to be attended by Prince Charles and Princess Diana, along with the prime ministers of both India and England, Indira Gandhi and Margaret Thatcher respectively. London society's A-listers, plus personalities with business links to India, each paid £250 to attend. A concert was directed by my friend Zubin Mehta, featuring the London Symphony Orchestra and Pandit Ravi Shankar as soloist. It ended with a rendering of the Indian national anthem, easily the most emotionally charged version of the 'Jana Gana Mana' I have ever heard, followed by 'God Save the Queen'. I think there was not a dry eye among the 3,000 or so guests, as a reverent silence marked the end of the music before the crowd rose as one with roars of 'Bravo!' and thunderous applause filled the auditorium.

A select few guests, including my family, were given the opportunity to mingle with the four VIPs at the reception and dinner that followed. I was excited at the prospect of meeting Princess Diana, but being heavily pregnant at the time, she departed soon after the concert.

Suddenly, in the midst of all this, I found myself face to face with Indira Gandhi. As I greeted her with an enthusiastic but humble namaste, I noticed that she was looking at me curiously. 'What is your name?' she asked. She must have used this opening line with all the guests who had preceded me, I thought.

'Bina Lalvani,' I responded. I wasn't sure what name I would adopt after my divorce, so in London I went by my maiden name.

'What do you do?' she asked, her eyes transfixed on my necklace.

'I am a designer,' I replied, feeling slightly unnerved by her interest in my jewellery.

'Did you make that necklace?' she asked, pointing to my chunky twist of twenty rows of garnets that ended in a cascading knot.

'Yes, I did,' I said. Now my heart was pounding nervously.

'Are you participating in the festival?' was her next question, and I began to feel as though I was at a job interview.

'I am actually based in New York, and I think this festival is only for people who live in England,' I responded with a smile.

Questioning me further, she came to know that I also lived in India part of the time. She then turned to Pupul Jayakar, one of the architects of the festival, who was standing beside her. 'Why hasn't she been identified as one of our jewellery designers?' she asked, and then proceeded to call over R.K. Dhawan, her personal secretary, who was standing nearby.

Deep down, I somehow felt that this conversation had displeased Pupul and that she, as the chief executive of the Festival of India, was in no mood to hear about my designing skills or to promote me in any way at this eleventh hour. I understood her predicament, and at that moment wished we hadn't been introduced. This long-awaited launch of India's biggest cultural event abroad was hardly the time to be distracted by a new entrant into her well-orchestrated programme!

But Mrs Gandhi had Plan B already brewing. She turned to Dhawan: 'Fix an appointment for this Miss Lalvani with me sometime in the next three days.' Her eyes kept darting to my necklace. It was all happening so fast, I could hardly contain the surge of joy, uncomfortably mixed as it was with a fear of stepping on sensitive toes.

'Oh, but I am leaving for New York tomorrow at 2 p.m.,' I said, as diplomatically as I could.

Madam was not to be deterred. She wanted to see more of my unusual treatment of semi-precious stones. 'Meet me at 9 a.m. tomorrow morning at the Claridges Hotel and bring along some of your jewellery designs,' she said determinedly. Then she instructed Dhawan to fit me into her morning schedule. For good measure, she added, 'I like semi-precious jewellery.'

She waved off her secretary's reminder of a 9 a.m. meeting with the BBC and gave me a warm smile, saying, 'I hope you can make it at nine? We are at the Claridges Hotel. Do you know where that is?'

'Yes,' I nodded. 'I will be there for sure.'

Of course I would! Sleep that night was elusive. I couldn't believe my luck.

Crowds of people and a whole BBC crew lining the corridor to her VIP suite met me when I arrived at the Claridges Hotel, red-eyed from lack of sleep, at the stroke of nine the next morning. I was immediately ushered into a luxurious drawing room. Mrs Gandhi walked in just two minutes later, greeting me with a brief and controlled smile. She examined me curiously, just as she had the night before. Then she offered me tea, which I politely declined, and we quickly got to the point. Respecting her crowded schedule, I pulled out my velveteen pouch that contained some twenty semi-precious fusion design necklaces. She examined each one, and then, without any hesitation, picked out four that caught her fancy. Her friendly approach in the way she examined each piece helped dissipate most of my nervousness. I had the feeling she liked me, and not only because I designed jewellery.

'Pupul, come out and see Miss Lalvani's collection,' she called out to the adjoining room.

Moments later, from one of the doors, in walked the woman who had given me the shivers. Her presence unnerved me. Mrs Gandhi, meanwhile, handled and examined each of the four necklaces with excitement and childlike delight. She picked them up, one by one, walked over to the mirror and sought Pupul Jayakar's opinion, getting a tepid response. But she refused to let her companion's indifference subdue her enthusiasm. She examined herself in the mirror and exclaimed, 'Oh dear, I think I'm too old for this, but I like it so much! Look—what an unusual design! How has Miss Lalvani managed to put such combinations together? Why don't we see more of these in India?' She tried to engage Pupul in conversation, but without much success. Then, in an attempt to put me at ease, she said in a warm tone, 'I wish you had more amber. That is my favourite stone. It gives me so much peace of mind.'

Her wistful expression was a sight to behold. To see one of the most powerful women in the world exhibit the same girlish vanities as any of us was a rare treat, and utterly delightful.

Fifteen minutes later, after some advice from Pupul, she finally picked out two necklaces with amethyst, rose quartz and silver beads. These were the simplest of all my designs. 'How much do these cost?' she asked.

'I am much too embarrassed to tell you,' I said. 'They cost so little. Please do me the honour of accepting them as a gift from me.'

She thanked me profusely, again reminding me of an innocent little girl. 'Do make some designs with amber beads in the future,' she pleaded. I promised I would.

Once I was sitting in the plane back to New York, I grasped the reality of the meeting. I soared higher than that plane as I thought about my charmed morning. And my good fortune was to continue in that flight across the Atlantic. The passenger next to me was a buyer of accessories for one of New York's most prestigious stores, Bergdorf Goodman (BG). She noticed the big colourful beads around my neck and wanted to know where I had got them. As we talked, she made it clear that she loved the East–West theme I had created and could not wait to get her store directors to do a 'programme' on accessories from India. My good fortune was beyond belief! I had never imagined that I could ever gain access to BG, and now it seemed that it was going to be my very first New York client! I was overjoyed. God *did* exist, and moreover, He seemed to like me.

I hadn't yet worked out a supply system in India, so I strung beads in a closet of my apartment that I had converted to a makeshift workshop. The buyers at BG were sympathetic to my plight and made exceptions by paying for the goods before the stipulated thirty-day period. Every time I had enough money to pay a couple of months' rent and buy a ticket, I would fly out to India to be in Sanawar.

20

The Interview

T HE FIRST FEW days after my return from India were always marked by a ritual I enjoyed. I would invite friends to drop in, and we looked forward to the occasion as an opportunity to exchange gossip, private and public. This time, many of them had also made it clear that they wanted to be among the first to own a necklace from my newest collection. A platter of cheese and wine was part of the ritual.

It was impossible not to share my unexpected and enthralling encounter with Indira Gandhi. For once, it was my story that dominated our ritual gathering. They were captivated by the part about Mrs Gandhi letting her guard down and revealing her feminine vanity. Josephine Lyon, who was the features editor of *McCall's Magazine*, apparently tucked the story neatly into her ticking journalist brain. The next morning, before I had finished my first cup of tea, the phone rang. It was Jo.

'Morning Jo, how goes? Are you happy with your new necklace?' I asked her cheerily.

'Bina, I love the necklace, but I have something of great importance to discuss. It's urgent.' She used a familiar bossy tone.

'What do you mean?'

'Bina, I shared your story with my editorial staff, of the unique insight you got into Indira Gandhi's feminine side, and they want to run an exclusive cover story about it.' She then continued in a rather officious tone that I had never heard her use before. 'You know, we are the world's largest women's magazine and reach twenty-two million women every month.'

'I had no idea,' I replied, suitably impressed.

'Well, here's the idea. We all think that revealing a glimpse of the soft, feminine side of one of the world's most powerful women, better known as the Iron Lady, would make excellent reading.' Now she softened her tone. 'The average American woman has preconceived notions about Eastern women, and we think this is a fantastic opportunity to show the American reader that deep down, all women have the same vanities, insecurities and desires.'

'Wow Jo, that's terrific.' I was delighted at the concept.

'So Bina, we need you to link us up with her. We think the first approach should start from your end, you know, almost like you are just continuing your dialogue with her at the Claridges Hotel.'

I cut her short right there. 'Jo darling, it's a great idea. But forget it. I'm not the one to make this introduction. I wouldn't know where to begin. Surely you have experts on your team who specialize in this sort of thing.' I paused. 'Sorry,' I concluded with finality.

She was persistent. 'Okay Bina, let's mull over this and figure out a way. I will drop by this evening.' Her office was only four blocks from my flat.

I spent most of the day trying to dismiss the conversation from my thoughts. I was not looking forward to Jo's visit that evening, but even as I considered calling her to postpone it, she was ringing my doorbell. She came in, breathless with excitement. Apparently, she and her staff had spent most of the day discussing the coup they would pull in the world of glossy magazine publishing if they could get Indira Gandhi to grace their cover three months hence.

'Nice try, Jo,' I said to her, after she had exhausted every argument to convince me to write the introductory letter. 'But here's the truth. I'm a hopeless writer. And besides, she most probably won't even remember who I am.'

Jo beamed a big smile at me, took a sip of the iced tea I had offered her and chuckled as she said, 'I have good news. We have already drafted something for you.' She handed me an envelope from her bag.

The letter consisted of two short paragraphs, rather cold and official in tone. It enumerated the advantages of Indian culture reaching the drawing rooms of middle America, and how good that would be for India's image. I couldn't possibly put my name to such a letter. But miraculously, I suddenly found inspiration and on the back of the letter I scribbled out a personal message. Then I reread it and rewrote some of it. Some mysterious power had come over me, and Jo's delight was palpable.

We burst into laughter. The whole conversion had taken about an hour, and I had begun to feel that the idea might actually be a good one. After we toasted each other with several glasses of chilled white wine, I assured Jo that I would give it serious consideration and let her know my decision within forty-eight hours. As it turned out, I did not need that much time. I was riding a wave of energy brought on by all the action and reaction from Jo's office in the past twenty-four hours. It suddenly made sense to me that writing to Mrs Gandhi within ten days of our memorable meeting, at someone else's behest, was possibly the best opportunity to open communication with her.

I tossed and turned until dawn, then simply put pen to paper and got on with it. I kept it brief. After a one-line reminder of my propitious meeting with her at the Claridges Hotel, I moved on to convey the urgings of this magazine that reached millions of American households, and the great platform they were offering to show India in a positive light.

I read it out to Jo in the morning. She congratulated me and remarked that I made myself sound like an earnest young girl, and certainly Mrs Gandhi could never turn down such a request. Suddenly I realized I had no address to send it to! So I simply addressed it to *Prime Minister of India, Indira Gandhi, New Delhi, India*. I called Jo to tell her, 'I have written the letter and put it in the mailbox this morning. Just prepare yourself for the disappointment if we don't receive a response.' I laughed. 'I'm already reconciled to that thought!'

'Let's cross our fingers,' she chirped optimistically.

With that task behind me, I plunged into my routines—the pleasant one of visiting my clients and the odious one of meeting with the divorce and custody lawyers. We were trying to see how best we could simplify my case and move it to India, rather than fight it in multiple courts in New York, Bombay and Delhi.

One morning, about three weeks later, I saw in the mailbox an envelope with a red embossed Ashok Chakra and the words: *From the Office of the Prime Minister.* The words and the emblem danced before my eyes as I carried the envelope to my apartment. I could barely contain my excitement as I opened it. The typewritten letter inside read: '*Dear Ms Lalvani: Thank you for your letter received yesterday. When are you visiting India to do the interview? With best regards.*' It was signed *Indira Gandhi.*

It took me a couple of days to digest the reality of receiving a response from the prime minister of my country. After much deliberation and discussion with Jo, I realized that I had to respond and set the record straight. Jo insisted that the response had to come from me, and not from them, as I would have preferred. I didn't know how to explain to Mrs Gandhi that she had misunderstood my request, and that it was not I who would conduct the interview but a writer from the magazine. Finally, in the humblest way possible, I wrote that I was not a journalist and had no writing background or skill, and that the interview would be conducted by Ms Josephine Lyons.

To my utter amazement I got another prompt response, saying, 'I find your style of letter writing quite adequate and would rather have you do the interview in your own natural way.' She asked me once again to advise her of my arrival date in India.

Stupefied by the response, I reread the letter several times and shared it with Josephine. Both she and I went silent on the subject for several days. She was not pleased, but she was not holding me responsible. She nevertheless lost face with her staff, and I believe they were all disappointed and rather annoyed. Realizing there was no point in pursuing it further, they concluded that if I did decide to do the interview they would consider running it, but not as a cover story.

■

It was with equal doses of nervousness and delight that I scheduled my trip to Delhi to coincide with the summer vacation at Sanawar. On the day of the interview I was recovering from a viral fever. But it was out of the question to postpone the date with Mrs Gandhi, as her calendar was unalterable. The previous week her secretary had already vetted my four-page list of questions and returned it unchanged. I had tried to strike an acceptable balance—I knew I had to be true to myself and keep the questions simple, with the result that some of them were somewhat naïve. I wanted to address personal issues that Mrs Gandhi had probably never discussed in an interview before.

I arrived with my little Binatone compact recorder in one hand and some fresh jewellery designs in the other, not forgetting the amber beads. I was seated in an informal drawing room of 12 Safdarjung Road, where I could see, through the window, a long stone path that led to a garden. The other end of the room, I thought, probably led to Mrs Gandhi's office, and perhaps a pantry, judging from the sounds emanating from that direction. The furniture was simple and the room was divided into two sitting areas.

Two or three men hovered around until she walked into the room, all smiles. Wearing a simple block-printed cotton sari, she looked like a quintessential Indian woman in her drawing room on a summer afternoon—except that her aura belied that image. Her powerful persona filled the room.

She seemed to sense my discomfort and nervousness at the task facing me, and decided to take the initiative of helping me through it. To put me at ease, she pointed to a picture on the wall at the far end of the room, in which her late son Sanjay was playing Holi. She then casually led me around the adjoining hallway and showed me many more family pictures, always looking wistfully at Sanjay's face. She told me how much she missed him, how lively he used to be and how he had the ability to fill every place he entered with a happy energy. The black-and-white picture of him playing Holi with a pichkari in hand was her favourite.

She had succeeded in easing my discomfort, and we headed back to the sofa near the garden door. She seated me next to a corner table, where I could place my tape recorder and the bag containing my latest jewellery designs. As I was about to open the bag with my jewellery, she reached out and stopped me.

'Let's finish the interview first,' she suggested, smiling.

'I have read your questions and they are charming. You do not need to be nervous,' she said encouragingly. One of her assistants came over and helped me test the tape recorder; a photographer entered and took pictures throughout the interview. I have to admit, I never managed to completely relax. My senses remained in a heightened state of excitement for as long I was with her, almost two hours.

My questions began with her early childhood years. I wanted her to recall her carefree times and days of innocence.

She surprised me by telling me that she did not recall any part of her childhood being carefree, because she was always torn between her father, who was in and out of jail as a freedom fighter, and her frail mother, who frequently suffered from ill health. 'My childhood got lost somewhere along the way, between the demands of circumstances,' she recalled wistfully.

On the subject of romance, she was quite candid in declaring that she was attracted to Feroze Gandhi as soon as she saw him, and he was the only man she ever loved.

About the turbulent days before and after the 'Emergency', she described the experience as akin to dipping one finger in ice-cold, and the other in boiling hot water. 'The peak of Emergency, and then the aftermath—both were extremities of numbness,' she said, sounding much the wiser for it. 'It was the need of the hour,' she summed up calmly.

In a profound moment she declared, 'It's one thing to grow up with instruction from one's elders and teachers, but altogether another when one has to construct one's own life in this world.'

We deviated from the interview questions a few times, and when it was over she turned the interview around and began to interrogate me. She wanted to know everything. My family, how I had managed to live away from India for so long (twenty-five years at this point), and was I ever considering moving back? She seemed to empathize with me for some reason and insisted I ask her secretary for any assistance I might need. I never took her up on this generous offer, though.

Once the interview was over, we finally got around to examining the jewellery and, to my delight, she loved the amber necklace that I had made especially for her. She was pictured wearing it on several occasions during the following year—the last year of her life.

I also showed her my scarf line in which I had used the parandhi tassles to secure the two ends of the scarf. She found it amusing, and I offered it to her as a gift for her daughter-in-law Sonia. She expressed discomfort when I insisted that these were gifts. She decided to invite Sonia in so that I could present the scarf to her personally. It was about 5.30 p.m. and we were alone. She rang the bell several times for the servants, but no one came. She tried again, and still got no response. Five minutes later, after another failed attempt, she shook her head as any housewife would do, complaining, 'These servants, they are never around when you need them!'

I smiled. 'Yes, it's a familiar scene, but I would never expect it in your home!'

Moments later, a servant appeared and informed her that Sonia memsahib was sleeping. So the last photo session that we had saved for the garden setting with Sonia, Priyanka and Rahul was never to happen. The photographer happily clicked away as we walked towards the big neem tree, laughing about the bird droppings. By now I had begun to feel completely at ease. The fever had miraculously disappeared, and a beautiful memory had taken its place.

I held on to the ninety-minute tape, which had run out during our conversation, as a prized possession. Josephine had lost interest in publishing the interview but by sheer chance I met Aroon Purie, who was delighted to run the story in *India Today* with a blurb on the cover describing it as 'Indira Gandhi's first ever personal interview'. Exactly three months after that interview, she was assassinated in that same garden into which I had gazed as I awaited her arrival.

21

Danny Boy

MALINI AND GITU had started to settle into school, and both were making their mark in sports teams, winning medals, making friends and writing enthusiastic letters. Their only complaints were about the strict regimental discipline and indigestible food. The two recurring items on their wish lists, other than wanting me to visit them as often as the school would allow, were American food and their little pug, Danny Boy.

The dog still lived with Andy in our big family house with its sprawling lawns in Dobbs Ferry, Westchester County. It had been the girls' home before they were kidnapped and admitted to Sanawar, a year earlier. I had moved to Manhattan, into the chic triplex pied-à-terre from where I had run my business before our separation.

I missed my nineteenth-century Dobbs Ferry home, which stood on two acres of lush green landscape adjoining an exclusive golf course and encircling a romantic pond edged with weeping willow trees. I had been unable to visit the house because of Andy's hostility, despite my primary financial support when we bought it.

Our maid Pasquin from Bombay, who had been with us for five years, left us at about the time I moved out of the house. Andy and his eldest nephew Zal, who had come to study in New York, now lived in this house as two bachelors. The men were away all day long, and Danny Boy was alone in the large fourteen-room mansion. I missed him enormously, as did the girls. We all wanted Danny Boy near us in a loving environment. Our erstwhile home in Dobbs Ferry was now a lonely house, devoid of love and attention for a little dog.

A plan grew in my mind with each new letter from the girls,

who pined for their pet. The urge to convert the thought into reality kept growing, and I conjured a plot to go pick up (dognap!) Danny Boy from the house some afternoon when Andy and Zal were away. It was so tempting that it began to feel feasible. It took a few weeks for the thought to crystallize into a firm plan—also, to build up the courage!

I was now about ten days away from my next trip to India. I needed a confidential and reliable accomplice. Andy was known to be in a foul mood those days, not at all pleased that I had established contact with the girls and even more displeased that I had made great strides with the stern headmaster and faculty at Sanawar.

My enquiries revealed that Pan Am Airlines would allow a lap dog to travel to India, and that there were no particular restrictions. His fare would be about $130; there would be a two-hour stopover at Frankfurt airport. It all seemed manageable. The time had come to carry out the plot and rescue Danny Boy from his lonely fortress.

After much deliberation upon who my accomplice would be, I settled on my friend Beverly Perry, who was rich, wacky and bored, and would be game for anything adventurous. She had been a good, solid friend all these years. In fact, it was her apartment where I had been the night I had received the horrific news of my children's kidnapping over a year earlier. She turned out to be the perfect choice as accomplice in my daring deed, and could hardly wait.

We picked a Wednesday, mid-week, when Andy and Zal would not have too much free time to go looking for a missing dog. By the weekend, I would be safely headed out of the US with Danny Boy, on my way to India with the best gift that Malini and Gitu could hope for. Emotionally, this would be a balm for their flagging spirits. With this grand plan churning in my head, I convinced Beverly—and myself—that our mission was a good deed aiming at harvesting happiness, therefore nothing could possibly go wrong.

I had not been at the house for a year, and wondered how Danny Boy would react when I found him. Would he even recognize me? As Beverly's car approached our destination, about a forty-minute drive on a sunny spring afternoon, I could feel my heart thumping. I was nervous, but I could not afford to let Beverly know that. She just assumed that I would open the door with my key, and the dog would come running out and literally leap into the car! Wordlessly, we drove up the front driveway of the house. Not a soul in sight. We rang the doorbell. No answer.

We waited for a few minutes. I took out my keys and tried to open the door. The keys wouldn't fit. To my horror, I realized that the locks to the house had been changed—the keys were useless.

'What a bummer!' I exclaimed. But we hadn't come all this way only to return empty-handed. We walked around the house until I found a bedroom window on the first floor, slightly open. It was about eighteen feet high. It looked daunting. My mind raced. I had to find a way in somehow. I vaguely remembered that our neighbours often kept a tall ladder outside their garage. I walked the two acres through a growth of tall oak trees and, as I approached, even before the house came into view, I spotted the old bamboo ladder leaning against a wall, waiting to be dragged away to serve my desperate mission.

Beverly's original enthusiasm had evaporated. She tried hard to cover it up with bravado, but I could see she was pale with fear. I did my best to calm her and assured her, 'Listen, this neighbourhood is always deserted. If we get on with our job quickly, we will be out of here in a few minutes! No one will even see us.'

She nodded weakly and mumbled, 'Okay, let's get it over with.' She told me later how terrified she was, imagining the worst and wishing she could disappear.

Once I placed the ladder under the window, Beverly held on to it with all her strength while I climbed up to the bedroom and made my way inside. I was overcome by a profound mix of feelings, very difficult to express. There was regret, remorse, a deep sense of loss and nostalgia—and an overriding fear of the consequences this action would unleash.

'Danny Boy,' I called out in a hoarse whisper, going down the winding staircase. I let out a nervous little whistle.

I reached the atrium, tentatively moving forward, afraid of being caught in the act by some unanticipated presence. And then I heard the delightful barking I had missed so much.

There was Danny Boy, jumping, barking, whining, romping ever so happily with doggy joy! I lifted him in a tight hug, rushed to the front door and ran out to the car, where I knew an extremely anxious Beverly was waiting. With Danny Boy safely tucked in alongside my accomplice, I dragged the ladder back to its original spot and made a breathless dash back to the car.

I stopped for one last longing look at the beautiful house that I had nurtured with dreams, love and hope. I was overcome with emotion, recalling much delight I had felt in decorating this house and making it a home, a little at a time. My eyes and heart drank in the contours of the house as I bid a painful final adieu to it, and to thirteen years of marriage. With tears rolling down my cheeks I put on a brave smile, pulled my pet close to me and Beverly drove us off.

After we had driven safely out of Dobbs Ferry, Beverly stopped the car, looked me straight in the eye and burst out, 'Bina, I will suffocate to death if I don't take some deep breaths and take stock of what we've just done.' She was indeed breathless. 'Gosh, Bina, I have never done anything so exciting or daring in my entire life.'

'Well, nor have I, Bev!' I beamed back at her. 'We are now successful partners in crime.' We laughed like kids until tears rolled down our faces.

Feeling like two stealth heroines, we congratulated each other and celebrated our success with delicious cocktails as soon as we reached my apartment. We swore that none of our friends would know this secret until I was safely out of the country.

There was one more obstacle to overcome before I left. I had arranged with Andy earlier that I would to go to the house on Saturday, the day before my departure, and pick up some of the girls' favourite clothes and belongings. I now had to keep this date while making sure not to betray my secret in any way. It was going to be a challenge, as I could be a suspect in Danny Boy's sudden disappearance. Beverly, riding high from our first escapade, drove me there like a daring warrior, eager for her next adventure.

Both Zal and Andy were home when we reached. Noting Danny Boy's absence, I asked after him. They pointed to his freshly-filled food bowl.

'He's probably out in the garden playing with the neighbour's dog,' Andy said dismissively.

'Since when do the neighbours have a dog?' I asked in disbelief.

'Oh, we have new neighbours,' he lied. 'Very friendly.'

I was afraid Beverly would not be able to conceal her laughter, but she performed like a pro.

Andy led me to the girls' room in his usual dry manner, watched as I packed some things and then curtly showed us out. The entire visit had taken less than fifteen minutes. More laughter and cocktails ensued. As she left, I warned Beverly, 'Don't get hooked on adventure, honey, I won't be needing a driver anymore!'

On Sunday I boarded the flight to Delhi. Alas, the airline insisted that Danny Boy be put in a carrier box and travel in the cargo section. I suffered terrible guilt and fear throughout the twenty-hour journey to Delhi. At Frankfurt airport, fortunately, they allowed a two-hour break for Danny Boy and for another dog, which happened to be travelling on the same flight.

Danny Boy, with his imperious Chinese, flat-nosed pug face attracted a lot of attention on the plane and at the Delhi airport. He had been a fantastic traveller.

Meanwhile, Malini and Gitu had received a letter from their dad with the bad news that Danny Boy had run away. Enclosed was a clipping of a 'Lost Dog' advertisement in the local newspaper that he had placed, hoping to appease them. When I showed up at the school with their dog—as it happened, the very day after they received their saddening letter—their expressions of joy gave me immeasurable happiness, more than I had felt in a very long while. I knew right away that this deed had contributed hugely towards the healing of their shattered faith in me.

I was promptly informed by the school authorities that pets were forbidden in school, and that I had already pushed my luck in bringing 'Tuck' from the US. 'The girls' vacation begins in a month and they can be with their pet soon enough,' I was told firmly.

One evening, my hosts in Delhi were entertaining a powerful politician for dinner. Rajan Nanda, in his customary style, was making a considerable effort to thaw the formal nature of the evening. Suddenly, Danny Boy entered and streaked across the room. The politician was spellbound.

'Where did you get this dog? It's a Chinese pug, isn't it?' he exclaimed.

'Oh, it's mine!' I said sheepishly. 'He has just arrived from New York.'

The politician melted. 'This is amazing,' he declared. 'My wife loves Chinese pugs and brought four of them from London just three months ago, one male and three females. But the male has died and she is inconsolable and in despair.' He was almost pleading as he continued. 'It would restore peace in my home if I were to bring a male pug as a mate for the three females. Nothing could make my wife happier.'

He begged to know how his wish might be granted. 'I assure you that your dog would get the best possible treatment, an air-conditioned room and abundant love.' He was willing to work out the dates to coincide with the girls' vacation in Delhi, at which time I could have Danny Boy back.

It was impossible to say no. Besides, it seemed to offer our dog a perfectly happy alternative all around. The Nandas saw nothing objectionable in the suggestion. I agreed. I was sure I could convince the girls about Danny Boy's three playmates and new air-conditioned home, something I was in no position to offer him.

During their vacation, the girls and Danny Boy enjoyed the best time they were ever going to have together. The amicable arrangement with the new adoptive parents worked for barely a few months before

Andy discovered the whereabouts of Danny Boy, who was then promptly removed from his cosy air-conditioned digs to the home of Andy's brother, Rummy. We eventually lost touch with him, as we could not see him at our convenience. He died at the ripe old age of seventeen.

22

Standing Up to Mr Das

During the following four years I felt like a tightrope walker, trying to maintain my financial stability through the unpredictable trends of the fashion business while fighting custody battles between courts in New York, Bombay and Delhi. Leading the life of a gypsy, I was ever prepared to move to the next emergency. Much like the British weather, gloomy clouds would make way for brilliant sunny spells. Meeting Indira Gandhi had been one such jewel, among a few others.

But the strain of creating an emotional and financial balance and providing stability in the children's lives was taking a toll. Andy was hell-bent on depriving me of the rights of motherhood and did everything possible to paint my character with a damning brush in the courts. He never visited the girls' school in the seven or eight years they remained there. He wrote them letters that were uneven in tone, sometimes full of loving fatherly affection and other times with negative stuff about me.

These were about the most difficult times of my life. During parent-visit weekends at the boarding school, I was among the very few who were divorced, and attracted judgemental glances from conservative parents. The narrow-minded provincial atmosphere was staggering. It must have been equally hard on the girls. I would have to conjure up ways of arriving at school with some good tidings for them. After some time, they settled into their places in the sturdy Sanawar fibre and both earned recognition from the tough faculty. In due course, with perseverance, I also rose above the stigma and made many friends, among them one of my dearest, Winnie Bedi.

Her daughter and Malini aggressively competed to be number one in gymnastics. Harpreet always managed to have a slight edge over Malini, and, in fact, she now runs a popular women's polo team in Singapore along with her young tycoon husband Satinder Garcha, also a Sanawarian. Gitu not only excelled in basketball, she also shone academically and went on to become deputy head girl in her final year.

Even though I wanted nothing more than freedom from marriage and custody of the girls, my court trial lasted five long years. It took the eminent lawyer Ram Jethmalani and his son Mahesh to finally earn my freedom. Due to our family friendship, they offered to take my case on a pro bono basis. It was thanks to Ram, who had the gift of embroidering words brilliantly, that we successfully derailed the verbal attacks by Andy's lawyer against me and won me joint custody.

Even as I breathed a huge sigh of relief, my instinct told me it was not over yet. I noticed Andy's ego take a dive and got a flash of the family court hearing in New York some five years earlier, when he had reacted harshly by taking the girls as far away as possible from me, to punish me. He had wrongly assumed that I would never give up New York for India. The déjà vu sent a slight shudder through me this afternoon, despite my victory in court.

Until that fateful day some thirteen years after we had been married, I had never really stood up to challenge to his abusive behaviour. I had allowed the bully in him to take power and control. The children had witnessed it and had always seen me as the weaker of the two parents, who couldn't stand up to their father's mood swings. He was in charge of all the decisions and he was comfortable in his narrow vision. In all my years with him I had dreamed of the day I would find the magical power to rise above his mediocre lifestyle and carve out my own path of creative freedom.

■

Andy decided that he would pay for the children's trip to New York for summer vacations. This meant that they would reside with him in the apartment he had moved into, which was in a low-income neighbourhood called Yonkers. I was to see them once a week. He simply laid out the rule, and I knew better than to argue. So I would take the forty-minute train ride or borrow a friend's car from Manhattan and visit the girls in the daytime when he was at work in another part of Manhattan, unbeknownst to him.

Within two weeks he announced that he had decided to remove them from Sanawar, and had already enrolled them in the local public school in Yonkers. The girls had been appalled by what they saw when he took them there for admission. They told me about the condom machines and signs saying 'No Drugs' and the graffiti on the doors and walls. Their schooling was to commence in a month, and we had to do everything in our power to prevent their transfer. Reasoning with Andy was not an available option. His action was aimed at getting into combat with me. He enjoyed confrontation. I wasn't going to give him that chance. After a mild attempt at showing my disapproval, I just backed down. But I had to find a way of saving the girls from Andy's disastrous move. The girls begged me to save them from this and find a way to taking them back to Sanawar, in India.

I resorted to the only option available: I would kidnap them back. I got full support from the girls, and I could not have succeeded without their help in fleeing with them back to India, via a short stop in London. I saw the possibility of failure in my grand plan, and was fully aware of the trauma it could cause to the girls' psyches, but the thought of them going to public school in Yonkers was even more frightening.

It took an entire month to prepare this escape, which was filled with trepidation and fear of being found out. As the process of making new passports for them took its time to play out, I would visit the girls every day to strengthen their morale and build their confidence. The stress of this devious exercise took a heavy toll on my health. I was suffering from occasional nausea and dizzy spells, but I ignored every symptom, including fainting spells and blood in my bowel movements. I could allow only one priority—to get us all out of New York safely by 31 August, the day before the start of the

Yonkers school term. The girls had already lost a month of school in Sanawar and they missed their friends sorely. I had no idea if they would be readmitted to Sanawar or not.

My plot for D-Day was simple. I had asked to be allowed to take them out for lunch on their last day before the start of school. It was a Sunday. Andy's sister Sheila was visiting from Bombay. I went to pick them up at the appointed time of 11.30 a.m., while my dearest friend since I was twelve years old, Leela Ellis, waited in her car downstairs. She had been a big athletic star on field and track, whom I had met during my all-too-brief career in athletics. Better known as Mary Leela Rao, she was in fact the first Indian woman to represent India in the World Olympics in the eighty-metre hurdles' race and hundred-metre run. She and Milkha Singh had represented India at the Melbourne Games. Several more followed. Leela and I had found each other in New York some ten years earlier, after a gap of about twenty years. We had discovered that our kids, then about four and five years old, were the same age, and Leela and I went on to become 'best friends forever'. She proved herself more than a friend in need.

Malini opened the door when I rang the bell and announced, 'Mummy's here to pick us up.'

'Call her in,' Sheila suggested.

We had barely said hello when Andy wanted to know, 'What time are you bringing them back?'

'By 3 or 4 p.m.?' I tried to appear calm.

'No, that's too late, I want them back by two,' he ordered.

Thank God for Sheila: 'Come on, Andy, what difference will another hour make? Let them go.'

'Okay, but not a minute later.' He looked sternly at Sheila. 'Back here by three!' he ordered me.

'Okay,' the girls and I chorused.

Malini dared to exercise her customary humour with her father, as both Gitu and I nearly fainted. 'Bye Daddy, we are going for yummy lunch, we won't come back—ever!' A big bear hug followed, showing that he was amused by her daring remark.

When we got into the elevator, the seventeen floors down were a silent, nerve-racking ride. We didn't utter a word. My heart was about to pop out of my chest. After we got into Leela's waiting car and drove out on to the highway, some two miles off, we breathed a huge sigh of relief and screamed for joy. We laughed and congratulated each other and sped straight to the airport. We hugged and thanked Leela for being our guardian angel. 'I will be praying for your safe landing,' she reassured us with her warm smile. Only when the Pan Am flight took off could we really rejoice in our freedom and success. But little did I know it was not over for me.

My family was aware that I had been facing some of the worst times of my life, but they did not know the extent of danger and stress I had gone through to achieve my daring goal. I had been tight-lipped with everyone during those dreadful months. Now, instead of rejoicing in my victory in bringing the girls out of 'captivity' and on a journey back to their school in India, they were aghast at my appearance.

My brother and sister-in-law, Partap and Padma, insisted on taking me to a doctor the minute they laid eyes on me. Partap told me, 'You look deathly ill. You need to see a doctor immediately.'

I could not see the difference in my mirror, though I knew very well that something terrible was playing havoc inside my body. By the next day, I was undergoing a series of medical tests in some of the best clinics at London's Harley Street, moving from doctor to doctor until we had found a specialist for my condition.

'You need immediate surgery,' I was informed by the doctors at the Princess Grace Hospital. 'You have colon cancer and the tumour attached to your intestine is already too large to remain there another day. This is an emergency.' We were recommended to London's most renowned surgeon, Dr Michael Clark, for the operation. But I would have none of it. The girls had missed two months of school already. I knew the headmaster would have filled up their spaces and it was going to be an almost impossible task to get them readmitted. I had to see them lodged back in school safely.

My future was suddenly unknown. I wasn't sure if I would survive this cancer. So I began to try to sort out a future for the girls, in the event that I succumbed to the disease. Getting them into Sanawar seemed imperative—at least they would be adults by the time they graduated from there. That seemed like the most promising path to their security.

'I have to reach Sanawar,' I declared to my family, with absolute determination. My mission was incomplete. I knew the fury and rage that was seething in New York. 'The kids have to be enrolled back into Sanawar School as soon as possible, out of harm's way,' I insisted.

My family had grown exasperated with my custody sagas and the dramatic twists and turns of my life path. Now, as if that weren't enough, they were horrified at my choice of priorities. 'You have to look after your health first!'

They were unprepared for my defiant response to their offers to save my life with the best possible medical care. My concern was that the girls might have lost the two seats they had vacated in their school. 'School already started two months ago. There is always a long waiting list for the enrolment of new students, and if they miss out they'll have no alternative but to go back to the Yonkers Public School in New York.' I tried to make my family see my point of view.

'But your health is far more important than the children's school status, don't you understand this?' they took turns in pleading with me.

'But you don't know what a dangerous journey I have just been through. I cannot abandon it so close to the end,' I beseeched them.

Both my parents had died of cancer-related illnesses, and my diagnosis had sent shockwaves through everyone. Panic-filled phone calls went back and forth to other members of the family residing across the globe. I had to rely on them for the entire financial burden of the surgery and medical care, so I needed to tread delicately in this matter. I knew that I was facing a great dilemma.

I could hear the whispering campaigns going back and forth between my brothers, sisters-in-law and sister Kiki, about their obstinate sister Bina. I held my ground, hoping to gain the female vote to win my argument.

Eventually, after a two-day period of deliberations, I got my way—against the doctor's advice. I showered them all with my deepest gratitude and promised them, 'I will be back in London, on the operating table and under the knife, within six days.'

What anguish or distress went through their minds I will never know, but I had to fulfil my mission. With my ominous medical reports packed in the top layer of my suitcase, I set out on the journey ahead. A twelve-hour flight to Delhi—overnight there—followed by a seven-hour drive to the school in the foothills of the Himalayas. Then back again.

I was simply going to show up at the headmaster's door in Sanawar, without an appointment, and force my will upon him. He was known to have turned away weeping mothers in the past. He was a stickler for rules and loved to exercise his power of discipline. But mine was a serious emergency, so I would beseech him and reach out to his parental sentiment and get my way. I psyched myself with these thoughts all the way up during the seven-hour drive.

The three of us arrived at the imposing gates of Sanawar School in total exhaustion. The girls were very nervous, yet excited to be back. The outcome of this meeting would decide their fate. This was my do or die moment. The prospect of rejection loomed large and scary in our minds. I was having trouble breathing the thin air at that high altitude, but our inner resolve got us all into the headmaster's office. He nearly fell off his chair at the sight of us. I knew immediately that I had to cushion this blow. He did not look happy.

This was to be my toughest dialogue ever, and the yawning gap between his unbending rules and my begging-bowl request seemed to have just become wider. I desperately hoped he would notice my frail condition and allow me the advantage of sympathy. So I looked straight into his eyes after he had me seated, asked the girls to wait outside the office and said quite simply, 'You know why I'm here, right?'

He simply stared back, displaying his annoyance.

'Mr Das, Malini and Gitu belong here and nowhere else,' I tried meekly. He continued to be silent, unnerving me.

'You know that I've nothing to do with their delay in returning.' I felt like I was blabbing because his silence seemed to magnify his annoyance. I managed to quickly fill him in about the drama of flying them back, my medical condition, etc.

Then, as if the savage awoke within me, I said, 'I just want to live to see my girls safe before I die.'

Not only did he turn me down, he scoffed at my audacity in turning up after two months and expecting to be accommodated. He shuffled through some files, pulled out a letter he had received from Andy and put it in front of me to read. The letter instructed the headmaster to remove the girls' names from his roster. He was not prepared to listen to any of my pleas. Even my medical reports wouldn't melt his resolve.

Unwilling and unable to take 'no' for an answer, I blurted in defiance, 'Okay, I'm staying on in this school. The children and I have nowhere to go, all our options are exhausted. I will work here as a maid, or a teacher's assistant, or even as a gardener. I don't care that I shall soon die, because then you will be responsible for the children.' In my desperate ranting, I even offered to buy two beds for the dorm, which was overflowing, according to him.

He had noticed my deteriorated health. But he made no attempt to look at the medical reports I placed before him. I just sat there defiantly.

At that moment, a little miracle happened. A couple of girls from Malini's batch spotted us in the headmaster's office and within minutes, word spread like wildfire about Malini and Gitu having returned to school. Another five minutes later, we heard a chorus of girls shouting out, 'Malini, Gitu—welcome back to Sanawar!'

Soon a commotion ensued. There were emotional outbursts, cries, laughter, hugs. Above all that ruckus, suddenly out boomed Mr Das's harsh voice: 'That is enough! I want all of you back in your classes immediately.'

'But sir, we have a break right now. Class starts after ten minutes,' one of the more defiant girls had the courage to answer him.

Malini and Gitu ran out and joined the others in the field, full of joy but definitely with lingering fear, I could see. I was watching Mr Das and saw quite clearly that this scene had had a transformational effect.

'You know that their dorms have no more space for another bed.' He looked me straight in the eye. 'Where will I accommodate them?'

'Oh sir, I bet if I went there, with help from the housemistress and some of the girls we could juggle a few beds around and surely find space for two more,' I offered. Then I briefly related the circumstances under which we had arrived all the way from New York, and how the girls had helped me in the daring bid less than a week ago to escape from a derailed future with their father, with its enrolment at the local public school.

'You know, if they hadn't been instilled with the gutsy Sanawar spirit, we could never have made it this far in our lives,' I added with a desperate attempt at humour. 'They have been little heroic accomplices in getting out of their father's flat with me, on the pretext of going for a lunch break with their mom.' Now his curiosity was a little aroused. I jumped at the opportunity and told him the details of the events of that morning. 'I had their luggage in the car already, which they had snuck out of the apartment early in the morning and left in the garbage chute for me to pick up before I came to the apartment to pick them up.' Then I added in a whisper, 'In other words, I have kidnapped them. I am dying. They have nowhere else to go!'

I saw a slight shift in his mood. Shaking his head slightly, with a tone of resignation, he said to me, 'The Ramani girls and Sanawar have faced a history of drama from the first time they arrived in this school four years ago.' It was a gentle reprimand he was throwing at me.

I shifted in my chair, uncomfortable. 'That was not my fault,' I countered in a whisper. I could see he was also softening his stance. I added, shaking my head, 'If only you knew how hard this struggle has been for me.'

His next words were, 'You do know that the school fees have gone up by 20 per cent. Can you afford that for your two girls?'

'Afford?' I had just heard the sweetest word. 'Oh, that is no problem,' I said, matter-of-factly. 'If I die, my family will take charge of their fees. If I live, I will have a new lease on life and get rich enough to provide a great future for my girls.' His smile was the magic signal that they had been accepted.

I stayed there overnight as a guest in the headmaster's own home. As I lay in bed that night, I reflected silently upon the last four months. I said a prayer of thanks and smiled in relieved triumph over accomplishing the daunting task of securing the girls' immediate future.

But even as I breathed a huge sigh of relief that night, alone in my bed, another disturbing awareness came over my newfound peace and my heart sank. While my immediate mission was accomplished, I suddenly felt weighed down by loneliness and the frightening load that was to stay with me all the way out of the Sanawar gates on to the road to Chandigarh and Delhi, and then all the way back to the London hospital. I would soon be under the surgeon's knife to remove the deadly tumour from my gut—would I awaken from the operation and find myself with my parents, whom I had lost more than ten years earlier? Or would I see my brothers and sisters in the hospital, standing by my side? If the latter, might there then be a relapse? What did fate have in store for me and for my children? I drifted into a hazy dream state from sheer exhaustion.

On the fifth day after my arrival in Delhi, I boarded my return flight to London to fulfil my promise to the surgeon, to my family and to my diseased body.

23

Under the Knife

I was forty-four years old, and not sure what life had in store for me—or how much life I had left. There were so many decisions to make: where would I live? Would I ever get my robust health back? What would I do? Or would I succumb and never wake up? I was overwhelmed by these questions and the fears of what this illness would mean in the long term. I wondered whether I would be the same after the surgery or if a part of me would be gone forever. I had never met anyone who had been haunted by thoughts such as mine, never spoken to anyone who had survived cancer. I had no idea how to articulate my fears. I was so used to wearing a mask of bravado that it had become like a second skin.

I stayed at Gulu's home on my arrival in London, the last night before my surgery. Though I was exhausted from the desperate mission of getting the children back in school, he insisted on my presence at his glamorous party for the ITV channel production of their *Lifestyles of the Rich and Famous* episode about him. He was a bon vivant bachelor again, having divorced his wife Vimla after ten years of marriage that gave them two lovely children. So now he was free to return to his favourite pastime of lavishing his wealth on his friends.

A number of Indian royals, all friends of his, happened to be visiting at the time. Thus, Gulu's beautiful villa on Bishop's Avenue, (also known as 'Millionaire's Row') had become more or less a palace that night. The combined presence of the glittering society crowd of London, the Indian royals and his A-list business friends promised that this would be the party of the year.

I was in no mood to attend, but at Gulu's insistence I put in my best effort, finding a quiet corner from where I could be an observer and remain unnoticed. At one point I noticed a ravishingly beautiful lady, looking alone and lost. I decided to play hostess and went up to her and introduced myself. She had arrived with a mutual friend of ours, Renuka Jain, and from her charming accent I gathered that she was Turkish. She also seemed to be a little hesitant to join the party and was pleased to be invited to share my quiet corner.

As we began talking, I learned that her name was Semiramis and she had just experienced the devastating death of her six-year-old son from cancer. She shared the ordeal of watching her boy slip away from her in agonizing pain. She spoke with a rare combination of grit and vulnerability. As if the loss of her child hadn't been bad enough, she told me that she and her husband had decided to part ways, torn apart by the ordeal and its despair. I couldn't believe what I was hearing. Her moving and painful story brought me out of my cloud of confusion and retreat, and I reached out and clasped her hands in mine. Fighting off tears, I told her what was awaiting me in less than ten hours. At that moment, my prayers had been answered—an angel had been sent to guide me through the myriad questions that I couldn't have articulated even if I had tried.

After the gruelling journey I had been through, I couldn't have asked for a better reward. Semiramis was enchanting, strong and composed, the epitome of feminine grace. She gave me hope and courage, the two things I needed most.

I was so overcome with her sincerity, I wanted to make her my sister. Quite irrationally, a thought crossed my mind and the matchmaker in me suddenly surfaced—she would make the perfect wife for Gulu! I had always suffered from a flaw of duality in thought and action, call it a relative of dyslexia. Perhaps it came from the two fish in my Pisces horoscope sign. They swim at cross-currents, opposite each other. So here I was, devoted to Vimla, Gulu's ex-wife, who had been like a sister to me. And on the other hand, I felt deeply touched by Semiramis's tragedy and candour and imagined her as a future sister-in-law.

Tossing protocol out the window, I dared to ask her if she had met Gulu. She hadn't. He was the busiest man that night, and I realized that this was probably the worst time for them to get acquainted. But that didn't stop me from asking for her date of birth and quickly juggling some calculations with Gulu's numbers in my head to establish their compatibility, based on my limited knowledge of numerology. She watched me in amusement as my face lit up like a 1,000-watt bulb. I didn't stop there. I took her hand and led her towards my brother. On the way I even declared, at the risk of losing her altogether, 'Semiramis, I think Gulu and you would have a very happy marriage together.' So meteoric was my declaration, she couldn't believe her ears! My clock was ticking, so I allowed myself this eccentricity. I just hoped that their destinies would do the rest.

The next morning, before I was wheeled from my hospital room into the operating theatre, along with all my family members who walked beside my rolling bed I caught a glimpse of Semiramis, blowing me a kiss and gesturing me good luck. She actually looked like an angel, I thought. Just before the nurses jabbed me with the needle and the surgeon took up the scalpel, I let my brain dance with hope of coming out alive to complete my newfound mission. Would I live to attend the wedding of Gulu and Semiramis? Was I delirious? I remember scolding myself, I should be praying for my life first!

I don't remember whether I drifted into deep sleep with a chuckle or with surrender. But I remember that I no longer had any sense of fear. I had firmly established in my mind that my most important role, which was getting the girls back to the security of the school that they loved, had been achieved. They were safe until adulthood. The rest was no longer in my hands.

■

Four hours later I was wheeled out of surgery. I was later told that my family was informed: 'She is indeed very lucky to be alive. We have removed 28 cm of her intestine, which had a 12-cm-long malignant tumour lodged in it. We are amazed that it did not spread.' It had remained self-contained, attached to my colon, and had not polluted any other cells. This was nothing less than a miracle, the doctor said. 'I have rarely seen a case like this. While all is well now, she needs to change her life pattern completely.'

However, the surgery itself had a serious impact on my system. I had to remain in hospital for three weeks, twice the normal time. 'You have received a new lease of life,' the doctor told me. But I had to take on a completely new disciplined routine and the medical team stressed its importance to me and to my entire family, many times over. 'For Bina it will be like learning to crawl again before she can take her first steps to walk.' They suggested four to five months of rehabilitation. Lying in the hospital, I was too weak to really understand or appreciate what this new regimen meant. There were days of excruciating pain, when only a sizeable dose of morphine would provide me relief.

As a form of denial, I also did not want to acknowledge what my real ailment had been. All I had understood from my first diagnosis was that a dangerously large tumour had attached itself to my intestine and it had to be removed very urgently. I did not want to know the name of the condition, nor any of the other details. I surrendered to the surgeon's verdict and left the rest to fate. I couldn't reconcile myself to the notion of being a 'cancer survivor'. I simply viewed this as a hurdle that had to be crossed. And I would do it, I promised myself.

I lost 20 lbs in weight and felt very frail in body, mind and soul. All my brothers and sisters had flown in and rallied around me, praying for me and offering every comfort to nurture me back to good health. I could see the worry and fear in their eyes during my three-week stay in the hospital, despite the doctor's many reassurances that I would regain my health and be able to lead a normal life in just a short while. They seemed to need a lot of hand-holding, a lot more than I did. On several occasions they had to be asked to leave my room because they tended to overcrowd it during their frequent visits. They talked in whispers, so I heard very little of what they said, but the fear in their tones pervaded the atmosphere.

Then there were days when I would awake to find that the angel Semiramis had slipped into my room—sometimes with a small teddy bear, a beautiful flower, or a personal and loving note, saying, 'I didn't want to wake you. I watched you in your sleep and said a prayer for you.' On certain days when I felt stronger, I lectured Gulu about re-evaluating his priorities. He was having too good a time with numerous beautiful women, burning the candle at both ends. He would tell me about his wild escapades with upcoming starlets. Even though he never actually ran into Semiramis in the hospital, I did succeed in playing Cupid and arranged a couple of dinner dates for them. At the time I had no idea whether their meetings were going to result in anything more serious, but I definitely knew that my healing process was being aided by this delightful mission.

There was a strong sense of security in surrendering my life to the care of my family, who had only goodwill in their hearts for me. I was still too weak to worry or think beyond that. I was so relieved to know that my girls were safe and on the right path for the next four or five years that I can remember feeling at times like I really didn't care if I lived or died. Walking that last mile after the daring kidnap had taken its toll, and some part of me felt too deeply exhausted to go on.

■

Two weeks after my discharge and being settled into Gulu's enormous empty home, most of my relatives began to depart for their own abodes in different countries. My sister Mohini, who had come from Kapurthala with a nurse to take care of me, stayed on for another month. But once she left, I was suddenly alone with a nursemaid and the odd relative stopping by for a visit. Even as I was healing physically, I started to sink into depression.

Being alone seemed to accelerate a crumbling of my strength. I had trouble walking, digesting food or focusing on anything like conversation, a book or television. All I wanted to do was sleep, perhaps never to wake up. I dreaded what the future held in store for me. I was no longer a whole person; for the first time in my life's ups and downs, I felt defeated and hopelessly alone. Fortunately, I had Semiramis's visits to look forward to, and these gradually helped pull me out of the weary depression I felt. Gulu's little black book of beautiful dates was increasingly neglected as Semiramis succeeded in filling that vacuum. Lying in my bed, day after day, my mind began to conjure up fantasies of the day when the two of them would get married. Such daydreaming, along with her visits, were the only bright events in my otherwise dreary and housebound circumstances.

Over the next few weeks, as the gloomy signs of approaching winter set in, sparks of motivation began to strike my previously dead mind. Gulu, caring brother that he was, ensured there was always delicious food being cooked to stimulate my appetite. He would bring me news about exciting events that were happening in London's social calendar. On the nights when he was at home, we spent long hours reflecting on his readiness to settle into a new family life and clean up his playboy image. He occasionally invited a few interesting friends for dinner.

During the two months of his nurturing me to better health, I managed to steer his romance with Semiramis towards a more committed relationship, gently drawing his attention to her mature values and unique feminine qualities. She possessed an uncanny wisdom and perceptivity that appealed to me. About eight months later, they were married. I was healthy again by then. They had a son the following year, whom they named Zoran.

In the last weeks of my convalescence, Gulu had thrown a couple of parties at his home that provided opportunities for me to realize I was prepared to face life again. I was still suffering from an immense trepidation about taking a decision of any kind. I had three choices before me. I could live in New York, a city I loved. But that would mean turning a new page and starting afresh. Or I could live in Delhi, which I didn't love, but which offered me proximity to my girls' school. Or I could remain in London where I had my family, my support system.

Despite offering me a comfort zone, living with my large and generous family on a continuous basis was not an option that appealed to me. I was never sure if it was the dreary London weather, a certain class of London's population or just old memories of feeling caged in which made me reject that option.

In the end, my girls were the determining factor. India it would be.

24

Pleasure Palace

ONE NIGHT, AS I was drifting off to sleep at Gulu's house in London, I had a clear vision of what my future was to be. Scenes of life in India began to form in my mind—the colours, the sounds, the smells. They were vibrantly alive and seemed to beckon and swirl around me. A celestial collaboration was carving out my new path, so strong was the vision. A sense of pure joy engulfed me, giving me a rush that seemed to wipe clean the slate of my forty-four years. I knew now that it had to be India. Doing something creative. No more microwave ovens or trading of diesel and coal. Beads and antique textiles it would be.

I had already experimented working with a few craftsmen in Chandni Chowk some three years earlier, albeit from Maya Virmani's sprawling home. This time I would start from scratch and establish my own roots.

The thought of working among artistic craftspeople was utterly seductive and I was impatient to get started. My imagination began to take flight, often keeping me awake and restless till dawn. For the first time in months I had an urgent sense of new purpose that overcame the depths of depression and listlessness I had plunged into. The doors of my willpower had been unlocked. I felt ready for any challenge now.

My brothers, feeling very indulgent towards me, for once welcomed my decision and unquestioningly offered me their blessings and support. However, they were uncomfortable about my choice of Delhi as the base. They were suspicious of its reputation as home to corrupt and self-serving politicians, power brokers and a society of nouveau riche who were beginning to flourish there. Overprotective as they were, they were worried about my naïveté being exploited. While I shared their opinion of the city, I knew that my place had to be Delhi, for practical reasons. It gave me the best access to visit the children in school and resources for my design pursuits were available in abundance there and in nearby Rajasthan.

The family agreed only reluctantly, but would not let me go unsupported. My sister Mohini chipped in and bought a three-bedroom flat with a full-size roof terrace attached, in Hauz Khas, the heart of plush south Delhi. She herself lived a seven-hour drive away in Kapurthala, Punjab, in a rambling luxury home with her husband and two children, both of whom had also graduated from Sanawar. She allowed me to use the flat for as long as I wished, rent-free. Once I arrived, I opted to decorate it myself and within days of settling in I unleashed my creativity and converted the roof into my design studio. I now had a charming safe haven of my own.

Soon I found, to my consternation, that my brothers had been right in not trusting the people of Delhi. While living in New York, I had set up an export business. My niece Ramona in Paris, who had lived with our family since she was four and was like a younger sister to me, had worked her magic and opened doors for me into the couture houses of designers such as Dior, Givenchy and Jean-Louise Scherrer, among others. I had even started my own factory, and used to work long hours to fulfil these exclusive orders. But due to my illness, this business had been shelved for almost six months now. I thought of reviving it, but to my horror, I found that all my unique designs that I had been exporting before my illness—to these leading fashion houses—had been stolen and copied and were being sold in the marketplace. They were shabby knock-offs being sold at heavily discounted prices. My clients would have been appalled to discover that the designs I had made for them, which they priced at $500–$2,000, were now being sold in discount shops in Delhi for about $30.

I found out that during my absence, the young manager I had trained and hired had betrayed me and started this 'side business' of his own. I was to experience a few other such heartbreaks and shocks before I realized that it was the price I was paying for not understanding or having a professional grip on the Indian mindset. My Western upbringing was proving to be a huge handicap here. I would have to make some adjustments if I was to survive.

I decided that I would open a retail boutique in Delhi, where I would create 'one-of-a-kind' designs with unique materials. This would make duplication difficult. I had to embark on a search for rare textiles and fabrics to work with, something that couldn't be copied. My quest led me to colourful bazaars, ancient marketplaces and remote towns and villages, especially in the state of Rajasthan and further afield to Gujarat. I found wonderful textiles, weaves, priceless old embroideries and block prints.

One day I discovered a cache of antique saris, and then became obsessed with collecting discarded old saris of every variety. They appealed to my creative senses and also to childhood memories. When one of my dealers brought me a horde of old satin brocades, sensual soft georgettes and silk tissues with intricate weaves, I was transported back to the magical wonder of afternoons spent playing 'dress-up' in our big house in Bombay at the age of five. It didn't take long before I could readily differentiate the unique and the valuable finds from the mundane ones. Before I knew it, I was converting these old saris, clearly from the wardrobes of affluent women, into jackets, skirts, dresses and pants with a Western sensibility. My collection had become a stylish and colourful bridge between the East and the West, an extension of my own personality.

Soon, I was creating a complementary line of semi-precious jewellery, shoes, bags and cushions. Clients were visiting my third-floor studio, which couldn't handle the crowds. It was time to search for the ideal boutique.

There were no boutiques as such in Delhi at that time. Women had their clothes stitched by their favourite tailors. Tailoring was a thriving business, with many housewives operating from their own garages, as well as the traditional tailor shops in every neighbourhood. Clients arrived with magazine pictures and lengths of fabric to have new outfits made, their measurements kept as well-guarded and valuable secrets in the registers of their chosen tailors.

I had just bought myself my first car, a red Maruti 800 for zipping around in when I went on my textile treasure hunts. Not far from where I lived in Hauz Khas was the hauntingly beautiful Qutab Minar. I was always drawn in that direction, down a tree-lined road that led up to the monument and the area around it, called Mehrauli. The Qutab Minar, an eleventh-century monument built by Qutab-ud-din Aibak, was created as a tower of victory. It stood proudly on the grounds where sacred Hindu and Jain temples and historic monuments had existed for more than a thousand years before being destroyed and used as building materials. In the midst of the remains of the old city, Qutab-ud-din Aibak erected what was then the tallest tower in the world, made of beautiful red sandstone with calligraphic verses from the Quran inscribed on its surface.

Driving my red car one drizzly monsoon afternoon, I passed by the tall structure and circled it to proceed down the narrow road that went into the ancient Mehrauli village. Just next to the Qutab, I saw a long columned building to my right. Its many doors and windows had long been shuttered. Quite eerily, the abandoned building seemed to beckon to me.

Spellbound by its mysterious shuttered façade, I stopped my car under a tree across the road and stared at the building for a long time, trying to hear what it was saying to me in its silent splendour. I heard peacocks cry out from behind in a chorus; I imagined them dancing in the rain as a welcome for me.

A shiver ran through my body. I was suddenly desperately curious to know what lay behind those shutters. But I could see no opening. Taking it all in, I drove around a second time, in case I might have missed a tiny opening somewhere, but saw no hint of any. That night in bed, the picture of the building lingered for a while in my mind, haunting me almost as if from some past life. I fell asleep, but not before promising myself another visit to that evocative structure.

Two days later, seeing that I could slip away for about a half hour without being missed, I left my workplace and found myself parked under the same tree again, staring at the building. If only I had X-ray vision! I might have seen the peacocks dancing. They sang out again. By the end of that week I had made yet another trip, feeling a little guilty that I might be wasting valuable time, as though I was going to visit some secret lover. Then lo and behold, on my third visit, I hit the jackpot! That day I noticed that a small door, which was built into a much larger door, was slightly ajar. I turned my car to face the front of the gate and then stepped in through it.

It opened into a huge garden with an ancient mango grove, a quaint swimming pool and several arched verandas facing the garden. It was charming, far beyond my expectations. A weathered old man with missing teeth and a wrinkled face greeted me, 'Namaste.' He looked at me, puzzled, wondering what I was doing there. 'Yahan to koi nahin hai.' He informed me that there was no one around, and that he was just the gardener.

'Yahan ka malik kaun hai?' I had to ask him several times who the owner was, and why such a huge building was empty, before he replied.

'Woh to Purani Dilli mein rehtein hain,' he explained reluctantly. The owners lived in Old Delhi in a neighbourhood called Daryaganj, and were not accessible. I finally cajoled him into giving me their address, which he provided hesitantly, with a look of suspicion on his face. That night I could barely sleep, with a constant replay of the little scene with the old gardener in my overactive mind.

The next morning, in a chirpy mood, I went on the adventure to Purani Dilli (Old Delhi), in a taxi this time. I didn't want to drive the long distance into an unfamiliar neigbourhood alone. My heart was pounding with anticipation, just like a child getting her first tricycle, as I sat in the taxi heading to the old part of the city.

Reaching Hindu Park in Daryaganj, where the landowner lived, I was charmed by the old tree-lined streets and the handsome mansions all around. Well-maintained footpaths lined the roads, unlike most parts of New Delhi, which had been developed in haste, leaving piles of rubble where sidewalks should have been. My taxi brought me to the door of one such mansion. It was apparent that these houses had been built in the early twentieth century during the British era, in collaboration with Indian architects, therefore retaining many traditional Indian motifs on the building façade. The street would have seen grander times in its prime, most likely housing nobility. Each block held about twelve large buildings with a garden square in the centre. It spoke of a history of gracious living. However, I saw no traces of that when I entered.

I rehearsed the opening lines for my conversation with the owner, a Mr Gupta, not knowing what to expect as I walked through the small door and up to the first floor. Bare walls greeted me inside, despite the ornate relief work on the exterior. Once I reached the first floor, I was overwhelmed by the sheer size of the interior. There was a huge courtyard in the centre, with randomly placed charpoys occupied by older folk. I stood on the balcony, which surrounded the full courtyard, forming a large square. It was divided by short partitions, separating the families that lived there. Each section was stuffed with furniture, utensils and bundles of clothes. At least eight families resided here, which gave me a déjà vu moment of my childhood when our home in Bombay had become a crowded camp for refugees from Karachi. I would learn later that there were at least 100 people living inside this building, with new births adding to the numbers each year. It had originally been built for the Gupta family, whose son, Diwanchand, I had come to meet. As I was ushered by my host into his rooms, I sensed suspicion and a certain hostility in the eyes peering at me from the adjacent balconies.

Diwanchand Gupta was a quaint-looking, wiry little man in his seventies. He had shrewd twinkling eyes, a jovial nature and spoke good English. He held a law degree and was looked upon as the most literate person in his family.

Gupta-ji's family occupied four rooms and a section of the balcony. He had two daughters, one who was happily married and lived out of town, and the other who lived in a separate room on the roof. His son, daughter-in-law and their two children lived with him. They greeted me very warmly, thinking at first that I was a foreigner. I'm certain they found me as quaint as I found them. I chuckled silently at their discomfort as they tried to slot me into a particular mould.

They were surprised and impressed by my command over Hindi, which had improved while communicating with my tailors and embroiderers. The daughter-in-law, covered from head to toe in a sari, tiptoed noiselessly back and forth, bringing an assortment of snacks and endless cups of tea, which she placed on a small table in the centre of where we sat. I felt a comfortable bonding with the elder Guptas. Finally, after much small talk, I got to the point. I told them that I wanted to see the inside of their building near the Qutab Minar.

'Why do you want to see it?' Diwanchand Gupta asked without ceremony.

'I am looking for a place to open a boutique,' I told him.

He hadn't a clue what a boutique was. He had little idea of anything I enthused over! But he was fascinated. His English was getting a long-neglected opportunity to be shown off, and he wasn't about to dismiss me. His eyes sparkled and his mouth spread into a wide smile, revealing crooked yellowing teeth.

The meeting lasted about two hours, because Gupta-ji would start wandering from the topic at hand to reminisce about the past history of the British Raj. He had fascinating stories to tell about his father, who had clearly been a visionary with a taste for the 'high life'. The father was the architect of the beautiful buildings in Mehrauli that had so fascinated me.

Exactly three weeks after my first meeting with Gupta-ji, I was given a personal tour of his two buildings with full commentary of the fascinating ninety-year history of the place, as the gardener watched in fascinated silence. I came away that day with a long-term lease for a sizeable space of 1,600 sq. ft for my first Indian boutique.

But before committing this to me, as if putting me to test, Gupta-ji asked directly, 'Do you know the recent history of this building?'

'No, I don't,' I stuttered, afraid to hear his answer.

'Well,' he hesitated and then continued in a sombre tone, 'it was a pagal khana—a madhouse for women. And many of them have died here!' He was either giving me an opportunity to back out if I wanted to, or he had changed his mind about giving me the space and was trying to scare me away.

Humorously, I responded, 'Gupta-ji, don't worry, you can consider me also a madwoman!' I quickly added, 'You know, I'm not exactly a normal person.' He was appalled, not amused, by my response. But I could tell that he had a certain sense of humour.

Taking on the air of a guardian, he explained that the Government of India had requisitioned his empty property at the time of Partition in 1947, with a view to house war widows and other destitute women. They remained there, often neglected, until most of them simply died. His property had remained vacant since then. He had opened up the shuttered building after many years just for me.

There was at least a ten-inch layer of pigeon droppings and dirt of every kind covering the floors. The odour was unbearable. Thankfully, my asthma condition was yet to take form. The building in which he agreed to lease me a space was a long colonnade with a Georgian flavour to its architectural style, very much like Connaught Place. It had been built some fifteen years after the one to which it was adjoined, which had been constructed in a haveli style and was used by the Gupta family members for their monthly picnics.

A quaint swimming pool was built in the yard of the haveli building. There was a shallower area with a platform for the ladies, and a large deeper section that would have been used by men. It reminded me of a scene from an Indian mythological painting. I felt like I had stepped into a storybook, where I was one of the characters. The two properties together occupied about 3 acres and ran 160 metres alongside the Mehrauli village road. Across the road in its full splendour stood the magnificent Qutab Minar and the first mosque of Delhi (a UNESCO World Heritage Site). Directly behind was the historic Lal Kot, Prithviraj Chauhan's city. It transpired that Gupta-ji's father, the erudite Banwarilal Gupta, had bought the property over a hundred years ago from a British landowner. This spot, which stood in the shadow of the mighty Qutab Minar, had witnessed some of India's bloodiest history over 2,000 years. When Banwarilal bought the original ten-acre plot, he assured the British owners that he would create the classiest pleasure palace to nourish their senses.

The architect then went about building a beautiful haveli, complete with a central ballroom-sized entertainment chamber for the legendary nautch girls. Several small chambers led out from the main dance hall. Almost every room boasted a spectacular view of the imposing Minar. The third floor had a private chamber with a terrace, from where one could see the Yamuna River. Walking down the rear staircase, I noticed a huge mango tree, which stood in a caressing embrace with another smaller mango tree.

Behind the entwined mango trees was the prized possession of this sprawling mansion. It was a well, rumoured to be 2,000 years old and 200 metres deep, which had witnessed many wars and housed hundreds of defeated soldiers over the centuries. The large well had several small nooks on the outside, divided by individual walls to provide shelter for the soldiers. An overgrowth of shrubs underscored the neglect that these buildings had suffered over the decades. I hung on to every word that Gupta-ji uttered as he related fascinating legends with candour and pride.

That night I was so overjoyed at my triumph in acquiring a place in this historic site to house my life's future that I decided to call my family in London and share the good news with them. Their response was, as usual, overprotective, transporting me yet again to the time I approached them with the news that I might soon appear in a musical talent show.

'You are taking on a mammoth risk.'

'You are in no state to take such risks.'

'You are in feeble health.'

'In a hundred-year-old building?'

'What? Are you dreaming?'

'What folly are you venturing into now?'

'Entering into a world of retail about which you know nothing!'

I was bombarded with negative reactions.

'Besides,' they pointed out, 'you are located in the far south of Delhi, where barely anyone ventures, except for a few tourists or school buses loaded with children. Who will come shopping for your fashion designs next to the Qutab Minar?'

Despite all my excitement and joy, a shudder of doubt ran through me. Indeed, what folly was I inviting into my new life? With my family's fears echoing in my ears, I began to wonder if they were right. How I would attract buyers? It was like living in New York and trying to open a fashion boutique next to the Statue of Liberty. Who would be mad enough to go fashion shopping there? Was my dream going to turn into a nightmare? Would I become the laughing stock of Delhi?

But I had already made my commitment and there was no turning back. Gupta-ji had given me a very long lease and, in the end, had virtually embraced me as a long-lost family member. I had to gather courage and focus everything on setting up my dream boutique.

Even as I was bracing myself to focus on this new path, a name flashed across my mind: 'Once Upon a Time'. That would be the name of the boutique. I debated with myself on the pros and cons of such a name. But over and over it came back, telling me that this was to be the beginning of my story. Still feeling a bit unsure of the choice, I ran into a stylish acquaintance, Romy Chopra. I confided my thoughts and apprehensions to him. Did he think Once Upon a Time might confuse a potential client in search of a fashionable ensemble? 'Or does it sound more like a shop that would sell wall clocks or children's clothes and toys?' I asked him hesitantly. 'Perhaps I should call it "Peacock Alley" instead, because there are so many peacocks strutting in the backyard?'

'Go with your conviction,' he suggested safely.

So it was that Once Upon a Time made its debut, exactly three months after I had taken possession of the space. I set aside all health concerns and pursued my goal as if fuelled by a new kind of adrenalin. Everything fell into place by the scheduled date, and I opened its doors with great fanfare at the end of December 1986, feeling full of vitality and enthusiasm. Strangely, all the important events in my life seem to take place at the end of December.

The opening happened to coincide with the annual Delhi International Film Festival. Much to my surprise and joy, many stalwarts of the film industry from Bombay, including Raj and Shashi Kapoor, popped into my boutique. Gulu and Semiramis came from London, along with Countess Bina and Count Nicolo Sella di Monteluce. I could not have hoped for a better opening night. I felt blessed. The boutique had been anointed and was now charmed. Within three days of the opening, Sonia Gandhi, along with Jaya Bachchan and Sunita Kohli, walked into the store unannounced and expressed admiration at the theme, the merchandise and the décor. Several others among the sophisticates of Delhi followed, gracing my store with their presence.

As I had been unable to find display mannequins to show my garments, I had come up with a daring idea that suddenly became the talk of the town. I had my carpenter make me T-shaped stands of full model height, almost in the shape of a cross. On these I draped gorgeous antique saris and then added a jacket or a skirt to its torso. On the top, instead of a beautiful mannequin's face, I placed an antique wooden horse's or a cow's head. I had become obsessed about collecting such life-size animal heads; they fitted in with the shop's fairy-tale name.

Mehrauli's century-long slumber was coming to an end. South Delhi was rapidly expanding. My boutique was drawing crowds from all parts of Delhi. Sales were brisk. Every evening the boutique turned into a party zone, with clients staying back to celebrate. I would play lively and nostalgic music of the '60s. My diplomatic clients would select their favourite dresses from the racks and pay me with a stash of cheese and wine. By 5 p.m., many of my new as well as older friends would show up to enjoy and share the day's booty of wine and cheese. Once Upon a Time was rocking within a month of its opening. I could barely keep the shelves stocked.

The long-abandoned pleasure palace had come back to life.

25

The Spiritual Path

THE THREE YOUNG American women who walked into Once Upon a Time about six weeks after its opening had a bubbly enthusiasm about them that I liked immediately. They spent a couple of hours trying on several garments, punctuated by many 'ooohs' and 'aaahs' of admiration. My brocaded jackets flew off the racks. By the time they were done, they had emptied half my store and bought twenty-six outfits. 'A testament to my designing skills,' I chuckled to myself.

Unable to contain my curiosity, I shot out questions one after the other: 'Are you buying all these for yourselves? Where are you from, and is it for a special occasion that you are buying so many?'

They looked at each other, obviously very pleased with their haul, and then one of them spoke. 'Actually, we are part of the advance team from New York for our guru, who is arriving here in a month.' I was a bit taken aback—they were so outgoing and stylishly dressed, quite unlike the usual 'ashram' types that I often encountered.

One of them pulled out a small flyer from her bag and opened it for me, pointing to a picture of a beautiful young woman with a divine smile, wearing a saffron hat. 'Here, this is our gurumayi's picture.' She handed the flyer to me and continued, 'She is coming to Delhi for the first time. The programme for her three-day visit is printed at the back. You must come!'

'I can't believe she is so young and beautiful!' I exclaimed. Followed by a teasing remark, 'No flowing beard, like most gurus?' They smiled, and almost in a chorus explained that Gurumayi was from the lineage of Baba Muktananda and had inherited his spiritual grace. She had movie-star good looks, but I didn't dare express that thought, lest I offend them. By the time they left, I had promised I would come to Gurumayi's satsang.

It turned out that their ashram was just a few kilometres down the road from the shop and quite close to my apartment. The young women came back at least half a dozen times, each time bringing more devotees. And my curiosity about the gurumayi heightened.

In fact, I had been in search of a guru ever since I had separated from Andy. I had read up on many of the current gurus and always eagerly listened to anyone who had a satisfying experience to share. Deep down, though, a touch of guilt nagged at me. As a Sikh, I was taught that there are no living gurus as such and that our holy book, the Guru Granth Sahib, is the ultimate guide in our lives. But I had thorny questions that needed answering. Questions I wasn't even sure I could articulate. I desperately wanted to experience the physical presence, the darshan, of a powerful spiritual being. My search had taken me from Swami Chinmayananda to Swami Rama, from the Radha Soami Baba in Beas to Sai Baba in Whitefields. I had also been to the Osho (formerly Rajneesh) ashram in Pune. My travels led to in personal darshans with several gurus at their ashrams, but none quenched my thirst for the 'inner charge' that I craved.

My last attempt had been four years earlier at Whitefields in Bangalore. At a friend's suggestion, I had waited for Sai Baba's arrival in a long line of diehard devotees. I was hoping for a magnificent current to pass through my entire being and elevate me to a higher state of consciousness. But even when the guru passed by me, I felt nothing.

I opened my eyes and prepared to retreat, doing my best to hide my disappointment. On the path towards the exit, an elderly man with smiling, kind eyes came up to me, his hands folded together in a namaste. He introduced himself and said he had been watching me.

'What were you looking for?' he asked gently.

'That's the point. I don't know,' I said. I trusted him instinctively. A thought flashed in my mind—maybe *he* is the one to be my guru!

He touched my shoulder, gracing me with a smile that radiated wisdom. 'You are too desperate, dear lady,' he said softly. 'You will never find a guru like this, you know.' He continued, 'If you are lucky enough in this lifetime, the guru will come and find you, or will send for you. Otherwise, it will be in a future life. Please do yourself a favour and abandon your search. It is good to be in the company of holy men, but please don't come expecting to find any enlightenment, else your life will be filled with disappointment.'

The man caught the gratitude in my eyes, bowed his head and said goodbye. Before departing he added, 'Don't be in a hurry. I sense that your guru will find you in your present lifetime.'

After that, every time these American devotees returned to Once Upon a Time to add to their wardrobes, I would feel a surge of hope. Before leaving they would always remind me of the time left for Gurumayi's arrival.

As it turned out, Gurumayi's first satsang in Delhi was set for 10 March. On my birthday! Surely this was an omen. I was certain that the Bangalore wise man's prophecy was coming true.

My parents had taught us not to dress in a flashy manner on visits to the Sikh temple. I grew up understanding that prayer time was sombre time. Therefore, watching these girls from the ashram pick out my colourful and dressy brocade outfits to adorn themselves for the guru's satsang had baffled me. Nevertheless, I chose to wear a comfortable beige cotton ensemble, understated but elegant.

By the time I reached the venue, which was at the opposite end of Delhi, some twenty kilometres away, the three ladies who had first walked into my store were waiting for me at the entrance of the large tent. They greeted me like a VIP and escorted me to the front row, where a comfortable seat had been reserved for me. The congregation was seated on the vast carpeted ground under a gigantic tent. Some 3,000 devotees, about 85 per cent of them Indian and the rest foreign, sat in silence, facing the large stage. On it was a beautiful silver chair with rust silk upholstery and several flower arrangements on either side. There were two large screens on both sides of the stage as well.

I was stunned to see all the glimmer and glitter of brocade, satin and silk in every direction! Several attendants walked about silently, ushering devotees towards empty seats and ensuring that everyone would have a good view of the guru when she arrived.

Soon, the lights dimmed in the big hall and the stage lights brightened as Gurumayi glided in, her hands folded in a namaste. She wore long maroon robes and a matching hat with some embellishment. She stopped a couple of times, then took her position on her throne. She was breathtakingly beautiful. I could see every feature of hers on the big screen to my left. Her skin glowed and her captivating smile revealed a perfect set of white teeth and, as she talked, I was riveted.

Within minutes of officially welcoming everybody she led us all into a chant, 'Om namah shivaya', which had a slow and gentle rhythm that everyone seemed to know. As the chant was repeated over and over again for nearly forty minutes, its powerful energy reverberated and dominated the whole tent, mesmerizing everyone, sending them into a trance. At some point the energy got so intense that I burst into an uncontrollable fit of tears. I wanted to keep my eyes open and watch Gurumayi, but I couldn't see anything through the tears streaming down my face.

The sound of the chanting had touched a nerve, releasing an ocean of tears stemming from years of hoarded pain. I was getting a spiritual detox, although I didn't quite understand it then. An ecstatic motion seemed to rise inside my psyche, which I couldn't comprehend. Every once in a while I would try to force it to stop, but I had no control over anything. Some deep, transformative mechanism was taking place. The seeker in me had found a path, and the gate to my inner journey had opened. It was as though I had been taken apart so that I might be fully prepared to receive the new vocabulary of the senses.

Once the chanting stopped, there was a fifteen-minute silence where everyone fell into deep meditation, including me. It was bliss. My wandering soul had found a place to rest.

Then, softly, Gurumayi's voice came through the speakers. In chaste Hindi, she started her discourse on the philosophies of the great sages of India. I was already experiencing a whole new expression emanating from my body and my soul, and was struggling with the articulation of it, even though I understood full well that I had now ended my search for the 'guru experience'. But my mind was still restless with doubts about embracing a living guru. I began to feel pangs of guilt. I had a vision of my parents, long deceased, showing disappointment at seeing me in this congregation.

As if Gurumayi had had an X-ray vision of my confused state of mind, she opened her discourse with the life story of Guru Nanak, the founder of the Sikh faith. With impressive articulation, she shared three legendary stories of his remarkable life, which I had heard before, but never grasped so well. She was, in fact, reciting the very verses from our holy book that I had been taught by my parents. Her translations were brilliant. I couldn't believe what I was hearing and seeing. I was in sudden harmony with my inner centre and in that tranquil state I knew that I had found my guru. And I just knew that I had my parents' smiling approval as well.

At the end of the three-hour programme, more than half the congregation had left. I was gently steered by my two guides towards the long line that was forming in front of the guru and stretching to the end of the long tent. I was ushered to the front, even as I tried to pull away, so that my swollen eyes and red face could have a reprieve that might make me presentable. But to my embarrassment, I was amongst the first few to have darshan with Gurumayi, which meant coming face to face with her, bowing at her feet and receiving her personal blessing. This might consist of a little conversation, or being presented with one of the many gifts that lay beside her. I could barely look up at her, I was so embarrassed about my appearance. She smiled warmly at me in an acknowledgement that needed no words.

'How does it feel seeing all your beautiful designs at the congregation here?' she asked. I was surprised that she knew.

'I am overwhelmed, as you can see.' I shook my head helplessly and gave a deep bow. I searched for words that refused to come.

'Stay a little longer. Watch the dance programme,' she suggested. Her invitation was my command.

I attended the satsang each of the next four days. I spent my days at the shop, and at a certain time started looking at my watch for the countdown to my exit at 5 p.m. For some reason I couldn't tell my staff where I was rushing off to every evening. It felt like I was going to meet a secret lover, and each day I came away from the satsang in a higher state of bliss. My staff noticed my transformation, but none of them had the temerity to question my mysterious behaviour. I'm not sure whether I kept the secret because I was embarrassed about submitting to a guru, or because I didn't want to dilute the powerful energy that was growing within me. I think it was a combination of both. According to one astrologer's reading, I had stepped into my 'golden period'.

On the last day, responding to the success of Gurumayi's discourses, which had drawn almost double the number of devotees, they decided to conduct a 'weekend intensive' the following week. I was informed that an 'intensive' was a two-day programme of meditation, starting at 8 a.m. and ending at 6 p.m. The thought of the required discipline was daunting. But the enthusiastic American lady guides succeeded in persuading me to enrol for this 'life-transforming' experience. Despite a twinge of guilt about neglecting my demanding workload, I signed up.

I wasn't able to sleep much in anticipation of the course, so during the first half of the first morning of the intensive I yawned continuously, staying awake with difficulty. Then, suddenly, I sank into a deep meditation just before the lunch break. It saved me from the embarrassment of trying to slip away unnoticed, a thought that had crossed my mind several times. Miraculously, during lunch—a simple vegetarian meal that 600 of us shared—I was infused with a new vitality. For the next five hours I was in a zone of enchantment during the meditation and chanting. In the last hour, when devotees were invited to share their experiences with the audience, there were mind-boggling stories to be heard.

I had been startled by the strange roaring sounds that emanated from some people in the midst of their deep meditation. Others experienced a fit of rapid circling movements in their bodies, appearing to be possessed by some supernatural power. I witnessed shaktipat reactions that ranged from the bizarre to the sublime. By the end of the two-day course, I came away feeling exhilarated. I realized I had absorbed a powerful energy—it was almost as though I had visited another planet.

The people had been warm and friendly, demanding nothing from me in return. It was the way of Gurumayi's devotees. Some were old, some young, and of many nationalities. Many of them were beautiful, like their guru, and all of them wanted to emulate her. So did I. Before I knew it, a new path lay open before me and I began to see my life and my future from a different, gentler, more giving and loving perspective.

■

My children were still in boarding school. I rehearsed in my mind all the wonderful experiences I was going to share with them, in order to give them a glimpse of this new protective divine path. I hoped they would appreciate the beautiful chants that now played on my music system throughout the day and filled my home with tranquility.

On 25 March, exactly a week after Gurumayi and her team left Delhi, I was drifting off to sleep close to midnight after a routine day, having completed my thirty-minute meditation, when suddenly I felt a cool breeze waft into my room from the window about ten feet away. Before I could register what was happening, a brilliant bright white light appeared, unlike anything I had known. I sensed myself levitating, being lifted into a space of pure beauty and bliss.

It seemed as if all my senses, even in that sleepy state, had sharpened. I was overcome with a force that was so overwhelming and exquisite, I started to cry and laugh simultaneously—something I had never experienced before, nor have since. I became aware that I had been caressed by a divine force and 'belonged' to a protective energy. I was never going to be alone or have reason to fear. I heard myself telling that force, 'Thank you! Thank you! Thank you God, for recognizing me as one of yours. I know this state of bliss won't last, but please, please give me the gift of being able to recall it for the rest of my life.' I must have remained in this state for just a few minutes—I have no way of knowing how long. It might have been longer. I wiped my tears as I felt myself return to my bed to ponder over this magical happening. I then sank into the deepest, most peaceful sleep ever.

When I woke up the next morning I felt an extraordinary glow within me and around me. My pace had slowed and I was savouring every movement of my newly harmonized mind, body and soul. I knew I had experienced my very own shaktipat journey. My kundalini had risen. It had opened up my personal chamber of higher consciousness.

This divine gift was the principal objective of the siddha yoga teaching, which manifested from the powerful two-day intensive. As a recipient of this gift, I now had to apply my new creative force in a more positive direction.

Only hours later, on the same day, the doors opened to my new destiny.

26

A Quaint Village

A NEW AND VITAL energy had entered my being. I woke up feeling radiant. Everything around me had an iridescent glow. When my maid brought my morning tray of almonds and tea with the morning papers there was a glow on her face, and the same glow radiated everywhere I looked. It was as if a divine energy had possessed both me and my environment.

My maid gave me a beaming smile as she placed the tray near my bed. 'Ma'am, aaj to aap bahut khush lag rahin hain. Kuch achhi khabar hai kya?' (Ma'am, you look very happy this morning. Is there some good news?) I responded with a wordless smile and nodded, thanking her, savouring this 'feel-good' moment.

As the day progressed I received similar reactions from everyone I met. The faces of my workers at the studio lit up when they saw me that morning. I could see them all reflecting the new energy that had entered me the previous night. It now seemed to be radiating out of me, touching everyone I met and giving new meaning to everything I did. At one point I shut my office door and meditated in a dialogue of thanksgiving with the newly discovered being within me. I had finally found my Self, opening up a vast reservoir of energy. It was to be the day that I would make my first foray into Hauz Khas Village.

The rising popularity of Once Upon a Time now required me to expand my studio. I had introduced what was Delhi's first fashion boutique and it had become quite the rage. Select groups of new clients were drawn to the boutique by word of mouth. It became a hit with expatriates, diplomats and other visitors who came in growing numbers. I urgently needed a larger studio and workspace to accommodate the increasing number of people working for me.

I had set my heart on finding a charming space, not unlike the enchanting building I had found at the Qutab Minar for my boutique—a place not too far away from home. There were other export factories popping up in distant Okhla, which was offering attractive incentives to garment manufacturers. But that was not what I envisioned.

I set out that very afternoon to look for a factory space to complement the unique boutique location. I climbed into my red Maruti to do what I loved most—explore the more rural parts of a rapidly expanding Delhi.

I wore comfortable clothes, boots to allow me to walk into muddy places if required and some good R&B tapes that I could sing along to. This was my personal adventure that I treated myself to every once in a while, discovering lesser-known parts of Delhi, usually within my neighbourhood. There were historical monuments scattered here and there amidst pop-up urban areas, the legacy of a long and turbulent history. This always filled me with a thirst to know more about them. Simultaneously, I was saddened to see these irreplaceable monuments in such a derelict state—heaps of garbage and discarded construction material were often dumped upon these exquisite edifices by new builders in their hurry to put up ugly blocks of buildings, often without official sanction.

On this day I followed my usual routine, with the difference that the CD player was playing Gurumayi's chants instead of the usual R&B. That didn't stop me from singing along. Music always sent an extra surge of energy through me. I was so mesmerized by the chants that I drove unthinkingly, semi-consciously taking a turn on to a narrow dirt road that I had passed many times before on my way to and from the boutique. In fact, it was quite close to my apartment-cum-studio. Today I allowed what seemed to be some outside force to guide me. I was curious to see how far the dirt road went, not knowing what I would find at the end.

It was about 5 p.m. I knew I had to return by 6 p.m. to close the studio. I drove along slowly for about two kilometres, past a few ancient dilapidated ruins and tombs on both sides of the road. They mostly served as home to stray cattle, dogs or the occasional donkey. These old buildings were interspersed with a few newly built villas, some beautiful green patches and piles of garbage. I continued through this incongruous mix until I came to a lush forest on my right.

I stopped the car. The short road ahead looked remote. My eyes wandered into the forest area and I shuddered slightly in a moment of déjà vu. Through the trees I spotted domed clusters of monuments, much larger and more numerous than those along the road I had seen up till now. Moments later I glimpsed a group of deer darting behind each other and, as I took a turn for a closer look, I noticed someone jogging on the narrow paths that were laid out. I debated with myself about stepping out of the car, knowing I might get distracted inside this peaceful green acreage and lose track of time. I promised myself another visit soon.

Allowing myself a few more minutes, I ventured a little further down the dirt track, looking for an opening where I could turn the car and head back. Before I reached the end, I noticed another park on my left, and saw a sign, 'Deer Park'. Once more, I felt like I was Alice in Wonderland—what an unexpected find! I congratulated myself on the good choice I had made, notching up promises to return another day. The road was about to end when I found an opening to turn back.

Just then I came upon a quaint little village. I seemed to have landed in a time warp! Men in white turbans, starched long kurtas and lungis, sat on two charpoys smoking hookahs. Women wearing colourful ghagras and kurtis, their heads covered with dupattas, were tending to their buffaloes. Children played in the centre of the open space where my road had ended. A tall, elderly man, dressed in a crisp white kurta, dhoti and turban, walked over to my car and asked me to step out when I told him I had lost my way. A moment of fear evaporated when I saw his warm smile. It was obvious that people here had rarely seen a car. I was now in the midst of a hidden village, surrounded by a burgeoning metropolitan giant, where time seemed to have stood still. I felt as if I had stepped back by a hundred years or more.

The man who approached me was Raghuvir Singh, the choudhary of the village. He was very friendly and rather handsome, except for his pockmarked skin. His eyes smiled and he displayed a perfect set of white teeth. Surprisingly, he spoke fluent English as he introduced himself as the village headman. He took me to be a foreigner and offered to give me a quick tour of the monuments ahead, where the gates were about to close at 5.30 p.m. I responded to him in Hindi, explaining that I was new to the area and would love to see the monuments properly another day. Instinctively feeling that I could trust this man, I explained to him my real reason for being there—I was in search of rental property for a workshop.

Leaving his companions on the charpoy behind, he walked me from the centre of the chaupal. We took a short right turn into a lane that had been hidden from view. It ran almost parallel to the road on which I had just driven. We were not alone. We had attracted a band of excited children, singing, skipping, giggling, who had decided to follow, with a few dogs in tow. Women sweeping floors stopped their work, stood erect, hurriedly covered their heads and smiled at me, catching my glance as I entered a gate behind the choudhary.

At that point the choudhary shooed away the children and led the way into a charming haveli-style stucco house. We had come to a long dark room that stretched from left to right about 30 feet and 15 feet across. At the end was a carved door, which opened into another such room, where a similar door opened out on to a terrace, sending beams of brilliant light from the setting sun to brighten up the rooms we had just crossed. I was struck with amazement the moment I saw the dazzling golden sun and the surrounds! The huge expanse of space held the lush green Deer Park to my right, the magnificent thirteenth-century monuments to my left, and in the centre glistened a large circular pond of water! The defining moment suddenly reduced me to a burst of tears; I couldn't fathom what my

eyes were beholding. I knew immediately that this was my calling! The
sun god was welcoming me with his glorious rays like outstretched
arms, saying, 'You can rest your soul, you have come home.'

Between sobs, I had forced a few smiles to signal to the choudhary
that he need not get alarmed. Nodding my head to disguise my
embarrassment, I let him know that I was in love with the place
and was ready to rent it right now.

With a radiant smile, he said, 'It is yours, immediately. We were
renting it as a storehouse to a salt dealer who paid ₹2,000 per month.
You can have it for the same price.'

I couldn't believe what I was hearing. I would have paid a queen's
ransom for it! I impulsively responded, 'I had a budget of ₹4,000, so...'

He cut me short, 'Okay, okay, let's meet in the middle. You can
pay ₹3,000, we make everybody happy.' Our deal was struck the
moment we shook hands, followed by a namaste.

This had been a hugely agreeable adventure! Rhythms were
beating in my veins by the time I reached home.

Within a month I had set up a spacious studio and separate
workshop areas for the tailors and embroiderers. It was more than
double the space that I had cramped them into on my roof. I ensured
that they heard their favourite Hindi music from speakers I installed
in the rooms. The lively ambience and bonhomie at 12 Hauz Khas
Village was indeed enviable from any perspective.

The residents' families took turns in visiting me. Some I liked
immediately, others I did not quite relate to. But in no time at all, I
had been adopted by them as their goddess of wealth, Mahalaxmi.

27

The Golden Days

In MARCH 1988, a group of twelve high-profile US senators' wives came to India on an official tour, with a thirst for some serious shopping. Since mine was one of the few boutiques in Delhi, and that too with a unique East–West flavour, it was always on the must-visit list for VIPs coming to the city. The US embassy arranged the day's itinerary for their guests and I was fitted into their second slot of the day—the first being reserved for an orphanage in north Delhi, called Palna.

From the moment they walked into Once Upon a Time, the ladies went into paroxysms of excitement, contrasting with the mood they had experienced earlier in the day. Even as they ran in and out of the dressing room, trying on their new Indian-fashioned booty, they recalled the scenes that had struck such a sad chord in their hearts. They were torn between the delights of the shop and the sad memories they had taken away from their morning's visit.

At Palna, these women had been deeply touched. Some had wept to see the hundreds of beautiful babies and children, most of whom had been anonymously deposited in the middle of the night into the little cradle that hung from the gate outside the orphanage. Many of these children were handicapped.

Soon, talking among themselves about the impact of their morning visit, they started mulling an idea. First they considered, then they drew me into their idea, and finally they all made a pledge— with my eager assent—that they would organize a fashion show in Washington, featuring my collection, for the benefit of Palna. If I agreed, they themselves would model the clothes at this high-profile function and sell them to raise funds for an annexe to be built at Palna for those special orphans with handicaps who had great difficulty finding adoptive parents.

By sheer coincidence, I already had a connection with Palna. I used to take my daughters there during their vacations, so that they could donate their outgrown clothes, as well as the food and candy we would buy en route to the place. This gave the girls a greater social awareness and an opportunity to appreciate their good fortune. It helped us all put our difficulties, such as the depressing custody battles and economic struggles, in perspective.

I welcomed the women's extemporaneous plan, and within seven months I was in Washington DC at the grand residence of the Indian ambassador, P.K. Kaul. All the senators' wives had kept their date with great enthusiasm, and had invited many more political wives and Washington society ladies. Over tea and cocktails, and wives strutting their stuff in my collection, we managed to collect about ₹30 lakh. It was sent as seed money for a facility at Palna exclusively for handicapped kids.

There now stands a building in west Delhi with an engraved granite that reads:

This Orphanage was Created with the Generous Donation of Wives of United States Senators.

It now houses more than 200 handicapped children. Many others have passed through the orphanage and found warm, loving homes in several countries. It continues to be run as a wing of the original Palna.

∎

By now, my life was starting to surpass my dreams. Besides the two boutiques in Delhi, in Mehrauli and in Hauz Khas Village, I now had two boutiques in New York, one on the west side and one on the east side of Manhattan. Both drew an interesting array of clients and celebrities. Within a couple years of opening we had been featured in several fashion publications. But the coup came when were we were featured on the cover of the Mexican *Vogue* magazine with five full pages inside. The editorial team had fallen in love with my collection when they had happened to pass by the store windows of the boutique on East 55th Street.

Quite by chance, an enterprising young millionaire who had just opened a new club in New York called the Reins Club happened to pass by and was drawn to the store. By the time we had packed the gifts he purchased for his fiancée, he had finalized an agreement with us to stage a fashion show at his new place. The hitch was that he gave us only four weeks to prepare for the event. The *Vogue* feature had put us in a celebratory mood, though, so this seemed like a good opportunity to leverage the celebration.

I went into fast-forward mode to pull it all together. This would require models—some professionals, some celebs—music, a choreographer, hair and makeup artists and a great collection to showcase. My host had assured me publicity and a great audience. Deep down, I knew I was taking on an overly ambitious task—and sure enough, I was driving everyone up the wall with the pressure of my energy in overdrive.

As luck would have it, I had struck up a warm friendship with Ronald Winston, son of Harry Winston and now the owner of the famous store named after his father on Fifth Avenue. I approached him with my conundrum to see if he could possibly lend us some of his fabled jewels for the evening of the fashion show. He generously agreed on the condition that two bodyguards would accompany the jewels and stay in close proximity to the models wearing them.

At one stroke, with a value of about six million dollars of jewellery on our side, everything seemed to fall into place. We managed to get a line-up of some of the top society clients to model for us, including Princess Elizabeth of Yugoslavia and actress Brooke Shields, along with some Broadway stars. I managed to design twenty-four outfits to showcase, twelve of which were shown with the glittering Harry Winston jewels. It was a great success.

■

The East Side shop was located in a charming brownstone four-storey building. It had a beautiful garden at the back, which became quite a regular gathering place, attracting friends, acquaintances and interesting people off the street. Some came in thinking we were operating a restaurant. Everyone who stepped in was welcomed with the fragrant aroma of jasmine incense, masala tea, classical Indian music and plenty of colourful designs to round out the sensual feast. On the rear thirty-foot-high boundary wall of the garden, during one impromptu all-night music and wine session, Malini and Gitu's friends from Sanawar, Vishal Dhar and Manjot Purewal, had painted a giant portrait of Lord Ganesh, the 'Remover of Obstacles'. It was in perfect proportion to the layout of our backyard garden and wall, and beamed with life. It was probably Manhattan's only Ganesh. It not only added character, but undoubtedly brought loads of good luck to our enterprise.

We attracted and entertained many from the worlds of cinema, television, art and entertainment, as well as other celebrity enclaves of New York. One afternoon Doris Duke, the reclusive tobacco heiress once listed as the richest woman in the world, pulled up in her limousine and bought out our entire rack of kaftans made from vintage saris. With a minimum of words she managed to express her delight, making a quick exit and leaving her female assistant behind to make the payment and inform us that she might get in touch with us periodically, if we could assure her of a wider selection. She was the kind of client that that every shop owner dreams of.

Other celebrities included Leela Luce—wife of *Time* magazine CEO Henry Luce—who married her childhood sweetheart at the age of sixty-eight after both had been married several times to others. It was our good fortune that she lived only two blocks from us, loved socializing and got 'hooked' on to our masala chai. She was a patron who added to our sales week after week, as long as she remained in New York. I wondered how many wardrobes she had and whether she herself wore all the clothes she bought from us. She loved sharing her adventurous past with us, which included passionate memories of an Indian lover she had lured away from a maharani on one of her trips to India.

Zubin Mehta would come by occasionally if he was passing through New York, often bringing his friends—Daniel Barenboim or Plácido Domingo or Luciano Pavarotti—to give them a flavour of an exotic Indian sanctuary, which he himself missed so much. The store was an international hub, a melting pot with new surprises every day. Our trendy Eastern ambience and my colourful and feisty friend Dora, who managed it, were the magnets. Of course, the weeks that I came to New York became even more exciting. Inevitably, something unexpected and wonderful would happen before the end of any given day.

One such day, a few months after the Mexican *Vogue* cover story had appeared, a providential gift from Mexico landed on our doorstep. We were already in a celebratory mood when an acquaintance of mine, Ivonne Abaki, walked in. She was a beautiful, energetic Lebanese-Ecuadorian lady, who taught art at Harvard University at the time. She looked more like a svelte stage star; it was hard to imagine her as a Harvard faculty member.

She had the predictable response of certain people with eclectic taste when they entered my exotic atelier. She had always longed to be draped in a sari and we got into that right away, fulfilling her dream. Then she raced around the store like a child in a candy shop. Within twenty minutes she had extracted a promise from me to put on a fashion show at Harvard University.

I had two months to pull it together. No professional models, just real people connected with India one way or another. I called on my artist friend Shakti Maira to add his creative brushstrokes to some of my fabrics, and we included some four-colour-splashed breezy chiffon capes in our collection.

Between some of Harvard's most attractive female students and other handpicked beauties, daughters of friends included, we put together a terrific fashion show for a very appreciative audience. There was a near stampede at the sale that followed after dinner. Our high-octane celebration took us to Harvard Square at midnight, where we invented our own carnival with friends, students and faculty members dancing to Hindi film songs on a cassette player!

That unexpected cocktail of joyous events leading us to Harvard Square remained deeply etched in Ivonne's mind. About a month later, I got a rather frantic call from her. She asked what I had scheduled for the next day and the following week. 'Nothing different than what I did last week, Ivonne, I'm at the store, doing what I enjoy most.' I was sure I had sensed an exciting invitation in her question. She was an adventurous Piscean like me.

I was wrong. What followed was *super* exciting! She happened to be a good friend of President George Bush Senior's daughter-in-law Columba Bush and her sister Lucilla. They were from Mexico and had married two American best friends who had visited their country for a bachelor holiday many years earlier. There they had met the two beautiful sisters with vibrant personalities and fallen in love. Columba, the elder sister, married Jeb Bush. His best friend John Schmidt, a powerful and successful businessman in Miami, married Lucilla.

Now, the tourism minister of Mexico had officially invited Columba, as President Bush's emissary, to visit Mexico on a state trip with her friends. There was I, suddenly and to my utter surprise, being invited by Ivonne Abaki to join them on this trip in the president's private plane! I was given four hours to decide; we were to leave in twenty-four hours. The plane could accommodate fifteen passengers and they had space for one.

Ivonne's invitation was too tempting to turn down. My main concerns were that I did not have an appropriate wardrobe for such a high-profile trip and that I didn't speak a word of Spanish. These apprehensions were quickly dismissed by Ivonne. She put a call through to Columba at the White House in Washington, who enthusiastically welcomed the inclusion of a 'friend from India'. That did it. Everything fell into place. I became the flavour of India in the predominantly Latin group, with my saris and Bina Ramani ensembles.

Our nine-day trip was planned by Mexico's tourism officials and took us to the grandest of hotels and homes in Mexico's many historic and storied places. Oaxaca and Huatulco, steeped in Mayan history, were our main destinations. The trip was filled with laughter, entertainment, hospitality at its best and a sweet little dose of romance. It could have spoilt me forever, but fortunately I had too many responsibilities and some more struggles awaiting me at home.

Mexico was certainly the flavour of 1990 for me, and remains my favourite country in the world, after India. When I married Georges five years later, in 1995, many of the friends from that trip came to India for the seven-day wedding. That occasion matched in many ways the joie de vivre and spirit of our Mexican adventure.

Ivonne Abaki, meanwhile, joined politics in her native Ecuador, where she went on to become the foreign minister. She spearheaded a global effort to preserve that country's unique ecology and is presently the country's most senior UN delegate. Based in Paris, she is as glamorous and youthful, adventurous and dynamic, as ever.

28

Embedded Memories

By the time I had comfortably settled into my new fashionable factory in Haus Khaz Village, I had become acquainted with all the village dwellers. Most had farmlands in Sohna, Haryana, some 40 km southwest of Delhi. The men divided their time between Hauz Khas and Sohna, where they harvested mustard, wheat, potatoes and such. The women and children lived in Hauz Khas, the small urban village, tending to buffaloes and eking out a livelihood selling milk in Hauz Khas and nearby Green Park. I had already been invited to attend a number of celebrations—births, marriages, religious ceremonies—in various households, each one with its own unique character. In some the women dominated, in others they dropped their dupattas over their faces and remained almost invisible.

Meanwhile, through my contacts and word of mouth, the news of the quaint village, hidden and forgotten, was spreading as the loudest whisper among the fashionable set. Every voyeur who made the bold foray into 'HKV' returned again with friends. The place held wonderful little surprises for everyone—not least being the view from my terrace. I took on the painstaking challenge of engaging anyone I could find with a creative talent, be it candle-making, leather craft, jewellery, painting, cooking, whatever. I visualized an eclectic mix of creative arts to satisfy the taste buds of everyone who took the trouble of finding their way into the village.

Once the international diplomats had found their way, the village was never the same again. It was the beginning of a vast transformation, from a sleepy rural enclave to the tourist destination it has become today. I even came to be referred to by some as the

'Godmother of Hauz Khas Village'.

Within a year, there were about twenty boutiques and a restaurant which filled rooms that had formerly remained empty, housed buffaloes or warehoused sacks of grain. With the support of the open-minded and erudite choudhary, I was able to chalk out the path of success between tenants and landlords. I would bring back pictures from my trips abroad, featuring artistically designed shopping malls in cities such as Santa Fe and Palm Beach, which would greatly inspire him. Our synergy led to desirable results. Celebrities from around the world began to visit, from rock stars to Arab sheiks. HKV was and is, more than ever, Delhi's most attractive destination on the tourist map.

Not everyone viewed the transformation in a favourable light—there have been critics over the years who disapproved of my enthusiasm to integrate these socially disparate worlds of villagers and the jet set. In my view, the main problem has been the appalling neglect by civic authorities of the infrastructure, especially walking areas, parking facilities and miles of unsightly overhead cables, not to mention sanitation.

Over the five years that I led the development of HKV towards the fruition of my vision, I witnessed several changes unfolding in the social dynamics of the residents. Inevitably, the new economic boom and fame had varying effects on different families. Some were a disappointment. I had two beloved families in addition to the erudite choudhary and his wife. My landlord, Jagjit Singh, and his family were good people and treated me as one of their own. Next door to them lived my favourite, the eldest couple in the village, Manbhari and her husband Buddha Singh. They would have been in their seventies. I rarely saw the rest of their family, but Manbhari had adopted a ten-year-old as her granddaughter and had two teenage grandsons, one of whom had a very foul temper.

These youngsters wanted no part of rural life. They were in a hurry to emulate the modern world now flourishing in Hauz Khas after my arrival. They wilfully avoided their duties in the fields, preferring to be enthusiastic witnesses to the rapidly growing fashion and café society that was manifesting itself in their village, day and night. The gruelling farm work was a harsh contrast to the glamour they were being exposed to. The father of these boys was obviously going to be the last farmer in the family—much to Manbhari's consternation.

I made it a point to take out a few minutes almost every day to call on her and share tea and cookies with her. I brought the cookies, she served the tea, and thus we tended to the little details of each day's programme. She must have been a great beauty in her youth—I could tell from her grey-blue eyes, firm but weather-beaten peach skin and high cheekbones. Her warm smile told me that she returned my affection. Her strength of character was clear in the way she perceived the changing scenario in HKV. In the midst of all those changes, within her four walls, she ruled.

Other women in the village readily gave out their homes on rent to boutique owners. Manbhari never gave up any part of her large home, which she considered sacred. Her husband Buddha would follow her around, bent over his walking stick; both chorused their disapproval of the rapidly changing attitude of their grandsons, who were slated to become their heirs. The HKV property was, by now, yielding much more income than their mustard fields.

One day, out of sheer disgust at their callow attitude, the feisty matriarch Manbhari announced that she was going to celebrate a rare, ancient tradition during the full moon of April on their farm. The grandsons' role called for making all arrangements with full fanfare, sparing no costs, to ensure that their entire biradari or clan (close to 1,000 guests) were invited to a lunch to celebrate the grandparents' death—while they were still alive! It was to be a replay of their wedding some sixty years earlier. It signified respect and thanksgiving, and assured the old people a grand funeral once the proper example had been set in the presence of everyone in their community. A mock throne was built in the form of a swing with decorated ropes. Colourful carpets covered a vast amount of ground. With great ceremony, relatives were garlanded with marigolds on their arrival. Manbhari beamed like a goddess with her million-dollar smile. She had ensured validation for her beloved Buddha and herself in the presence of a thousand well-wishers, who sang and danced around them in all their finery and with great merriment all through the day. It was a delightful assault on the senses.

They would both die peacefully a year later.

The great Choudhary Raghuvir Singh died in a tragic accident shortly thereafter, and a few years later so did my young landlord Jagjit Singh, from sudden heart failure in his fifties. Suddenly my three heroes of HKV were gone, leaving a great vacuum.

Meanwhile my workforce grew, as did the number of my clients. Goodwill was pouring in from many directions. Within months of discovering and renting a space in HKV, I had bought a lovely, spacious three-bedroom garden apartment in Neeti Bagh, a beautiful new neighbourhood. Everything seemed to be falling in place.

The Russian exodus and American arrival in Afghanistan caused enough upheaval to bring thousands of refugees from there and Iran pouring into India through a United Nations initiative. I was among the lucky ones to be offered a few skilled tailors and embroiderers for employment by the UN agency for refugees. This turned out to be a godsend. The tailoring skills of these refugees was far superior to that of my Indian tailors, providing priceless finesse to my collection and adding gravitas to my reputation in the industry. In my heightened state of confidence, I experimented with unisex cuts using delicate saris, resulting in a unique look that caught the imagination of international buyers. Both my vital energy and my earnings were soaring.

On the home front, my social network was growing. I was receiving positive media coverage across the country. In the meantime, the National Institute of Fashion Technology (NIFT) had produced its first batch of graduates. Among that group were Rohit Bal, Ritu Beri, Suneet Varma, J.J. Valaya, Rina Dhaka and dozens more who would quickly go on to carve out successful niches with their individual styling. The idea of fashion designer boutiques had caught on, and HKV became a role model as a delightful fashion hub, inspiring other village areas to open up to the fast-growing fashion and café society. Delhi, which was hitherto stuck with the reputation of a provincial town, had suddenly become a metropolitan magnet attracting artists, architects, foreign designers, theatre, music, dance and culture—indeed, a hub of modern thought.

My daughters had by then graduated from school and were in college in New York. During their vacations in Delhi, our apartment was a vibrant party zone for artists, designers, musicians and the likes. The late fashion designer Rohit Khosla was one regular.

One of my favourite guests was Protima Bedi, who would come periodically from Bangalore to raise funds for her project, the dance village Nrityagram. It had seemed like an impossible dream in the beginning, but her dogged devotion and faith led to its unprecedented success during her lifetime. Her life was tragically cut short at the age of forty-nine in an avalanche during her pilgrimage to Mount Kailash.

Protima's daring honesty was a source of great inspiration for me. We often talked into the wee hours of the morning, sharing dreams and discussing the hurdles that faced our respective village projects. 'Bina, my dearest,' she said to me one night, reflecting on the canvas of our mutual vision, 'you should have no trepidation about your village. It's a commercial, income-earning village. Whereas I have to rely on a begging bowl for mine. I'm constantly thinking of innovative means to raise funds to support my dance students.' She was right—her challenge was much greater than mine. But the reality was that we both had made a daring, voluntary commitment to realize our dream villages, and in each case it was a daunting task.

I had to constantly maintain equilibrium between the village landlords and my hand-picked choice of tenants. It was easy in the early years, but once the idea had proven itself and so many interesting people poured in, it triggered a greed among the landlords. They started to indiscriminately rent out spaces to anyone who was willing to offer a higher rent. Quality gave way to quantity and, with the sudden death of Raghuvir Singh, my carefully planned oasis for hip and happening designers, artists and connoisseurs began to deteriorate into a crass commercial agglomeration of whoever had the deepest pockets.

Sometimes my all-night talks with Protima would end with a drive to HKV, where we would take a brisk walk in the Deer Park and watch the first rays of the sun come up. On such mornings we would end our walk at Choudhary Raghuvir's charpoy under the peepal tree and have a hot glass of chai, served up by his attentive wife. One morning, feeling rather a strong equation with us, the choudhary reflected in a heightened state of wisdom, ' You two ladies who are conquering your village dreams have been blessed with the might of Goddess Durga, the gifts of Goddess Laxmi and the intelligence of Goddess Saraswati.' Then, for good measure, he added—aimed more at Protima—'No one will dare to block your path or harm you!'

Truly, though, Protima's task was a tough one, to raise funds for her dance school, which she had built herself with a group of volunteer friends. It was located an hour out of Bangalore in a remote field, requiring a 10 km drive on dirt roads. She managed to organize power, water and charming lodgings. Her students came from all over the world, and they helped support the place by making jams and juices with homegrown fruits. I have followed this labour of love and devotion with enormous admiration through every stage of its growth. The Nrityagram group, now run by star students and Protima's great friend Lynn, gives spectacular performances all over the world to appreciative audiences. They are easily the best of India's Odissi dance troupes.

■

Another memorable event that took place during my seven years in Neeti Bagh began when my friend, the maestro Zubin Mehta, called me from Israel. He wanted to inform me of his upcoming concerts in Delhi and Bombay. He was conducting the new 'Youth Orchestra of Europe', a 120-piece orchestra made up of young men and women between twenty-one and twenty-five years of age. They were all excited to visit India, and Zubin wondered if I could possibly lay my hands on 120 white kurta-pyjama sets for them to wear. I agreed, and was given just one week to arrange for them. He was to arrive from Tel Aviv; the orchestra was coming in from Frankfurt.

The next day I visited Lajpat Nagar, where the little shack shops were only too keen to fulfil my order within five days. They would deliver an assortment of sizes in pure white cotton with elastic waistbands, for a price of ₹300 per set. Zubin couldn't believe his ears when I told him the price.

He checked into the Oberoi Hotel a day before the orchestra arrived and wanted to visit the bazaar and see the miracle for himself. When he got into the hotel limo, he gave the driver my address. The driver promptly said, 'Oh, you want to go to Ms Bina Ramani's home?' Zubin was at my door fifteen minutes later, and entered with a beaming smile. 'I've just flown in from Israel, where every person on the street knows me. Here, not one person has recognized me in the hotel or at the airport. It feels strange, but it also gives me such a sense of freedom!'

Before I could say anything he continued, 'It seems that here in Delhi, everyone knows *you*. The driver just looked at your address and knew your name. The hotel receptionist knew your phone number and connected me before I could give her any details. I'm very impressed!' We embraced and laughed like two kids. Then we sat down over a glass of lassi and reminisced about the early days in Los Angeles, when Mira and I had searched from pillar to post to pull together an Indian-themed fashion show for his mom.

A bit later, we headed to Lajpat Nagar market. By the time we reached the central square, Zubin threw his hands in the air enthusiastically, jesting, 'Now I feel at home!' 'Look,' he further exclaimed, gesturing towards the shop hoardings, 'there is a Mehta Crockery Store, and further up Mehta Shoes, and look to the left— Mehta Kurtas.' He was enthralled. 'I've come home,' he joked. 'Even though they are probably Punjabi and not Parsi, I don't feel like a stranger anymore.'

The kurta shops between them had managed to come up with 180 sets, much to our relief. Zubin took them all. The extra sixty sets would be distributed to his fans in Israel.

When the young Europeans walked on to the stage in their starched kurta pyjamas, at Bombay's CCI and Delhi's Siri Fort, it was indeed a brilliant sight. Their symphony soared to a crescendo and so did my pride in India's craftsmanship and ability to deliver.

By coincidence, when Zubin made his brief visit to the Hauz Khas Village, we met the French ambassador's wife, Anna Merrimee, a frequent visitor, who had come with a request to place a French flag outside my shop facing the reservoir. She said poignantly, 'Bina, I told you two years ago when you first showed me HKV that it would become a roaring success. We have just been informed of our transfer out of India and I would love to fly our little French flag here as a symbol of my appreciation, and to let you know that we will send you many French friends!'

Life presented beautiful surprises like this almost on a daily basis. I felt blessed and grateful. And the French promise has been fulfilled manifold. In HKV there is now a wonderful little guesthouse owned by an enterprising Frenchman, along with several French eateries and boutiques. Not to mention that flags of almost every country hold pride of place there now.

29

Georges Walks In

HAD I CONSULTED an astrologer in the early 1990s, I would have most likely learnt that my planets were shooting romantic beams from their orbits. During that period I seemed to be drawing a lot of attention from interesting men, on all my travels. I had no intention of getting married, but the prospect of romance was always titillating. I nurtured dreams of getting Malini and Gitu married—the Indian mother's perpetual mission. But they were happily preoccupied in their chosen careers and, as thoroughly modern women, not open to the idea of 'arranged marriages'. Malini, after a stint of dabbling as a columnist, had begun designing clothes and accessories and was attracting positive attention. Gitu had graduated in journalism from New York University and had a great job at a top TV news channel in New York. They both enjoyed 'dating games' and that was fine by me, as they understood their priorities.

On a drizzly September evening in Delhi, I was invited by a friend to the Golf Links home of a Canadian management consultant, who was working on a project to set up a support office for the Canadian government's aid programme in India. He also happened to be an artist. He was in the process of wrapping up an exhibition of his paintings that evening, and I was persuaded by a friend to see his collection before he closed up.

His home in Golf Links revealed a man of eclectic taste and imagination. Two very large rooms were dedicated to his art studio space and one was styled as a makeshift theatre, attracting creative people, principally Indian and Canadian, from all the arts. They were invited to come and feature their art and talents, while he generously provided drinks and food. He referred to this passion as 'Canada's unofficial cultural programme in India'.

The large outdoor terrace had a fascinating variety of plants that were cunningly layered over rocks, creating a dance of their own. A third of the terrace was devoted to a carefully cultivated bonsai collection, creating a pristine, Zen-like Japanese landscape. The rest of the space harboured armchairs and tables placed between exotic potted plants, with bits of sculpture and found-objects peeking out. Georges's reserved demeanour did not fully reveal his fertile mind.

The living-room walls were lined with books from end to end, on an eclectic array of subjects, including history, philosophy, economics, biology, art, India, Japan and so on. This was a different ambience from the world that I had been accustomed to. This unassuming but warm person was a man of few words, but a thinker who seemed to have balanced his yin and yang very capably. His unusual combination of traits appealed to me. I received a personal tour through his art collection, which was among the most colourful I had ever seen in one space. I was instantly charmed by his reticent reaction when I admired his artwork. Georges was tall, attractive, soft-spoken, disarmingly knowledgeable and a talented artist and sculptor to boot. Very different from the artist who had stolen my heart in San Francisco some twenty-five years earlier. But he was definitely not shy when dealing with vibrant colours. I booked one painting that I liked and he generously offered me a 50 per cent discount, thereby securing his position on my 'new best friends' list. I didn't stay long, as I had a dinner engagement elsewhere. But later, reflecting on our meeting brought cheer in my heart. I notched up a thought in my head about adding him to the list of guests for an upcoming Diwali party the following month.

■

During Diwali festivities each year, I tended to feel a little lost and lonesome, like hundreds of single people in Delhi who were left out of traditional family festivities while the country was consumed in days of celebration and religious rituals. It felt much like being a non-Christian in the West during their Christmas season.

Years before, I had started creating my own type of Diwali celebration with my children and a small circle of foreign friends in attendance. The day before Diwali, at sunset, we would perform our customized version of a puja, which developed over the years, with the help of a pujari. Our evening would take on a great spirit of bonhomie in the casual atmosphere I would create, covering the entire floor of my living room with mattresses and white sheets. Food and drinks were plentiful, and new visitors were added to each year's celebration. We would continue into the wee hours of the morning after engaging in raucous sessions of teen patti (a traditional Diwali card gambling game), which went down well with foreigners once they got the gist of it. This annual event at my home had styled itself into a popular tradition of its own. Between the NRIs, the foreign expats and a few Delhi singles, we had a wonderful mix of guests to assure us a memorable Diwali, Bina-style.

This particular year, 1993, Georges was one of the new guests. In no time at all, not only had he grasped the essentials of teen patti but he had cleaned out the bank. His embarrassment and humility at having to sweep up his winnings of ten, twenty and fifty-rupee notes into a big bag attracted everyone's admiration. He had earned himself a firm position in the inner circle of my enviable group of friends, and he had unknowingly charmed me.

We began to go out on dates with close friends. On one such date with Italian resident friends Valeria and Franco, who had also just found each other, we all took off spontaneously on a November weekend trip to Pushkar during the world-famous 'Camel Fair'. Amidst the hectic chaos, noise and crowds of camels, nomads and tourists, George and I found ample opportunity to discover each other's interests. We were very different. As the phrase goes, we got drawn to each other's opposite characteristics. He was an intellectual and a man of few needs, who got his high from exploring historic, scientific, biological and philosophical facts. He talked wistfully of achieving the goal of living like a forest dweller. I derived my highs from experiencing sensual, emotional, spiritual and esoteric layers. But we both shared a spirit of adventure, and Pushkar offered a huge dose of it.

At our last lunch together, Valeria and I managed to whisper into each other's ears, when we saw that the men were distracted, that the trip had been a life-transforming one. The magic of romance had struck. Nine months later, Valeria and Franco had a beautiful baby daughter, Gaia, who became my goddaughter. Georges and I returned to Delhi as a starry-eyed pair, having left as new friends just a few days before.

As our circle of mutual friends expanded, Georges' home in Golf Links became a centre of impromptu gatherings. A typical evening could start with just two or four of us having a drink and chatting wistfully, till we sensed the first rays of dawn on his charming terrace. An unexpected visitor or a couple of phone calls could quickly balloon into a group of fifteen to twenty. There might even have been a live guitar or sarod player. During such evenings, Georges's studio would be abuzz with activity. He had a gentle but powerful knack to persuade even the shyest of guests to put brush to paper and have a go at making a painting.

There were several large paint books already half-filled with the efforts of sundry visitors. Tubes of colour and brushes were spread out on three large tables, and numerous cans of ready acrylic paint and dozens of brushes stood upright in other cans. It was always amusing to see the initial reluctance to participate in virtually everyone. But once Georges had succeeded in nudging them into putting the first stroke of paint on the page, there would be no stopping them. I recall Rajmata Gayatri Devi, who flatly refused to even touch a brush until she saw Naveen Pattanaik have a go. She watched his initial reluctance evaporate as he splashed colour on page after page. This inspired the rajmata to have a try, and soon others joined. Vasundhara Raje needed no persuading as she attacked the page with her usual zeal, imagination and fearlessness. Before we knew it, at least ten guests were sitting at tables with their own pages, paints and colours. Meanwhile, music filled the space, glasses clinked among friends, food materialized; some guests danced on the terrace and bonhomie spread across the house. There were many such memorable evenings.

Great Indian and foreign artists such as Anjolie Ela Menon and Bryan Mulvahill left their artistic marks. The beautiful wife of a leading Delhi editor protested that she could do anything except paint. Yet, she gamely took brush to paper and produced a notable piece. She signed off, 'Thank you for the worst evening of my life', but everything about her demeanour testified that she was quite pleased with her effort. These large painting-filled books are now among our treasures, filled with beautiful memories and images from a lovely synergy that we created among our charming circle of friends. And to this day in Georges's studios, one in Delhi, the other in Goa, where the atmosphere is always conducive and inspiring, guests are invited to paint.

My own interest in painting developed at this time, encouraged by Georges. One year after we married, he and I held a joint exhibition in New York at Trump Tower. It featured work that we had produced that summer in a studio, which he then maintained in the Big Apple. The exhibition was quite a success and it opened up a wonderful new path for me. I still love painting, and more recently it has led me into photo art. I even have a couple of exhibitions coming up!

From the beginning, Georges and I had always candidly discussed our values, our pasts and our visions for the future. Above all, we agreed on our mutual love of freedom and independence. When his three-year contract with the Canadian government was over, Georges opted for early retirement and decided to stay on in Delhi. He moved into my flat, and we were officially a 'pair' with the understanding that there need not be a marriage. During that period one of my brothers came visiting from London, and even though he enjoyed meeting Georges, he did not appreciate the fact that we were living together. Another brother soon followed with a visit, and before I knew it, my four brothers had expressed their disapproval of my open relationship with a 'foreign man' in India while I still had two daughters of marriageable age.

Meanwhile, Georges had very much become part of my inner circle of friends in India, and got along well with Malini and Gitu. Given the pressure from family elders, we reconsidered our situation. We were each financially independent, dedicated travellers (together or independently), and had similar life values. We mutually agreed that marriage need not destroy our individual interests and aspirations—it was to be a marriage of great companionship.

It was a good decision. Our wedding celebrations drew our friends and family from all corners of the globe, and while it was originally planned to last for four days, it grew organically out of our control and stretched into nine glorious days. Such a contrast with my first, over-in-the-blink-of-an-eye wedding! Years later, that gala is still brought up with nostalgia among friends as one of the happiest wedding celebrations.

Georges was now at a crossroads, with many choices facing him. He had sold his home and was starting life afresh in India, with no idea of what the future might hold. After thirty years of supporting himself as a teacher and management consultant, with his focus primarily on the needs of others, he now had the opportunity to turn his attention to his own interests—study, travel and art. Nevertheless, he was open to using his lifetime of skills, combined with mine, if some opportunity arose that would not grow into a 'full-time job'. We hit upon the idea of synergizing our talents and starting some business.

Around that time my old landlord, Diwanchand Gupta, came by my shop and told me that he planned to sell his building, a small part of which I was already occupying. He offered me first right of refusal if I wanted to buy it. The timing could not have been better. His offer gave articulation to our dream, and before we knew it, Georges and I had launched one of Delhi's most interesting commercial and cultural hubs, sandwiched between the UNESCO World Heritage Site, Qutab Minar, and the ancient ruins of one of Delhi's early cities, Lal Kot. Calling it Qutab Colonnade, we set about to fill it with eleven handpicked boutiques. At its centre lay our special project, a beautiful café in the courtyard under an ancient tamarind tree. We named it the Tamarind Court Café. It was in effect, India's first 'shopping mall', albeit a miniature in comparison to the mega-malls of this millennium.

30

The Orbit of Stars

ONE COLD FEBRUARY morning in 1998, the phone rang and a friendly male voice asked, 'Am I speaking to Bina Ramani?'

'Yes,' I replied. 'Who is this?' I was totally unprepared for the answer that nearly made me drop my mobile phone.

'My name is Richard Gere,' the man introduced himself. 'Please, don't hang up. It's really me,' he continued quickly, responding to my incredulous silence.

'You are joking, right?' I asked with some hesitation, presuming it was a prankster. But the voice at the other end definitely had a vague 'Richard Gere' ring to it.

'No,' came the reply, 'this is not a joke. This is Richard Gere, and I'm used to this kind of a response. Your friend Bhagwanti Mohan was at the Kalchakra meditation camp in Bodh Gaya, from where I have just come, and she gave me your number.'

'Gosh! How amazing is this,' I gushed. 'How did this come about? And what a lovely surprise...'

He cut me short, saying, 'She is a very fine lady and a true friend of yours. She was supposed to call you to explain why I'd be calling. Did she?'

'No, but I've been expecting her to turn up soon, because I know she has been at this camp for the past ten days. She truly is a great friend of mine to spring such an amazing surprise on me—'

I was gently cut short again, not because he was rude, but he was aware he had this impact on people and they tended to ramble when in conversation with him. He explained his reason for calling: 'I have been coming to India for many years, mainly to Bodh Gaya and Dharamshala. I have derived so much joy and fulfilment from my Buddhist practice and I feel indebted to India for offering me this opportunity. I want to give back something meaningful. As a gesture, I thought I could offer some of my free time to a fundraising event for some cause...' he trailed off for a bit. 'We need to meet up and discuss this further. I happen to have about four–five days free in early April. Bhagwanti tells me you are the best person she knows in India to organize something unique for a charitable cause.'

I was aware that Bhagwanti had attended the camp, because we had had dinner in Delhi the night before she left. I wish she had warned me! What I managed to say was, 'Oh, that was nice of her.'

Soon enough I managed, 'I'm really flattered that you've taken the initiative to call. Yes, I have pioneered a few successful fundraisers here and in the US. I think we ought to meet.' Then I quickly threw in, 'Bags, as I call Bhagwanti, is a truly loyal pal.'

'She is a very special lady', Richard purred in his warm voice.

His time was very limited, so we arranged to meet within two hours at the Qutab Colonnade.

Richard arrived with an Italian fellow-Buddhist friend, Fabrizzio, oozing charm and humour, wearing a crushed blue jacket, a casual shirt and trousers. He was shorter than I had expected but had an electrifying presence. We sat down at my favourite spot under the huge shady branches of the tamarind tree, on the small first-floor terrace. Over two glasses of ginger lemon fizz, we discovered that we shared the same sentiments about the cause of HIV/AIDS awareness.

Although Richard's first choice of causes was to help raise funds to assist and provide better shelter for senior citizens of the Tibetan refugee community, I managed to convince him that given the short span of time (six weeks) he was offering me to organize a top-notch fundraising event, we had a slim chance of success, since Tibetan issues ranked low in popular consciousness. I had recently been giving lectures at a small NGO in Delhi called Naz Foundation, using my experience as a voluntary worker with advanced AIDS patients at St Luke's Hospital in New York. We thus settled on his second, but equally passionate choice of AIDS.

We learnt that both of us had suffered the loss of the same person to AIDS in New York in the previous year. She was Sandra Isham to me but Sandra Vreeland to him. She was the daughter of a very special friend, Sheila Isham, who was like a godmother to me. Sandra had married Alexander Vreeland, the grandson of legendary queen of style Diana Vreeland, who was one of Richard's best friends.

After a tragic road accident in Puerto Rico, Sandra had been given transfusion with infected blood, which had led to a very painful and untimely death from the AIDS virus. Richard and I had both, separately, sworn to do everything in our power to help raise awareness about this dreaded disease—it's ironic how Sandra brought us together from remote worlds.

By virtue of this coincidence, we leapt into making plans for two separate events to involve the media and notables of Delhi and Bombay. While spreading awareness and sensitivity on the subject, we also wanted to raise large donations to provide funding to NGOs who were struggling to survive in India due to the terrible stigma which accompanied the disease.

We both agreed that while Richard Gere's name would attract much of the attention we needed, we should balance his presence with an Indian actor. I suggested Shabana Azmi, with whom he was not then familiar. In fact he was not conversant with any Indian cinematic names at the time, other than Shekhar Kapur, Deepa Mehta and Mira Nair.

We agreed on goals and objectives. There was no time to lose. Richard gave us exactly six weeks from the day we first met. He was offering five free days from his cramped schedule. He managed to attend the first meeting I called with the committee ladies, where he inspired them all before leaving for New York, promising to return later in time for the event in Delhi. Our five-day window was from 3 to 8 April 1998. The event in Delhi was to take place at the Qutab Colonnade, which we would contribute to the cause. The Bombay event would be held two days later at the Oberoi Hotel.

From that moment on we worked like maniacs to put together a great show. We first created an NGO called 'The Art of Giving' to organize the event, receive the benefit funds and to distribute these to other NGOs already involved with AIDS.

Six weeks later we held a charity fashion auction at the Qutab Colonnade, where a select group of young fashion designers donated an outfit each. The models were celebrities, including a prominent politician, the feisty ninety-year-old mother of a former Delhi lieutenant governor Romesh Bhandari, Sharmila Tagore and many others.

The auctioneer was none other than Richard Gere at his humorous yet humble best. That evening is still remembered as one of Delhi's most glittering nights by those who attended.

A similar show followed in Bombay, with Bollywood stars as models, and Bombay designers and a few from Delhi donating outfits. In the end we raised almost ₹1 crore, the largest amount ever in such a short time for a new cause.

While we had succeeded in launching the first AIDS awareness programme as part of our efforts, the idea itself attracted plenty of negative response and opposition, especially from conservatives and government lobbies. They saw the word 'AIDS' as something dirty that might inflict on them an incurable sexual disease if they even uttered it. I had been appalled at the ignorance of some of those resisting this function, days before our event. A typical anonymous caller said, 'Why are you interfering with God's process of controlling our population problem?' In other variants, we were accused of interfering with God's just punishment for sinful behaviour.

Fortunately there was plenty of goodwill, too, especially when the event moved to Bombay, which has a more broad-minded society and where the topic of AIDS was openly being raised as an alarming issue. Of course, Richard Gere's endorsement was key to our success. His main objective was to sensitize people about the HIV virus and spread awareness, and to help raise funds for those afflicted by it who were being treated as social outcasts.

His contribution paid rich dividends. The somewhat reticent Bombay celebrities came out with hearts outstretched. From every top star of Bollywood to the powerful business houses and society women, we received unconditional support. The event not only raised a large sum, it opened up a whole new vocabulary for AIDS awareness overnight.

Having observed first-hand the daunting task of spreading awareness of this dreaded disease in its early years in the US, I had understood that if we were ever to make a breakthrough in India, we would have to use the same fashionable platform to launch the idea. Then we would be able to extend it, through NGOs, to where it was most needed. The events in Delhi and Bombay were a huge leap forward in establishing our goal. The funds collected were distributed to many NGOs across India, which had virtually been operating underground so far. Because of the stigma attached to the disease, many of these NGOs had to work covertly, so as to avoid the wrath of difficult neighbours, antipathy from hospitals and government officials, not to mention the risk of hostility being directed at the workers and their families.

Initially, we faced difficulty in locating worthy NGOs across India because it was also essential to keep a low profile to attract the shame-ridden patients. Soon, however, they emerged—happy with this new support, financial and moral. It gave them some much-needed validation, and well-deserved too. They were really the original heroes who had had to fight off aspersions in a country steeped in orthodox religious beliefs and judgemental attitudes. Without the support generated thanks to our efforts and the generosity of Richard Gere, they may never have overcome the stigma of being associated with a 'dirty sex disease'.

Today, almost fifteen years later, huge strides have been made in the field and there are affordable drugs that are saving the lives of millions. Even the stigma has been reduced; this had seemed unthinkable back then.

The events were not just a big leap forward for the cause of

AIDS, but the fortunate association with the revered Buddhist Rimpoche, Lama Zopa, who is among Richard Gere's gurus and a close aide of the Dalai Lama, brought me some personal spiritual benefit. And the timing couldn't have been better. I learned some important doctrines of the Buddhist path to peace and the power of being a silent observer and letting the dust settle, thus allowing the bright truth to surface in its own time. The beauty of this simple but powerful message permeated the atmosphere among all the Buddhists I had the opportunity to meet on subsequent visits to Dharamshala. The Rimpoche's blessings brought me a sense of much-needed peace, but my hectic work pace, multitasking and social commitments to other causes continued in overdrive.

■

Our fashionable galleria, the Qutab Colonnade, had become one of the most stylish gathering spots for the Delhi elite. The charming Tamarind Café was our biggest draw, where I was able to indulge my taste buds, developed from years of restaurant-roving in New York and Europe, and create an ever-evolving menu offering a fusion of flavours.

By 1998, I had opened a boutique in New York in partnership with my good friend Belle McIntyre. We had a large space in New York's fashionable Soho district, showcasing collectibles from India and Asia. We named it The Asian Opera (TAO) and it featured an eclectic array of stylized East–West products. We worked our magic into making it a rich cultural experience, and very quickly attracted an enviable influx of lucrative clients.

One day in early December 1998, an attractive young man walked in, looking for a present for his mother. His fascination with our merchandise was evident. After an hour or so of browsing, he told us shyly that he was Sean Lennon. My partner, good old Dora, who came in to help out occasionally, recognized him immediately as the son of John Lennon and Yoko Ono. He called his mother and described our store and merchandise to her. After listening to his description, she asked him to invite one of us to her home the next day with some shawls and jewellery.

Since both Belle and Dora had previous engagements, I had the good fortune of visiting the legendary apartment in the famous Dakota building where John and Yoko had moved after their marriage and where John was tragically shot to death in 1980.

Armed with two shopping bags from TAO containing our best shawls and a few pieces of jewellery, I arrived. A group was gathered at the street entrance, some people with bouquets of flowers. After being admitted by the doorman, I rang Yoko's doorbell on the twelfth floor. She opened the door personally and greeted me with a warm smile. 'Hello, Bina. Sean was so charmed by your store and your two ladies that I couldn't wait to meet you. And thank you for taking the trouble of coming all the way uptown for me.'

She wore dark glasses and looked very slim in her fitted black pants and beige cashmere sweater.

'It's my pleasure. Your son is adorable, he had us mesmerized,' I replied.

We made small talk as she led me to her large open kitchen. A chessboard was laid out in the centre of the long table. Her companion, Scott, brewed some fresh tea. She lost no time in shifting aside the chessboard to make room for the goodies I had brought to show her. She asked several questions about India as she made her selections, choosing almost all the shawls and expressing her delight about gifting them to her friends for Christmas, which was some two weeks away. She said she was keen to visit Varanasi and asked me if it was possible to organize a discreet trip where she would not be recognized. She was wary of the media.

I assured her that I would look into it. I was impressed by her unaffected warmth. She spoke softly and chose her words carefully. Then came the bonus. She offered to give me a tour of her apartment, which I accepted with enthusiasm. She chatted gently, almost like an old friend, as she walked me through the pristine white, starkly furnished drawing room. As we strolled, I took in the breathtaking view of Central Park, where, directly below, a small commemorative plot, 'Strawberry Fields', had been dedicated to the memory of her husband.

She pointed to a white cradle in which there was an Egyptian mummy of a child. This, she explained, was a prized possession. She explained how much controversy it had caused when she and John had acquired it, but I had heard none of it, I told her. On one of the walls near the cradle was the famous Andy Warhol portrait of John Lennon. 'They seem to enshrine each other,' I commented.

'I think so too,' she said, and continued to walk me through all the vast, mostly white spaces of her apartment. I sensed her loneliness and could see that she craved anonymity. She asked me to take off the jacket I was wearing so she could try it on. She loved it so much, I promised I would make one for her, from the same Kashmiri shawl, when I returned to India. But I didn't get to fulfil my promise.

I sensed that we could become good friends. She was lonely, and my Eastern descent combined with modern thought seemed to appeal to her Japanese sensibilities. But some instinct held me back; I restricted my enthusiasm and held on to my reserve.

When we returned to the kitchen, she opened her fridge to offer me a snack and apologized profusely when she found nothing she thought worth offering. Then she opened several cabinets and picked out a beautifully packaged box of Japanese green tea. Even as I protested, she pressed it into my hands, asking me to accept it as a token of her gratitude.

As I was taking my leave, she accompanied me to the elevator. She suddenly had an afterthought and asked me to wait. She rushed back to get her coat, and with a hasty explanation to Scott she wrapped one of her new shawls around her neck and entered the elevator.

Then she looked at me, with seeming embarrassment, and asked, 'Bina, do you know what day it is today?'

'Yes,' I reflected for a moment, 'it's 8 December.'

She lifted her glasses to her forehead so that her eyes were exposed for the first time since we'd met, and said, 'It's today John died, eighteen years ago.'

'Oh my god,' I gasped. 'I'm so out of it. Forgive me. What a significant day.'

Overwhelmed with emotion, I held her hands, closed my eyes for a moment and said, 'What a great man the world lost.'

She nodded in agreement.

As we reached the ground floor and stepped out of the elevator, we ran into the actress Lauren Bacall, Humphrey Bogart's widow, who was about to take the same elevator up to her own apartment. The two ladies gave each other a peck on the cheek and Lauren's eyes darted from the shawl on Yoko's neck towards me. 'Aha, you've done some hot shopping.'

Yoko made no comment, nor did she introduce me; instead she chuckled and held my hand. This unexpected gesture made me swell with pride. We stepped out into the courtyard on 72nd Street. I had been treated to a revealing moment of a small vanity war between two legendary women.

'I'll walk you down the block, but be ready to be stopped several times along the way,' Yoko warned.

As we turned right towards Broadway, past the security guard at the gates, we were caught in a mild mob of well-wishers gathered outside. They had come to pay their respects at the gates of the Dakota where the historic tragedy had taken place eighteen years ago today. The last thing they had expected was that Mrs John Lennon would herself be present and greet them all.

She stopped and shook hands warmly with each and every one who had come. This continued intermittently all the way down the block. Our conversation was continually interrupted, but she did most of the talking and made a point of telling me how much she appreciated my visit. She reminded me that she awaited a jacket, more shawls and information about the trip to Varanasi, and we parted ways with a warm hug. I was very moved by her spontaneity.

TAO would become one of the fatalities—along with Yoko Ono's special jacket and her Varanasi trip—of the Jessica Lal tragedy, which radically changed our lives forever, barely four months later. It had to be closed when I was barred from leaving India, a fate which is too often imposed on civic-minded witnesses.

31

The Fateful Night

It was the last Thursday of the month, 29 April 1999. With torrid summer around the corner, this would be the last party of the season. That Thursday night at the Tamarind Court Café was the most happening night in Delhi. It was to be a multiple farewell party. We were closing for the four-month slack season, and also hosting a farewell for Georges, who was to travel to Canada the next morning for three months. His bags were packed and the driver was on standby for a 3 a.m. departure—which was not to be.

Our restaurant used to draw distinguished visitors from all over the world, because it was also Delhi's first shopping mall of sorts, albeit housed in a charming heritage building surrounded by 2,000 years of history. It boasted eleven chic boutiques, including an art gallery, which showcased the best works Delhi had to offer. And, of course, the trendy Tamarind Court Café, where guests would frequently be treated to live jazz, blues music and impromptu guest performances while they dined on Mediterranean fare.

Malini had started the 'Thursday Night Private Party' theme some six or seven weeks earlier, when her friends had persuaded her to put aside one night of the week for them to get together and enjoy a private-party atmosphere rather than having to go to the crowded clubs that were popular among the affluent young at the time. They settled on Thursday, since that was the night hip youngsters usually headed to the Djinns nightclub at the Hyatt Hotel. Unable to afford the weekly trips to Djinns, they decided to create their own little club among close friends, styling a new theme each Thursday. Invitations were restricted.

This idea started out the first night with eight girlfriends bringing their own wine, ordering dinner at the restaurant, playing their favourite music and just 'hanging out' together, having a good time. The concept caught on, and every week it increased in size as its reputation spread by word of mouth. By that Thursday, it had evolved into something bigger. Some friends had started calling me, saying, 'Our kids are raving about your place on Thursdays. Can't we come too?'

I could not believe what Malini had created. It resembled New York's nostalgic El Morocco or Copacabana, with even a touch of Studio 54 in it. The parties took place in a large courtyard with a tamarind tree in the centre. Part of the courtyard would be turned into a bar, part into a dance floor, with lots of casual tables and seating, while under our grand staircase Malini would create a new themed area every week where the guests could hang out to see and be seen. Models, designers, young business tycoons, foreign residents, Bollywood and Hollywood stars, artists, musicians—all turned up to join in the festive atmosphere. On this Thursday of the seventh week before the summer season started, several hundred people came and went during the course of the evening.

At that stage we still didn't have a liquor licence, though we had received notice a few days earlier that the last barrier had been cleared so that there was 'no objection' to the final licence—the end of a long and frustrating ordeal. The growing success of the Thursday night parties had become rather alarming for us, because it had passed beyond the original 'private party' concept. A sign at the gate announced 'Private Party' but by now, word was out and few paid heed to the sign. We didn't have adequate controls at the entrance—only a single guard.

On that April night I was busy the entire evening, rushing up and down and greeting people between the courtyard and the upper terrace where Georges's farewell party was taking place.

As it happened, the World Economic Forum was meeting that week in Delhi, and most of India's prominent businesspeople had gathered in town. Some had got wind of the party and decided to come down and check it out for themselves. I was shocked when I started to see faces that I usually saw only in the business pages of newspapers and on television, several with their wives. I was rushed off my feet, greeting them, being introduced, making new acquaintances. They were amazed at the beautiful atmosphere, wanting to know who was who, what was going on, what the night was all about. However, most of them departed before 12 a.m.

At one point I glanced towards the gate and saw another group walking in. A tall, handsome man, who I later learned was the Hollywood actor Steven Seagal, came walking in with a group of ten or so Tibetan friends, some of them in Tibetan wear. We showed them up to the upper terrace to shield Seagal from unwelcome attention, and spent a good part of the evening with them. Seagal, a teetotaler, also left well before 12 a.m. We wonder to this day, having seen him in action in his movies, how he would have responded if he had been the one to encounter the scene that was to confront me at 2 a.m.

Everywhere I turned I saw celebrities and radiant faces; the weather was perfect. The people, the music, the cool bursts of wind blowing and the crisp, star-filled sky all combined to create magic. Perhaps it was because the crowd was so much larger than we expected, perhaps the night felt too perfect—a strange premonition flashed through my mind, which I shared with a couple of friends. I told them that the night felt so unbelievably good that something terrible might happen and snatch it away from us. They both responded with, 'Shhh, don't utter such negative words.'

By 1 a.m. the food and drink had run out and, much to my relief, the crowd had largely thinned out as well. By 1.30 a.m. there were some forty people left, mostly regulars and the younger lot. The staff, as always, had completed their cleaning up, sweeping, washing; the bar and counters had been dismantled; the garbage had been hauled away. They were eager to finish the work because the place would be reopening in eight hours and had to be spic and span, ready for business. They all had to be back for work at 10 a.m.

On my way up the stairs, turning around to take one last look below me, I noticed, through a window across the courtyard, that a few men had walked into the restaurant and seemed to be arguing with the cleaners. This part of the building was intended to become the formal dining room when the restaurant was refurbished. It contained the kitchen to the right, through a blue door, and a small unused bar. It was out of bounds for the guests while it awaited refurbishment.

Just before 2 a.m., I descended the stairs and started across the courtyard towards the restaurant. Before I could get there, Malini came running out, visibly shaken, saying, 'Mummy, some men have just walked into the restaurant and they're using foul language.' She didn't go into the details but looked unnerved.

I comforted her, saying, 'That's exactly where I'm going, to get everyone out of there.'

Malini later said in her police statement that a man (who would later be identified as Siddharth Vashisht aka Manu Sharma) had burst in with some friends and demanded some drinks. Sharma even offered ₹1,000 for a drink. Malini explained that the place was shut, that there was nothing left and that he would not even get a sip for ₹1,000. He responded that he would give ₹1,000 for a sip of her. Irritated, Malini had left the restaurant, then I had met up with her.

Malini's designer and model friends used to take turns to act as 'celebrity bartenders' at these evenings. Jessica Lal was one of them and was there that night, helping out. Her work was over by then, as the bar had long since been taken apart. She had been chatting with Malini and Shayan Munshi, another 'celebrity bartender' who was present in the restaurant. They had been reflecting on the success of the evening and were hoping to find something to eat from the fridge when these men had walked in.

I started up the four steps that led to the restaurant entrance. As I climbed the third step, I heard a pop. It sounded like a balloon bursting but then, after another step, I heard another pop and this time I saw Jessica, who was standing amongst the men, now outside the bar, some fifteen feet away from me, fall to the floor. Immediately, the blue kitchen door beside the counter swung open and a light-skinned, stocky young man burst out into the restaurant from behind the counter, in front of me.

I thought I saw him put something shiny into his pocket, which might have been a gun, though I did not see it clearly. I blocked his exit even as I saw his friends make a hasty departure past us to the door behind me. Simultaneously, both Shayan and my electrician Shiv Das pointed towards the stocky man (Manu Sharma), saying, 'He did it!' Everything was happening in seconds.

Blocking the man's exit and with my eyes focused on him, I shouted instructions to Shayan, 'Run outside and ask everyone with cell phones to call the police, the ambulance or the nearest hospitals.' He ran out and announced to the remaining few guests, 'Someone shot Jessica!'

Meanwhile, I continued blocking the young man's exit as best I could, and demanded to know who he was. I kept blocking him in a side-step that must have looked like a dance rehearsal, as he tried to leave through the door. He just kept shaking his head and repeating to all my questions, 'No, I didn't do it.'

'Everyone is pointing at you, saying you did it!' I glared at him, my adrenaline at its peak.

He shook his head and said, 'No, it wasn't me.'

Then, mapping my vulnerabilities, 'Hand me the pistol,' I risked, pointing at his right-hand pocket, where I thought I had seen him hide something shiny.

I didn't dare take my eyes off him, because I was acutely aware that I needed to keep him on the back foot, in case my gamble failed. Following the example of Rajmata Gayatri Devi, I remember thinking, *One of us is going to win this.* I decided I had to overpower him somehow. I was hoping someone would come and capture him while I was buying time to delay his exit. I now know that this is not the approach police recommend, worldwide, when dealing with a gunman!

The man showed no signs of aggression or of reaching for a gun; his sole purpose was to escape. Then, after some very long three or four minutes, he suddenly shoved me aside and made briskly for the exit. He snaked his way with high speed through the hurried exodus of the last guests. I chased him closely for seventy-odd metres till he reached the main gate and the street exit. No one made any attempt to assist me. By the time we reached the gate, I'd managed to grab his T-shirt a couple of times, but he shook me off and won the chase. I yelled out to the few guests that were still hanging around, 'Call a hospital! Keep trying the police! Someone go look after Jessica!'

The man then exited through the gate and rushed to the right, towards Mehrauli village. His companions were long gone.

By this time, Georges was at the front gate. He went after the man into the night, where he lost him after some 500 metres at Mehrauli village. He thought he spotted the man climbing on the back of a scooter, with a driver. It later emerged that he had hidden in Adham Khan's tomb, a monument at the entrance of the village, where he may have hidden his weapon as well (it was never retrieved). Georges then ran on to the Mehrauli police station some 150 metres up the road, where he attempted to report the murder. He was told to sit and wait but he refused, stating that there had been a shooting incident at the Qutab Colonnade. He then ran back a kilometre. By the time he returned about thirty minutes had elapsed, and the Colonnade was empty.

During this time I had returned to the restaurant. Several of the staff had surrounded Jessica, who was lying on the floor. One of the guests, Rohit Bal, had reached Dr Alok Chopra on the phone, who happened to be on night duty at Aashlok Hospital.

I told him, 'We've had a shooting incident and I am bringing in an injured girl.'

'I'll have a stretcher waiting at the entrance,' he assured me. 'I will attend to her personally.' Meanwhile, two of the staff had slipped a white tablecloth under Jessica, wrapped her in it and were already carrying her out into the courtyard. There were no more than fifteen people left in the place as we rushed towards the main gate.

I called out, 'Anyone with a car and driver, please get them ready at the gate!' At this point Jessica was still breathing, though unconscious. As we crossed the courtyard, Malini, who was standing in a state of shock with some of her friends, saw me leading two of the restaurant supervisors, who were carrying Jessica's body. She exclaimed 'Oh no!', let out a terrified scream and fell down in a faint.

'Someone, please take her upstairs and take care of her,' I yelled, hoping some of her remaining friends or staff would take charge and revive her. My mind was racing.

A young friend of Malini, who was visiting from Hong Kong, had volunteered his sedan car and driver and it was now waiting at the gate to receive us. We placed Jessica on the back seat. I sat in front with the driver, with my two helpers, Jitender Raj and Madan Kumar, cradling Jessica on the back seat, wrapped in the tablecloth. Looking out into the quiet empty roads of Hauz Khas and Green Park as we approached Aashlok hospital, an overwhelming flood of thoughts consumed me. The events of the previous twenty minutes or so played in a continuous loop in my head, especially the couple of minutes of confrontation with the man who ran away. Another premonition replaced the devilish one from earlier in the evening: 'What if they were sons of politicians?' A sweaty chill ran through my body.

We arrived at the hospital about twelve minutes later, in record time, with Jessica breathing very heavily and coughing. Some blood was trickling out of her mouth, and she was making heavy gurgling sounds. We couldn't see where she had been shot. Her face was ashen but clean, showing what looked like a small bruise on her forehead.

As promised, Dr Chopra was waiting on the street with a stretcher. Jessica was taken into the operating room immediately. We waited outside and prayed. Within minutes, a few stragglers from the party started to trickle into the hospital lobby. Among them were Rohit Bal and a few close friends of Jessica, as well as her sister Sabrina, who had not attended the party that night but had been called. Rohit started to cry out loud and others followed. I suggested that we do some collective meditation. I optimistically told them that Jessica was still breathing, and that she would be fine. I didn't know that she had only hours to live.

The doctor came out of the emergency room about thirty minutes later and said, 'The bullet is a one-way wound with no exit and it has a created a lot of haemorrhaging inside. I'm afraid my hospital is not equipped to deal with this kind of complication. I suggest that you take her to Apollo Hospital.' Wasting no time, her sister and a couple of friends took her, in the Aashlok ambulance, to Apollo Hospital.

I got a call from Georges, who was at Qutab Colonnade, informing me that a police team had finally arrived. I returned immediately with Jiten and Madan. Georges and I gave our statements to the Mehrauli Station House Officer (SHO) and mapped the entire incident, walking the police team across the scene. We gave them Jiten's bloodstained shirt, in which he had cradled Jessica's head in the car, and offered that they take Jessica's shoes and handbag, which had been left behind.

We then noticed a black Tata Safari parked outside our building. Being convinced that the killer had left on foot but certainly had not come walking, Georges and Jiten wrote down the licence number and handed it to the police, suggesting that it could be the killer's car. By daylight this vehicle would be driven away by the killer's friends, unmindful of the police.

We took the police to Aashlok, by which time Jessica had been taken to Apollo in an ambulance. Shayan was waiting at Aashlok to give his personal account to the police. I was with them during the thirty-minute interview, filling in the missing pieces of the puzzle. The police had now recorded the full First Information Report (FIR) from Shayan and were equipped to go forward and fit in the missing links.

By the time Georges and I drove to Apollo Hospital, the first rays of the sun were up and we learnt that Jessica had passed away. Many young friends of Jessica, along with her parents, were present.

Malini had recovered and was also there, but unable to speak, like most of the others. A sense of shock prevailed.

At 5 p.m. we attended Jessica's cremation, one of the saddest experiences of our lives. While returning from the cremation in the car someone told us that the rumour was that the killer was Manu Sharma, a person unknown to us but known among the younger lot. He was the son of a prominent politician. My thoughts wandered back to the encounter from earlier that morning. Manu Sharma—I now knew his name. I recalled his face from the previous night and tried to fit that name to it. From the beginning I had identified his arrogant behaviour, including the carrying of a gun, to be that of a privileged youth, perhaps the son of a politician or business tycoon. I resolved that given the opportunity, I would identify and accuse him, if it's the last thing I ever did. He would be made to pay for his crime. Georges, Malini and I had clearly seen him and had all observed his behaviour. Our statements to the police, as well as our testimony at the trial, would unwaveringly support what we saw.

Then my thoughts turned again to poor Jessica. Neither Malini nor I were close friends of hers, but we liked her. I had once helped her secure a lease for a little boutique she had opened below my shop in HKV. She had walked in requesting that I introduce her to the landlord. It was the first time I had ever interacted with her, and I had liked her immediately. She was pretty, and had a directness and sincerity about her. She smiled easily and seemed to have a lot of friends. There wasn't much communication between us, but her warmth and friendly nature had left a memorable impression.

In the coming days, witness statements, including Malini's, filled in the picture as to what had transpired in the restaurant after the entry of the Manu Sharma quartet. Manu had done most of the talking. Jessica, Malini and Shayan had been having a late-night chat. Manu and his friends had suddenly walked in at about 1.50 a.m. Manu wanted a drink. Learning that there was nothing available, he spoke crudely to Malini. She walked out and came to inform me about the men.

Manu then went through the blue door behind the counter and looked into the refrigerator—empty, no drinks. He stood behind the counter, next to Shayan, from where he addressed Jessica. She said something to Manu to calm him down, after which he drew his pistol and said something like, 'Now we'll do it my way.' He shot once towards the ceiling, then, at point-blank range, fired another shot, which hit Jessica's forehead. Then he dashed out the blue door towards the exit, putting away his weapon.

That was when I had entered the restaurant.

And that was the motive for killing Jessica Lal—she had refused him a drink that wasn't available.

To those who find this unbelievable (as one defence attorney later claimed it was), we offer the following facts:

- On 13 May 1999, two weeks later, the sons of a policeman and of a member of legislative assembly (MLA) walked into a Baskin Robbins ice-cream parlour in Lucknow and asked for cassata ice creams. When they were informed that there was none, one drew out a pistol and killed the attendant.
- On 6 November 1999, six persons were involved in a shootout at 1 a.m. involving three pistols, which left one dead and three injured, at a wedding party in a Delhi banquet hall. The argument this time did not involve drinks or ice cream, but the choice of music. The venue did not have a liquor licence. Guests had all left by the time the police arrived.

That venue was not closed down. The Tamarind Court Café was. As was our entire building.

32

The Investigation

THE CASE HAD a memorable beginning for us.

Georges, Malini and I were summoned, virtually every day, to
the Mehrauli police station, where we mostly sat around all day as
the police made exhaustive lists of every person we could recall as
being present the night of the party. The last list had amounted to
about 180 names. Our personal phone books were taken away and
never returned. This lasted several days, giving ample time during
which the suspects covered their tracks. To me, it appeared that the
police were behaving like a dog going around in circles chasing its
tail, instead of grabbing the meat that lay right in front.

Everyone on the list was summoned and interviewed by the police.
Most of them truthfully claimed that they were not present when
the crime occurred at 2 a.m.; some stated that they had not been
present at all; most had nothing material to report. This exercise did
not reveal anything much about the crime, but it grabbed headlines
for several days, giving the false impression that hundreds had been
present at the time of the shooting.

On a Friday just eight days after the tragedy, the SHO showed
up at 9 a.m. to take us all to the police station. He assured us a
swift return home after a short formality. Malini was unwell and
depressed, and I was deeply stressed and exhausted from all the
police and media visitations, but the SHO and his team refused
to leave our home unless we accompanied them. After arriving at
the police station, we were ushered into a small dusty room with a
table and two chairs and, with no further explanation, ordered to
stay there. An hour later, a police officer brought in a paper with

two paragraphs handwritten in Hindi. He asked me to sign at the bottom. I asked him to translate it. He said he couldn't. So I refused to sign. He shut the door again.

A couple of hours later, Malini received a cell-phone call from Priti Paul, a friend in Kolkata. Priti had seen a 'Breaking News' item on television that we had been arrested! Suddenly, it all seemed clear to me. They were holding us at the station on a Friday afternoon until it would be too late to arrange bail, and we would face a weekend in jail! We immediately went into high gear, calling friends and pleading for their help.

My lawyer friend Rani Jethmalani came to the rescue and sent her junior, Baldev Malik, to court, where we were taken in an open jeep by the cops. Our loyal friends and family members were already waiting with appropriate papers in hand. Also present was a swarm of media cameras and reporters, ready to capture the event. We pressed and shoved our way to the courtroom and within the hour we had secured the required bail of ₹25,000 for each of us. We also had to surrender our passports. But we were free to go home, much to the disappointment of the police and the media.

Unfortunately, after this hugely publicized incident we had become 'suspects' in the eyes of the public. Our reputation as witnesses had now earned a black mark, putting our integrity in doubt. It looked like a larger plot was being hatched. Our lawyer later explained that in the Hindi document I had refused to sign we were being asked to confess to violations that might well have led to imprisonment.

∎

We became increasingly aware that we were inconvenient witnesses, and that there was a relentless effort to not only damage our credibility but possibly make us disappear.

First and foremost was the issue of our not yet having acquired a liquor licence. Two bottles of wine (one half-full of cooking wine) had been retrieved by the police from the kitchen. This formed the basis of a charge against Georges, Malini and myself under the Excise

Act. The case would drag on for several years and eventually result in a small fine.

Within days we received show-cause notices, all in line with threats we had started receiving—the purpose of which was to immediately revoke our visas and deport us from India for 'violating the laws of the land'. We responded that we had not even been charged with any crime, much less convicted, and thus must be considered innocent until proven guilty. The matter was dropped.

An action was then initiated against us whereby our restaurant licence was revoked. Meanwhile, the Municipal Corporation of Delhi (MCD) was announcing that our building would be seized by the government through acquisition—a totally bizarre proposition which, as it turned out, went nowhere.

Other municipal and federal departments soon joined the fray until a total of around forty actions had been launched against us, in the process effectively destroying our business and ultimately causing our building to remain idle for almost thirteen years. It also kept us going to courts and lawyers' offices for more than a decade. In India, conviction rates are abysmally low, but the judicial process itself is a much-feared and casually inflicted punishment. Unfortunately, that process punishes the innocent as well as the guilty.

We and all our tenants were then served with show-cause notices by the Delhi Development Authority (DDA) to the effect that we were doing business illegally, though everyone held legal shop licences. We would all find ourselves in court for years on that charge. In the meantime the MCD, refusing to produce any legal document to justify the action, ordered our building to be sealed, along with twenty-three other properties. Our tenants had a couple of hours to vacate their shops—forever. It took seven months in court to reverse the spurious sealing order, but the tenants never returned. We hit financial rock bottom. The desired damage had been done.

Next, the DDA went into overdrive and served us a vague demolition order on the grounds of illegal construction. That action stretched over a decade of costly court hearings, but eventually led to a happy outcome for us.

In 2000, the income tax sleuths made their appearance in a raid (a 'survey', they preferred to call it) of all our premises. The café had been closed for twenty months by now. Most of our tenants had long been driven out by the MCD. The remaining few were not paying their rent. In short, our business had no income whatsoever. Despite all that, we merited a raid. The Income Tax Office then initiated hearings that dragged on for thirteen years. These cases were all won by us in the end, but still imposed endless frustrating visits to tax tribunals and huge legal bills.

The same year, at the first Fashion Week in Delhi, which happened to fall on 15 August, Independence Day, Malini decided to wear a dress inspired by the Indian flag as a patriotic gesture. It was a snazzy off-shoulder fully sequinned dress in a stylish cut, the cynosure of all fashion observers. But suddenly, within hours of the launch, we got a call from a friendly policeman, warning us about trouble. A police team was on its way to confiscate the dress and Malini's collection, and arrest her. Someone from the fashion fraternity had apparently lodged a complaint that Malini had violated the code of respect to the national flag. Acutely aware of the kind of trouble that police involvement could cause, Malini removed her collection from her stall and left. The dress was seized by the police.

Within three days, she became the target of national and international media. She decided to keep a low profile. However, the end result was that she became noteworthy overnight, resulting in phone calls of concern and goodwill from all over the world. The flag dress was featured in prominent international magazines such as *Time* and *Newsweek*, and newspapers including *The Times*, *The New York Times* and many more. The articles in general derided India's archaic law that resulted in a jail sentence for wearing something that should have been a symbol of pride.

At the time Georges was in Bangkok airport watching the opening ceremony of the Olympic Games on TV, where team after team marched into the stadium, many wearing uniforms inspired by their national flags. He was surprised when he saw the news and learnt that Malini had drawn the ire of the nation for the very reason so many were being feted at the Games.

At one point, when we were buckling under the daily police and media pressure and were at an emotional low, some friends who had a spacious home in Lutyens Delhi invited us to stay with them, to unwind and get some peace. We continued to respond to summons from the police for questioning even while there. It was a welcome sanctuary, but within a few days the police had traced our whereabouts.

■

Meanwhile, shifting the media focus on us had provided the defence team and Manu Sharma a protective shield. Bina-bashing had become quite the fad. Even though most of the actions against us seemed to have the sole purpose of punishing us or destroying us as witnesses, this fact caught no one's attention. Everyone was busily engaged in this appalling new trend.

Through mutual friends and acquaintances, attempts were made to get me to sign an affidavit saying that I had not seen either Manu or Vikas that evening at Tamarind Court. I was told to develop symptoms of amnesia, to forget what I had seen. More chillingly, I was warned in a friendly manner that every time I read in the papers about a girl being gang-raped or having acid thrown on her face, I should heed it as a warning about what could happen to Malini. Another frequent threat came by way of trying to scare us into leaving India. These kinds of communication often evolved into indirect offers or bribes in an attempt to silence us. Several friends warned me against taking on powerful politicians.

One evening, at a busy intersection in Delhi around 6 p.m., Georges and I were in our car, returning home after a meeting.

Suddenly we heard a very loud, shattering thud.

The driver exclaimed, 'We've been hit!'

We looked behind to see our entire rear windscreen shattered. I was stunned to see a bullet-sized hole directly behind my head, with a web of cracks radiating from it. Luckily, the projectile had bounced off and we were spared. We feared that someone was making good on their threats.

We headed for the nearest police station to lodge a report. The officer on duty took down the details, until he heard my name. He then stopped abruptly and made a phone call to someone, and moments later told us we were in the wrong precinct.

Off we drove to the next precinct. Incredibly, we encountered the same reaction there! Finally about three hours later, we reached a third police station and insisted on an enquiry. We were told to leave our car behind as evidence. When we returned for our vehicle a few days later, the police told us they had found nothing. They closed the case, but assigned us three security officers round the clock. These soon proved to be a nuisance, so we requested that they be recalled.

■

We were interviewed by the police countless times, and they certainly were not courteous to us. However, they clearly appreciated that we were not wavering from our original statements, and that we had not tampered with evidence. A senior officer at one point candidly revealed that they were under great pressure to arrest us.

Manu Sharma's defence team, meanwhile, worked at destroying the police investigation. Their tactic of eliminating real witnesses and creating new and more convenient ones was extraordinarily successful, as became apparent when the case was finally brought to court and the accused were acquitted.

33

The Big Lie: 'Wiping Blood'

T HIS ASPECT OF the case may seem trivial, but I've singled it out for special treatment because the final outcome of the case, as it turned out, hinged on it. And also because it has caused me so much grief over the years. To this day, I am occasionally asked, even by well-wishers, 'But why did you wipe the blood?'

The issue casts light on one of the standard tricks used by lawyers to convert a witness into an accused, thus neutralizing them. It also shows the appalling reluctance of the media to do their own thinking and expose the truth—especially when false statements serve them so well, providing sensational headlines.

Let me categorically state, at the outset, that I did not wipe any blood from the scene of the shooting, nor did I order anyone else to do so. I had no motive to do that. Nor did it have any bearing on solving the crime.

Initially, the police thought that we knew Manu Sharma and were trying to protect him (though it is not clear how wiping blood from the scene would have helped his case in any way; it would have been much more useful to pick up the empty bullet casings and dispose of them).

Hours after the shooting, a senior inspecting officer, Vivek Gogia, had set up a small table in the courtyard of the Colonnade. Two other officers were searching the restaurant (they would find one of two empty bullet casings, with Georges looking on). The first question the police asked Georges was, 'Who wiped the blood?'

Georges was surprised at this question. It seemed somewhat trivial compared to the many more serious questions he was expecting.

Nevertheless, he accompanied the officer into the restaurant and examined the spot on the floor where, for a couple of seconds, he had seen Jessica's head lie. The area showed no sign of blood—but neither of having been washed. It had been trodden upon by several feet. Jessica's bleeding, as Dr Alok Chopra pointed out, was mostly internal due to the one-way wound.

Georges enquired why such importance was being placed on the absence of blood. Surely there was no question that Jessica had been shot, that she had fallen there, had been wrapped in a white tablecloth by the staff and then rushed, by me, to a waiting hospital. Gogia insisted that the killer had been a frequent guest and that we knew him. We were equally adamant that we did not.

On the drive to the hospital, some blood did issue from Jessica's head, which was being cradled by our employee Jiten. His bloodstained shirt was subsequently given to the police. This shirt was never heard of again.

I had no motive nor opportunity to wipe any blood from the floor when Jessica was shot, nor was I ever charged for it. But the media, in their misjudgement, tossed it out repeatedly as their bestselling headline for the longest time. It worked as the best bet for the defence in eliminating me as a witness.

Regularly, newspaper items would bray on about my destroying evidence by 'wiping blood', keeping the notion alive. Only four voices in the press spoke out about this conspiracy against us—the venerable Khushwant Singh, ever alert to police chicanery; the feisty Tavleen Singh; *The Hindu*, which has always shone for its honest reportage; and finally Tarun Tejpal, whose riveting sting operation changed the dynamics of the case forever (detailed in a later chapter). These people helped sustain our courage and hope.

34

The Trial at the Sessions Court

Just over two years after the murder, the trial commenced in the sessions court. Manu Sharma's lawyers began by arguing that he had not been present at our restaurant on the night of the shooting.

Deepak Bhojwani, a guest, was the first prosecution witness to give evidence, and he identified several of the accused. Almost all the other guests from that night had claimed that they left the party early, or that they were never there. Unlike us, he was spared harassment for his honesty because he had moved out of India to South Africa.

Then the nation watched aghast as the defence team's tampering began to bear fruit. Three key witnesses, who had seen and heard everything, 'turned hostile'. Shayan Munshi, Shiv Das and Karan Rajput, who were the main eyewitnesses to the entire encounter that evening, reneged on their original statements to the police. A daring lie of a 'two-gun theory' was introduced by one of them. They all gave various excuses for going against their original statements, and each of them failed to recognize the accused in court. They perjured themselves, and twenty-nine other witnesses also changed or invented their testimonies. The case was about to crumble.

During testimony, it was noticed by us that the senior lawyers from the defence team appeared to be dictating the terms of the proceedings to the court clerk, who dutifully wrote down whatever they instructed. They seemed to rule the scene.

Next, Malini testified, sticking to her original police statement. She went over to Manu Sharma and identified him by touching his shoulder.

I was summoned to testify after that. It was the day I had waited for to help vindicate Jessica's tragic loss. The atmosphere was highly charged. The small court was packed and stifling. I was the last eyewitness to the shooting and its immediate aftermath, the only one whose account mattered in challenging the hostile testimony of the three key witnesses. Facing a powerful group of lawyers on my right, a weak prosecutor and dozens of hostile media persons on my left sent a shiver through my body. I was almost frozen with fear, overwhelmed with a flood of memories of the threat-filled interludes since Jessica's murder.

With all the courage I could muster, I responded to the prosecutor's vague and sketchy questions, relating the actual facts I had given in my police statement. I recounted the entire incident in detail. I was then asked to identify Manu Sharma and to go and touch him. As I turned right to face the defence crowd, I couldn't see Manu's face.

Then I heard the judge say, 'Step out from behind and make yourself visible.' I suddenly saw Manu, the shortest one in the group, emerge from behind a tall man. He was now in the front row. He looked different from the night I had first seen him—he seemed darker and had added a short beard and glasses. But it was definitely him. Trembling with emotion, I went over and, without hesitation, touched him, and then Vikas Yadav, a second accused. I muttered something to myself, which was immediately seized upon by Naseem, the head defence lawyer. The defence side sprang into action, shouting that I was not certain. I protested to the prosecutor, insisting that I was certain; I had simply muttered involuntarily to myself that his appearance had changed. However, my request to be heard was refused. The prosecutor did not ask for clarification (he would later be criticized by the High Court for this). Instead, I was brusquely ushered out of the courtroom with an order that my testimony was over, leaving the defence to project their own interpretation on what had happened.

Next, Georges began the first of four testimony sessions, during which he was questioned about the case and many other irrelevant matters regarding his past, our relationship and so on. Georges ended his testimony by identifying Manu, placing his hand on Manu's shoulder, just as Malini and I had done earlier.

The defence would later introduce two witnesses who testified that Georges was not present at the party (one of these, a waiter, Madan Kumar, later admitted that he had been paid/forced to lie).

■

On 25 January 2002, Manu Sharma was granted interim bail by the High Court, with Ram Jethmalani acting as his advocate. A month later, co-accused Vikas Yadav, who was out on bail, and his cousin, were remanded for the brutal killing and burning of Vikas's sister's boyfriend, Nitish Katara. On 11 November 2002, Manu Sharma's interim bail was cancelled by the High Court, which stated: 'There is a long chain of circumstantial evidence linking the accused with the crime which is inconsistent with his innocence and consistent with his guilt.'

On 21 February 2006, Georges and I were in our car in Delhi when we heard the news: All accused had been acquitted and released by Additional Sessions Judge S.L. Bhayana. His ruling stated that the only clear culpability lay with Georges, who, as two witnesses had testified, was not at the party and thus had perjured himself; Deepak Bhojwani, who had also identified the accused, was declared a planted witness because his name had not appeared on the guest list prepared by Georges. Manu had been framed by the police. The two-gun theory was credible. The police had failed to create a credible link of events.

Our jaws dropped in incredulous shock.

The very next day, 22 February 2006, S.L. Bhayana was elevated to the High Court. The appointment met some resistance on its way to confirmation by the president of India, who returned the list, unapproved.

35

Public Outcry and the SIT

W E WERE NOT the only ones to be stunned and outraged by the verdict. The news came as a sobering insight to the nation.

Almost immediately the airwaves were buzzing with protests and calls to action from the outraged public. The printing presses rolled. The law-bending rich and powerful would have to be held accountable for their arrogance and their brazen flaunting of the law.

A tongue-in-cheek SMS, penned by Tarun Tejpal of the investigative newsweekly *Tehelka*, reading 'Nobody Killed Jessica Lal' went viral. (It was later adapted as the title for a movie based on the incident.) Hundreds of thousands of people across the country forwarded it and TV channels in all languages flashed this line.

Candlelight vigils and protest marches were held across India throughout February 2006. A new precedent of public demand for justice across the nation had been established. The powers that be at the highest levels were listening. Very quickly, a retrial was ordered by the Delhi High Court. The orchestrated acquittal, which had allegedly involved several government departments and important power brokers, had been exposed, and their plan to free the accused had misfired.

The media played a crucial role in demanding justice and arousing public ire. The public outcry dimmed once an SIT, under then Delhi Commissioner of Police K.K. Paul, was set up to carry out a fresh investigation. Ironically, a large number of the arguments that were made in the document that called for the reinvestigation and High Court review were based on us as key witnesses.

To us, it became immediately apparent that my testimony would now have to be considered in a new light and given its due importance to achieve justice. But that would not be convenient for our powerful detractors. I feared that I/we may be targeted again, and my intuition told me that my journey was about to get very rough. I tried to brace myself for the road ahead. My family shared my jitters.

The police chief, K.K. Paul, decided that a team including officers from the Economic Offences Wing (EOW) of the Crime Branch would reinvestigate the case, focusing on any improprieties that might have been committed by the original police investigation team. Nobody questioned why the EOW was chosen to investigate a murder crime case. Special attention, he said, would be given to any tampering of evidence. Fresh charges might be laid. They were to report periodically, and in confidence, to the High Court.

On 6 March 2006, seven years since the murder, the first bulletin issued by the SIT to all the news channels announced: 'The Ramanis have been served with a lookout notice. They cannot leave the country.' This kind of notice is usually served to hardened criminals, terrorists or persons who pose a threat to the security of the country! A campaign to defame us had now been put in motion.

I started receiving calls from the media asking what kind of 'notice' the police had served. They were surprised to hear that no notice had been served to us, but none followed through to investigate why this bulletin had been issued. Alarmed calls came from family, friends and loved ones all over the world as the news spread. We were unable to comprehend what this could mean. It turned the notion of 'witness protection' into a farce.

Unable to bear the pressure of the damaging media reports, I decided to speak to Sabrina Lal. I thought that she would be the best positioned to explain to the SIT that they were barking up the wrong tree.

Sabrina's reluctance to meet came as a surprise. After much persuasion, she agreed to a meeting at a coffee shop in her neighbourhood in Gurgaon. She was visibly surprised to see my distressed state. 'What's the matter, Bina?' she asked.

'Sabrina, why is the police team hounding us?' I asked. 'Don't they know that we are their main hope if they want to solve the case?' I added, 'You know it too, don't you?'

I was amazed by her chilly response. She basically shrugged her shoulders and said, 'I can do nothing about it. Why don't you speak to K.K. Paul himself, he's the man in charge. I can do nothing.' She gave me his number. 'I don't know how else to help you, Bina; just get in touch with him, he is handling the case now.'

I broke into tears several times during our conversation and told her that I had become a bundle of nerves at home, that Malini and Georges were alarmed and couldn't bear to see me in this state. Strangely, these very dialogues were to appear five years later in the film, *No One Killed Jessica* (2011), which painted us Ramanis, especially me, in a very damaging light.

One day, Malini and I made a quiet appointment to meet with K.K. Paul to offer our full cooperation with the investigation. I had brought my niece's wedding invitation as well. She was to have a big Indian wedding in Phuket at her father's (Gulu) marina. I wanted to ensure that we would have no problem travelling there, and had even commissioned a couple of colourful cultural troupes to take along for entertainment. Paul refused immediately, explaining that we had foreign passports and that he feared we might run away and never come back. All my pleas to him that I had lived in India for almost sixteen years and had no intention of running anywhere, fell on deaf ears. He could offer us no explanation as to why we, as key witnesses, were being portrayed as 'suspects' in negative press releases to the media. By the time we left his office in shock and disappointment about twenty-five minutes later, we were astonished at the sight that awaited us downstairs.

A sea of media persons, TV cameras and photographers blocked our exit. All of them demanded, 'Did the commissioner call you in for interrogation?'

'No,' we answered, 'we have come here voluntarily to offer our support.' They were incredulous. I believe that that was the first time some of them caught the hints of a conspiracy.

The next question they all had was, 'What kind of notice did the commissioner issue to you?'

'We have never received any notice to date,' we chorused, trying to snake our way through the crowd of people. They, however, wanted all their questions answered. Some of them followed us home in a convoy, too, still seeking answers.

■

The SIT soon showed up at the Qutab Colonnade to interview the three of us. They went through the sequence of events at the murder site in a cursory and mechanical way. The questioning immediately launched into our personal and financial affairs. Georges was quite indignant that the SIT seemed more preoccupied with matters unrelated to the murder case—and besides, all these matters had already been thoroughly investigated earlier. When they finally did turn to the murder, their first question was, 'What happened to Jessica's clothes?' We were dumbfounded. What did they mean? Were they suggesting that Jessica had been taken to the hospital unclothed? We received no explanation.

Sabrina Lal later confirmed that when the SIT examined her, they had asked so many questions about the Ramanis, she had had to remind them that they were shifting their focus, as it wasn't Bina who had killed her sister.

We were the only people in the case with any credibility. It was this credibility that was going to challenge Manu's acquittal, yet every move was being made to demolish it. I even wondered if the powers that be might have me eliminated. Years of pent-up memories were now piercing me like toxic shots. For the first time in the seven-year ordeal, I was crumbling. One day, unable to see me so brittle, Georges asked me, 'What is it about this whole episode that is bothering you the most?'

I thought hard. 'It is a series of things,' I told him.

'But,' he insisted, 'what's the scariest part?'

'Well, the scariest part is not that they might kill me, I'm not afraid of dying.' I then continued without pause, 'The really scary part is that they might arrest me on some false charge and put me in jail. I'd rather die,' I choked.

He put his arms around me and held me tenderly, feeling my pain, and comforted me. 'We are all in this together. Besides, they need us and our cooperation to solve the case. They won't do something so stupid.' That didn't console me, somehow. My premonitions were too often true.

Later that day, while I lay in my bed reading a book, Georges walked in and presented me with a packet containing two new books he had bought from the neighbourhood bookshop. 'I brought you a present that might be useful,' he said, tongue-in-cheek.

They were books on palmistry. I found it amusing and burst out laughing, but I was actually happy to have them and thanked him for his thoughtfulness. Promptly I started leafing through the pages, studying diagrams of palms, looking for markings and descriptions that signified 'jail term' or anything similar. To my surprise, I found that there were several different markings on a palm which one could interpret as signifying a jail term. I certainly found a couple of those on my palm. Then, on examining Georges's palm, I found patterns signifying the same result. While I was confused, I was also relieved in a way and arrived at my own conclusion. It all seemed so trivial in the larger picture. I was reminded of the fact that each of us had our personal journey and reserve of power. Reflecting further, my spiritual journey from an earlier past came alive, reminding me of the reservoir of strength I held within me, which would never let me down. I suddenly felt a rush of power and made a commitment to myself—I would not be swayed into delusional, negative thoughts. Strangely, these palmistry books with their confusing interpretations had strengthened my resolve. I had been chosen by the gods to be witness to such a tragic murder. Was there a purpose? Did I have a karmic debt? Was I ever to understand the rationale behind it? Life is tough, but I am tougher, I decided.

On 6 April 2006, Georges requested written permission from the SIT to travel to his only brother's funeral in Canada. He did not even receive a reply, despite several requests. We held a small memorial service in our garden instead.

On 22 April, in his newspaper column, the lone voice of Khushwant Singh accused the police and media of making a scapegoat out of me.

In July, the High Court, after reviewing the Progress Report, termed the SIT probe 'an eyewash', raising doubts about the SIT's true intentions in the case. It would prove to be worse than an eyewash.

By September, the SIT had prepared an FIR against me for 'forgery and cheating'. One item related to a ration book that was supposedly forged. The basis of the allegation was that the number was not correct. It may be that we were among the many thousands who mistakenly held a false ration book at the time (what police have described as a 'minor offence') but if so, we were the victims and not the perpetrators of the crime. The other allegation related to supposed forging of documents related to obtaining a licence for our restaurant, based on the presumption that we were tenants of the property, rather than the owners.

The SIT then proceeded to Goa, where I was staying at the time. On 6 September 2006 I was arrested with great fanfare and flown like a criminal to Delhi early the next morning, where I was kept in police custody, pending a bail hearing.

36

Arrested!

For the next seven days I was held in police custody in Delhi. There were no interrogations, no explanations given, no questions asked. I was stripped of everything except the clothes I wore, my glasses, and my asthma inhaler. We were issued a gag order, meaning that the media could only get updates about me from the police, not even from my lawyers.

Imagine that!

Our lawyer was told that I had been charged with forgery. Each day I would be taken to the court, and each day nothing would happen. I was just their prisoner, sitting in an office all day and sent to a horrible dark cell each night. They were determined to punish me, break my resolve, smear my reputation and finish me as a witness.

I sat on a chair all day long, some days with thoughts crowding my mind. On other days, my mind was blissfully blank.

By the seventh day, instead of being released for lack of any evidence, a grander conspiracy unfolded. Their smear campaign against me hadn't worked out to their satisfaction. It had to get darker! I was sent to Tihar Jail. It was all being played out for the media and lawmakers. To the few insiders, it was clear that the conspiracy was so gigantic that, indeed, crores had been spent to keep Manu Sharma out of jail. The first chapter of this book relates it all.

Barely twenty minutes before I was bussed away to Tihar, along with other convicts, my family showed up from behind the barbed-wire wall carrying shopping bags full of food and drink. Gulu had flown in from London and was doing his best to stay strong and offer me confidence. The pain in his eyes belied his strong words of comfort, though. My heart broke to see him so dispirited. He was living a nightmare, watching his favourite sister's terrible plight. Malini, Georges and Nafisa were my beacons of light. Steadfast in their goal to get me justice, they stayed positive and their tenacity gave me amazing courage. Their determination assured me I would not be let down.

That searing last vision pierced my heart for days.

The obvious injustice of the hasty proceedings and the real motives behind my arrest and captivity had finally become clear and created the right kind of shockwaves among the public. The thick, dark cloud of seven years of derailed justice, casting a doubt on my integrity, was finally lifting. The media woke up to re-evaluate the situation and finally saw my real role in it. It now dawned on them that I was the victim.

It was 5 p.m., time to travel to my new abode for the night, Tihar Jail. I was the last to enter the bus with about twenty-two other women and children. A quick glance at their faces sent a rush of compassion through me. I offered them a warm smile, and realized that this was the first time in days I had done so. A strange joy and confidence lifted my spirit. I started to see the mission ahead of me. My destiny had brought me here for good reason. There had to be a larger purpose in all this. All of a sudden I became comfortable. I distributed the sandwiches, samosas and drinks that my family had brought me. My appetite was long dead. The miserable seven days in police custody made going to jail feel like heaven.

The 'check-in' procedure at Tihar took over two hours. Uniformed matrons were assigned to do the work, and they were assisted by plainclothes women, who, I later learned, were prisoners who had 'earned' their jobs and positions. A lengthy interview followed, and forms had to be filled. My thumbprints and footprints were taken, and I was photographed from three angles. I had only seen this happening in the movies—I couldn't believe I was living it!

∎

Malini had passed me a message when she gave me sandwiches through the barbed wire to look out for a woman inmate named Reva. She assured me that Reva would take good care of me inside. Indeed, Reva lived up to her reputation when I met her and was warm and friendly, appearing very much in command. She was respected by the inmates as well as the authorities, and was in charge of several administrative jobs. She was serving time for supposedly signing fraudulent cheques on her sugar export business, and had completed ten months in Tihar by the time I arrived. Reva did everything possible to make my stay there bearable. I remain utterly grateful to her and to the NGO friend who passed the message through Malini.

By 8.30 p.m. I was shown to my new home, Block 8, which had around sixty cells housing about 300 prisoners. In the four furthest corners of the block's concrete central courtyard were four large rooms, called barracks, each packed with approximately seventy women and children of all ages and sizes. They shared three toilets between them. My cell, Number 17, was about six feet by nine feet, with a partially walled Indian-style WC and a water faucet. I was informed that each cell was normally shared by three inmates, but I was privileged to get one to myself. I later learned that a wealthy businesswoman, Rita Singh, who had made headlines about five years earlier, had been in there for three months. Even Sushma Swaraj, currently the leader of the Opposition party in Parliament, had once spent a night in the same cell I was in.

All the cells had iron-barred doors, which were locked for the night. Nevertheless, Reva came to visit me and quickly made me feel at home, introducing me to numerous women in charge in my block. In addition to the two sheets, two thin durries, a steel plate and a glass that Reva generously arranged for me, I got a toothbrush, toothpaste, shampoo, a bottle of Dettol, a bottle of water and a set of laundered pyjamas from her personal closet. I was informed that there was a thick bureaucratic blanket laid out at every step of the way, but that I would get used to it.

By 8.45 p.m. I had been locked up in a cell with iron bars,

open to the air. There was a light and a fan that stayed on 24/7. The fan did nothing to alleviate the sweltering humidity. There were mosquitoes galore, from which I had no protection. The floor and bed felt incredibly hard under me and I had only the thin, pokey jute durries and coarse sheets for cover. I tossed and turned endlessly, praying to God to somehow protect me from mosquito bites. I was terrified that rats would come through the bottom of the door, so I placed my water bottles and my chappals against it, hoping to block them out. It was a restless night, with a chorus of screams and abuses echoing for long, especially from the four barracks.

At about midnight, silence finally descended and I drifted off into sleep, but not before a deep meditation, asking God to give me some sign that He was with me and protecting me in this entire episode, and that my fight for the truth would triumph and He would never let me down hereafter. The buzz of the mosquitoes miraculously stopped. I fell into a deep slumber and woke up at 4 a.m. to the delightful sound of rain. A cool breeze wafted through the bars of my door and window. My thoughts came into focus as my senses came to life with the divine sound of falling rain and the nostalgic fresh fragrance of wet earth. My heart leapt with this acknowledgement. This was clearly my sign from God. He was telling me that He was guiding me through this ordeal with His hand in mine, and there was going to be a rainbow at the end of it all.

■

At exactly 5.30 a.m. my door was yanked open with a noisy clink of gigantic keys. I heard the same sound continue on to the next cell and the next, as it moved away to the far side of the compound. The next hour remained silent. By 6.30 a.m. there were voices and noisy footsteps passing by my cell, moving towards the central courtyard to await the morning chai. A few women stopped by my door, inviting me to join them. I looked out to see a huge unruly crowd of women, each with a steel glass in hand, sitting on the floor and awaiting their tea. Someone brought me a steel glassful, but I could barely swallow the first sip. It was watery and very sweet. I could taste no tea in it. I poured it down my toilet.

Reva appeared, bright and chirpy, from Block 1. She had assigned a young inmate from Nepal in my block, Renu, to look after me. Renu's cell, which she shared with two other Nepali girls, was a few cells away from mine. They had all intended to go to Kuwait for domestic jobs but landed in jail instead, thanks to a corrupt travel agent. Devotedly, Renu tried to provide me with every comfort. I never had to wait in any line for my daily needs. Like a faithful retainer, she visited me at least six times a day. She swabbed and cleaned my floor twice a day and moved my floor mat around to avoid the rays of the scorching sun. She brought me fresh bathing water, food, cleaned my plates, laid out mosquito coils and basically spoiled me thoroughly. Hardly any words were exchanged between us, because she understood no English and very little Hindi. I thanked God for bringing her into my life and dreamt of taking her back home with me so I could repay my gratitude to her for her care. But that was not to be.

There was no sign of my bail order, but I had surrendered to a higher state. The 'me' no longer existed. I was at peace with my inner being.

Twice a week, prisoners were allowed visitors in a highly guarded section of the jail. My fellow prisoners were excited for me when it was my turn. I would be allowed two visitors, and I longed to know who they would be. I couldn't wait to let them know that I had finally moved into a zone of peace and relative comfort after the horrendous days in police captivity.

After passing through layers of bureaucracy I finally got to the visitors' centre, where I saw my sister Mohini, and Malini. Behind them stood Munawar, my driver. They had been made to wait two hours to get inside, and our meeting lasted only twenty minutes. I noticed Munawar looking at me with deep pain in his eyes and tears on his cheeks, even before I made eye contact with the family. He was struggling to accept that his boss was 'behind bars'. I quickly tried to console him, smiling as hard as I could, telling him I was okay. He wiped his tears and shook his head. Mohini and Malini were thrilled to see me, but complained about the rude treatment they were subjected to just to get in. They brought me fresh sheets, a pillow, delicious homemade food, some magazines and toiletries and two new sets of clothes. My friend Shirin Paul had sent my favourite Sindhi dish, sai bhaji, specially for me. We talked excitedly, and they couldn't believe their eyes when they saw me genuinely happy. I wanted my anxious friends and family to know that I was doing fine. I was thrilled to learn that the media had finally woken up to the truth about the conspiracy to demolish me as a witness.

During the course of that day, while the cell door was open, women from the neighbouring cells lined up outside my door. They seemed to think I was a political heavyweight who could help deliver them their due justice. There was a line-up of nine or ten women of all ages, sitting outside my door, relating their tragic stories and the causes of their downfall.

Many were genuine cases of injustice, and my heart went out to them. I was told that more than half of the inmates were in on false charges. I talked to many of them, and can write a book on some of the grave injustices they narrated. Some of the women had endured horrific atrocities at the hands of their employers, the police, their husbands and even their lawyers and local politicians. Others were clearly lying to me, especially regarding cases of dowry disputes, where they had caused death or grievous injury to their relatives. I was rather amazed at my intuitive reaction to each one's story. One woman even confessed she was lying to me when I challenged her story.

Later in the day, a message arrived from the chief superintendent to curb my movements because the media had been calling, wanting to know how I was being treated. Apparently, the media had gone into overdrive to report the real facts of the hitherto false reports from the police. Guessing games about my status 'inside' occupied front pages.

In the outside world, Malini, Nafisa and Ravina, a friend of mine, worked tirelessly to get me out of Tihar as soon as possible. Ravina's companion, Aryaman Sundaram, was coerced by Nafisa to appear on my behalf before the magistrate of the criminal court. With a flourish of eloquence lasting four hours, he got me bail. The magistrate had to take a two-hour recess while writing her order, which had become quite complicated. At 7 p.m. on the third day, my bail was announced and all my new friends in jail who had earned the privilege of watching TV in their cells came running to hug and congratulate me when they saw the news.

On Friday, the fourth and final day of my custody, I was on tenterhooks because my bail order had still not arrived at Tihar, and if it didn't come through in time I'd have to spend the whole weekend in jail. Even though the familiar melodious sound of rain delighted me during my waking hours each morning, I missed my own bed desperately.

That day, the NGO run by my friends Rani and Neera had come to rehearse a play with the inmates of the jail, which was to be staged in two weeks for the president of India. I was invited to attend the rehearsal. Sure enough, the chief superintendent was there. She gave me a disapproving look because I was out of my area of confinement, but decided to ignore my trespass. I was worried that I might annoy her in some way, as she was the one who would have to approve my release.

Suddenly she sent for me and asked, 'Aren't you a designer?'

'Yes,' I responded hesitatingly, wondering how that was relevant to my being here.

She gave me a pen and paper. 'Can you design an elaborate and elegant costume for my daughter-in-law? She will wear it for Karva Chauth. She is slender and tall like you, and quite beautiful!' she said warmly, surprising me.

I sat uncomfortably on the floor outside for lack of an alternative place, and came up with a design that I hoped would please her. I sketched a three-piece lehenga set, which brought a momentary smile to her face when I showed it to her. She asked, 'What colour do you suggest?'

I pondered, then recalling that the daughter-in-law was a new bride, fair and slender, a vision of peaches and cream came to me. As soon as I had finished explaining the palette of colours, she took the design sheet in one hand and with the other, she slipped me the folded court order as she shook my hand. What a trade-off!

I couldn't conceal my joy on seeing that piece of paper. I had nothing to pack. I had given everything away to Renu, along with the unused coupons I was allowed against money while there. I was ready to walk out, but before my enthusiasm got the better of me the chief superintendent explained that the checking-out procedure would take two hours. Those two hours were the longest of my life.

A wonderful surprise awaited me on the other side of the gate when I emerged: Gitu had just flown in from New York and had come to fetch me for the long walk to the street. Once out, we were greeted by a battalion of photographers and journalists. Nafisa and Ravina helped us duck between the eager paparazzi, jump into our waiting cars and speed off.

Some of the paparazzi chased us home, but my car managed to lose them en route when we made a sudden turn into the Bangla Sahib Gurdwara, in accordance with the instructions that Gitu brought from my family. The next stop was a visit to see Georges, who had lived in secrecy for the previous five days, as per our lawyers' advice.

That night, a priceless scene awaited me at home. All my sisters, who had arrived from other parts of India, and several close friends had gathered to give me a truly hearty welcome. The house was filled with flowers and well-wishers. A feast was laid out on the dining table. What a delicious assault on my senses! The phone rang incessantly as my brothers and other family members kept calling, celebrating my stand for the truth, telling me how proud they were of me. We all acknowledged and toasted to the role of our parents, who had laid our foundation stone of truth and integrity above everything else.

The start of the High Court review was now only three weeks away.

37

High Court Review

The High Court's role was to review the evidence and testimony that had been gathered in the initial trial, and to see whether the verdict reached was consistent with that material.

It also had to consider any additional material gathered by the SIT's reinvestigation of the case. It had been showing increasing annoyance with the SIT and its leaked progress reports. In early October, it had begun its deliberations and lost no time in putting SIT in its place. It refused to accept the SIT's final report, calling it 'not worth the paper it's written on.'

On the second day of the review, 6 October 2006, exactly thirty days after my highly publicized arrest in Goa, the High Court, having reviewed my testimony, declared me not just a 'key witness', but 'the star witness'. It stated that the prosecution initially took the right decision of using me as a witness, rather than succumbing to pressure to make me an accused for 'destruction of evidence'. I was declared to have shown valour and guts in confronting the killer. Malini, Georges and I, they said, were the ones who had stuck to their statements, refusing to turn 'hostile'. They made a point of mentioning that my husband, a man of mature age, had chased Manu in the night.

To the SIT, the court posed the question: 'Why are you browbeating your own witness? Stop going after Bina Ramani.' And they stopped.

The media finally awakened to reality, taking a 180-degree turn in their reporting. The SIT ceased its activities against us and we stood vindicated after years of abuse.

As the court's deliberations continued, *Tehelka* conducted a sensational sting operation directed mostly at the witnesses who had perjured themselves. It revealed in stark terms the audacity and depth of the Manu Sharma defence team's tampering with witnesses and evidence. The sting was shown on prime-time national TV and created a sensation. But no legal action was initiated against the perpetrators.

In the sting, Shayan Munshi was lured into an interview, purportedly for a role in a film, which revealed that he indeed spoke good Hindi, validating his original signed statement to the police.

Karan Rajput had died of alcohol abuse, probably brought on by the plentiful sums that had been provided to him by Manu's father. It transpired that he had also been milking Sabrina Lal for funds. Several friends and relatives described payoffs and parties at Sharma-owned hotels.

Shiv Das Yadav, the electrician, also spoke of bribes and intimidation.

Madan Kumar admitted that he had been beaten up and forced to lie about my asking him to clean blood from the floor, and about Georges being absent from the party.

The exposé caused a sensation on national TV and forced the resignation of Manu's father Venod Sharma from the Haryana cabinet, rumoured to be at the insistence of Congress party President Sonia Gandhi herself. He had already been forced to resign as head of the Punjab Congress Party in 1999 when the case first made headlines.

The sting also vividly brought to the public consciousness what the murder case was really about—massive defence tampering with witnesses and evidence, not police incompetence. In his column, Khushwant Singh again deplored the treatment I had received at the hands of the police and media.

Ram Jethmalani then began his defence of Manu Sharma, spinning and repeating a litany of alternate 'theories' and stressing that he was conducting the defence pro bono: Manu wasn't present at the party; there were two gunmen, not one; a tall Sikh man had shot Jessica; Bina had destroyed evidence; the Ramanis were in a conspiracy with the police to frame Manu; the motive for the murder was not a refused drink, but refused sex.

Ram was immediately assailed by the media, by protest groups, by colleagues and even by his family for having taken the case and for having introduced such blatant fabrications into his arguments. He bowed out of the final proceedings in the High Court before the defence arguments were concluded.

In a TV interview with Karan Thapar, Ram once roared, 'Lawyers never lie. Only witnesses do!'

On 18 December 2006, the High Court delivered its verdict in the review: Guilty. The court went on to severely criticize the trial judge, S.L. Bhayana. The lower court, the order read, had erred. The trial verdict and acquittal by Judge S.L. Bhayana had been 'a miscarriage of justice' and the verdict was 'positively perverse'. The bench went on to say: 'In the totality of the circumstances adduced from material on record, the judgement appears to be an immature assessment of the material on record, which is self-contradictory, based on misreading of material and unsustainable.'

The key witness, Shayan Munshi, came in for serious criticism: 'He is now claiming that the said statement was recorded in Hindi while he had narrated the whole story in English as he did not know Hindi at all... We do not find this explanation of Munshi to be convincing.'

Regarding the 'two-gun theory', which Munshi supported in court, the judgement reads: 'In court he has taken a somersault and came out with a version that there were two gentlemen at the bar counter. We have no manner of doubt that on this aspect he is telling a complete lie.'

The prosecutor also earned severe remarks regarding his performance and motivation. He was deemed not to have performed his role properly regarding his witnesses. His questioning was often irrelevant, aiding the defence more than the prosecution. He was particularly criticized for allowing the defence to dismiss me without clarification after I had identified Manu Sharma in the court, and of not having pursued the fabrication of the 'two-gun' theory.

On 20 December 2006, Manu Sharma was handed a sentence of life imprisonment and a fine. The other accused, Vikas Yadav and Amardeep Singh Gill, were fined and given four years' rigorous imprisonment. Vikas Yadav was already serving a sentence for the murder of his sister's boyfriend. A plea for Manu to be sentenced to death was rejected on the grounds that the murder, although intentional, was not premeditated and Manu was not considered to be a threat to society.

The court then cited thirty-two of the witnesses for perjury. At the time of writing, Shayan and the ballistics expert had been charged.

Manu's lawyer announced that they would file an appeal in the Supreme Court because the judgment was wrong in holding me to be a witness. The court subsequently upheld the High Court's judgement.

38

The Media Circus

One problem that has come up in recent years (in India) is 'paid news', in which the media are compensated for favorable coverage. A 2010 study by the Press Council of India, a statutory body, noted, without naming names, that some of the country's biggest newspapers and TV stations practiced paid coverage. The report called corruption in the industry 'pervasive, structured and highly organized.'
—The New York Times, 23 April 2013

I AM NOT SUGGESTING that every negative treatment or blackening of my name by the media was paid for. Obviously, when someone is involved in a murder case, doesn't have a liquor licence and is being vilified by people in power, much negative media coverage will result. Fair enough.

However, when I single out my treatment in what I call 'The Big Lie'—the notion that I wiped blood off the floor and should thus be treated as an accused rather than a witness, I believe there was a clear bias against me in sections of the media. Herein lies a case study for some enterprising journalism student—we have all the clippings. Consider what I have written in Chapter 34, all of which was available to any journalist who wished to apply intelligence rather than ape others.

Astonishingly, the defence hit the jackpot, in that the entire nation bought into this false charge against me. For the first few years, I was looked upon as a criminal in people's judgemental eyes. As things transpired, had the defence been successful in their attempts to eliminate me as a witness, Manu Sharma would be a free man today.

I felt stifled and angry as I watched my character assassination on a regular basis in the front pages of the dailies. It was a bitter pill to swallow. Not one publication or TV channel talked about the heroic way Georges had run on foot in the dark night to apprehend Manu, or of how I had confronted him at the risk of my life, nor that we drove Jessica to hospital—all this in an effort to do the morally correct thing at split-second speed.

I, on the other hand, felt that too many falsehoods were going unchallenged. Looking back, I regret that I did not react more quickly to the harsh, sensational and false headlines suggesting that I wiped bloodstains from the scene of the crime. I wanted to call a press conference and refute the ridiculous charges and fabrications publicly, explain the facts and rectify the record, and end the one-sided bashing. But my lawyers and my husband would hear none of it, saying that I would be fanning the flames, and that these false accusations would die a natural death. As a result, the country judged me cruelly on falsehoods perpetuated by the media. It was a very unfair and difficult time.

Twenty-four-hour television news channels had just begun. They filled a large part of their broadcast time with the Jessica Lal murder case. In fact, even now, more than fourteen years later, anything remotely connected with this case occupies prime-time territory on all the channels, so pervasive has been its drawing power in recent history.

We observed that some papers were consistently publishing damaging headlines against us and simply inventing sellable material, while others presented measured reporting about the case.

A friend suggested I hire a public relations firm he knew, giving me examples about how they had succeeded in polishing and lifting images of certain individuals with a tarnished reputation. Alas, the publicist, when he met me, simply declined, saying, 'You don't stand a chance.' He just shook his head. 'Nobody will go against the tide and give you a positive editorial. Your money won't be important enough.' That came as such a blow.

My self-esteem often hit rock bottom, but my inner truth and integrity kept me going. I had to show some optimism and confidence in the justice system. Moreover, Malini needed to believe in it. My daughter Gitu in New York was worried sick for our safety and simply grabbed on to any tidbits of good news that she could receive from us. Georges was our Rock of Gibraltar throughout the ordeal.

39

Aftermath

THOUGH THE HIGH Court judgement was a vindication for us, our troubles continued. The SIT had not yet disbanded, so their oversights continued—especially if one of us had to travel abroad.

During this period, Gitu had found the man of her dreams, David Ruff. They got married. A year later, 2005, I became grandmother to a lovely baby boy, Kai. Two years later I was blessed with another grandson, Kaspian! To be with Gitu during these special times we had to go through punishing procedures at the police station, then post a surety bond in court of anything from ₹25,000 to ₹200,000; plus there were our lawyers' fees and, of course, the media fanfare that still accompanied our every move. This process would repeat on our return, when we had to submit our passports and collect the surety amount.

Every time Malini had to travel abroad, Georges had to hand in his passport—once, it was only after six weeks of arguments in court that the police sheepishly returned it. It was half-eaten by rats, and of course, the page with Georges's India visa had been all but chewed up. The court was appalled, and ordered the SIT to organize a new passport and Indian visa at their expense. They did no such thing. Georges ended up paying for it.

In April 2007, the High Court opened its perjury case against Shayan Munshi. Justice Sodhi (who had delivered Manu Sharma's sentence) dropped a bomb when he announced that he had received an anonymous letter which pointed to a nexus between a rich accused, a certain lawyer, hostile witnesses, the prosecution, the police and an expert from the forensic lab (CFSL) in four murder cases (including the Jessica Lal case), and the promotion of a 'two-gun theory' which led to acquittal in each case. Justice Sodhi openly wondered if there was a collaboration to destroy the justice delivery system. The letter was turned over to the SIT for investigation with a request that they report back in three days.

In July, in a scathing commentary, the court pronounced the entire SIT exercise and reports as not only useless, but intended to help the accused.

Within months, I was invited to Singapore to receive a Bravery Award from the powerful World Sindhi Congress: 'In recognition and appreciation for her indomitable courage and relentless pursuit of justice.' It was presented to me by L.K. Advani—he had been home minister at the time of the crime. Other prestigious awards followed from magazines, clubs and the like. I was invited to speak at seminars and women's groups in London, New York and parts of India.

Congratulatory letters poured in on Facebook and blogs. Random people, mostly women, would come up to me to shake my hand in recognition of my courage. Magazines lined up to get my story and basically to glorify my stand, which I turned down. This was in total contrast to the reaction I had faced during the first few years of the tragedy.

About four years after the sentence, the Supreme Court of India heard the defence appeal by senior advocate Ram Jethmalani and affirmed the sentences, stating: 'The High Court has analysed all the evidence and arrived at the correct conclusion.'

The appeal was dismissed. Manu Sharma is serving a life sentence in Tihar Jail.

Recently, I got to know from a well-heeled political acquaintance that Manu's family was inconsolable after the verdict. He added, 'You better be careful…' Then for good measure, as if embellishing a bad cake with a cherry, he added, 'Actually, you played a very courageous role and set an example, and I can tell you with confidence that you are admired by many in the higher echelons of government.'

This line has been echoed by many friends and well-wishers since. I realize upon reflection that God's justice is the final justice, and I am not going to let any fear come back to haunt me.

40

The Movie

I<small>F</small> W<small>ALT</small> D<small>ISNEY</small> were to make *Snow White and the Seven Dwarfs* today, he would probably subtitle it with 'Based on a True Story'. So many movies today make that dubious claim.

Thus it was with *No One Killed Jessica*, a Bollywood movie 'based on a true story', which released in 2011. There was no mystery as to which 'true story' the film was based on.

My lawyer, Aparna Bhatt, called me one day to say, 'Bina, I just saw a mention in the papers that someone is making a movie on the Jessica Lal story. Have they contacted you for any material?'

I wasn't surprised; I knew somebody would make a movie of it someday. 'No Aparna, I've heard nothing about it. I'm sure they will call when the time is right.'

Two weeks later, she called again. By now, the announcement was popping up in all the papers. She said, 'You know, Bina, I think it might be a good idea to offer them support. They must get the record straight.' The director was a man named Rajkumar Gupta. I decided to follow her suggestion, found his number and called him one day.

'Good morning, Mr Gupta, I'm Bina Ramani. I see that you are doing a movie on Jessica Lal, and I just thought I should call and see if you need any support to get the records straight.'

There was only silence from his end. 'As you know,' I continued, 'we have been key witnesses to the whole episode. So we could perhaps help you with material for your script, if you wish.'

When he broke his silence, he was nervous; I could almost hear him sweat. 'Don't talk to me,' he said, somewhat rudely. In a shaking voice he muttered, 'I have nothing to do with the script, I have only been hired as a director. Speak to the producer!' And with that the phone went dead. I was not prepared for this response. It was a crushing revelation.

I felt the familiar shudder again. My intuition told me there was danger lurking. I called my lawyer immediately and related the conversation; she also saw it as ominous. That evening at dinner, I told Georges and Malini about the strange conversation. We knew instinctively that we had to brace ourselves and count on our strength. Sure enough, when the movie was ready for release, almost all the dailies printed the same headline, 'Bina Ramani is *not* invited to the premiere'.

When we later went to see the film it became clear why—the movie was libellous. Jessica and Sabrina Lal got to keep their names. Georges, Malini and I were given fictitious ones, presumably to protect the film-makers from legal action.

The basic proposition of the film was that I, a simpering wimp of a woman convincingly played by Bubbles Sabharwal, had ruined the case by not giving evidence, so that the killer and the other accused went free. There was then a media/public outrage, led by Sabrina and a fictitious female TV reporter, so that the case would one day be heard by the High Court. Conclusion of the story: Bad Bina, Crazy Georges, Over-reactive Malini…Good Sabrina.

Many who saw the film were left with a very confused impression. I emerged as the greatest villain in the piece, surpassing even Manu Sharma, whose name is obliquely mentioned as supposedly having been sentenced based on a fickle witness account!

Georges was moved to respond with an article, 'No One Killed Jessica, but what about Bina?' which appeared in *The Indian Express* (11 January 2011). It sums up our reaction. He strongly refuted my characterization, saying:

> Bina's character provides one of the few comic elements in the movie. Anyone who has met Bina must laugh at the simpering, hand-wringing, indecisive, weepy-aunty persona

she is given in the film. This is not the Bina we know and love. The film's director Rajkumar Gupta would do well to meet her some day.

He further clarifies:

> Bina, Malini and I all stuck to our original police statements during gruelling court testimony. All three of us separately identified Manu. [...] For good measure, Bina also identified Vikas Yadav—an intimidating experience for a woman. No, I did not rush over to strangle Manu as shown in the film (I suppose they needed a borderline psychopath for further comic relief) [...] At what point does a 'fiction' become a lie and a slander?

And the final nail in the coffin, 'The film conveniently ends with the appeal to the Delhi High Court in 2006. They thus avoid Bina's pivotal role in that case.'

Epilogue

Life seemed to return to normal, despite several compromises we had had to make in our routine. Our Qutab Colonnade income flow had stopped. We managed to live a comfortable life on diminishing savings and Georges's pension, though luxury was not an option. In the years that followed the tragedy, we became closer to Jessica Lal's family and visited her parents on Jessica's birthday, Diwali and Christmas, and 30 April, the anniversary of her tragedy. Malini's creative talent fast-forwarded her in the fashion business.

We found plenty of comfort in the love and goodwill from a few friends, but there were still some who were not going to let us live in peace.

I had taken to going to Osho's ashram in Pune as an escape from Delhi's harsh atmosphere. Seeking respite from excessive media attention, Malini decided to join me on the second visit. Together we both discovered that this was one place where we could feel free and merge ourselves into a spiritual universe. What came as a soothing balm for our wounded psyches was the mandatory format of entering Osho's ashram—you had to leave your identity at the door and shed all the mental, emotional and psychological baggage that came attached with each entrant's persona. For the entire duration of one's stay there, one had to wear maroon clothes, which depicted the purity of a vermilion essence. Once we had registered ourselves, we were steered to the local boutique, where we selected our robes from an array of styles. Changing into the new attire and walking into the spaces created for the spiritual programmes, we heaved sighs of relief. We had shed our shackles and found a delightful sense of freedom. We were no longer the 'notorious Ramanis'. No one knew us here. It was the United Nations of the spiritual kind, and we were lost in this divine space every time we went there. It was a truly freeing experience that we desperately needed. Here everybody was equal, seeking a path to connect with the inner self.

I was so enamoured by the sheer spirit of this place that I began to visualize a new life for myself in Pune. I was already hunting for a residence near the ashram so I could get daily nurturing with some of the programmes offered—painting, singing, writing, gardening and cooking were just a few, along with several esoteric courses in the healing arts, raising one's consciousness levels and much more.

Malini sounded alarm bells when she noticed my heightened enthusiasm for a permanent life there, suggesting that I check out the possibility of settling in Goa instead, which also offered some degree of spiritual enrichment. She already had a little apartment and a boutique there. So the charming duplex apartment I had eyed a block away from the ashram, and hurriedly put a tiny deposit on, had to be put on hold. Her suggestion turned out to be the perfect prescription.

We took a twelve-hour overnight train journey to Goa along the scenic ghats and the sparkling Arabian Sea—the sea of my childhood. My reflective mind after meditative days at the ashram seemed to sing in harmony with the fleeting glimpses of the water. Never a good sleeper on trains, I watched the early morning rays of sunlight pierce through the horizon. They seemed to whisper a thousand secrets into my soul, as I watched Malini sleep in her newfound state of peace. I wondered if she had indeed led me on a new path where the sea and the rocks would collaborate to give me back my lost destiny.

We settled into Malini's flat on Candolim Beach and after a delicious meal consisting of our favourite Goan dishes with fresh coconut water, took a long lazy walk into the sunset along the shore, allowing the surf from the waves to soak our legs. A wonderful sense of freedom filled the atmosphere around us and we reflected on how we could both almost taste the flavour of happiness here.

The next day, an acquaintance of Malini took me to see some properties. Malini had requested him to show me half a dozen, so I could find at least one that would appeal to my fastidious taste. He was nervous about the choices he had lined up for me to see. However, to my utter delight, the first property he showed me won my heart. Just a seven-minute drive from Malini's apartment, we reached a narrow lane with charming, weather-beaten homes peeping out from leafy old jackfruit trees and, to my surprise, I caught a glimpse of a flowing river running behind them. We stopped at a small gate in front of a cottage which was being renovated. As we walked through the uninteresting site into the rear garden, my jaw dropped at the sight of the charming river flowing along the edge of the property! Unable to hide my joy, I said, 'This is it. I'll take it!' It seemed to beg for my finishing touch. I asked Malini's acquaintance to cancel all the other appointments he had made for me. My choice was made.

He was in shock. I was to learn later, after the deal was struck and I had given my first deposit, that in Goa such cottages on riverbanks were meant for fishermen who caught fish for their masters, who lived on the upper side of the road in bigger properties. I was over the moon at the prospect of living at the edge of a flowing river, and by the fact that Malini's apartment was so close by. The silver lining was the timing. I managed to buy the property at the tail end of an affordable period. Property has been on an upward spiral since then and prices have skyrocketed. Now, about twelve years later, almost everyone I knew in Delhi and hundreds of others have bought homes in Goa.

Living in Goa opened up a newer, more tranquil way of life. Within six months I had moved into the new cottage, which I designed with a nostalgic Portuguese theme. Anyone who came visiting wanted me to find them a house just like mine. If I had had a slick business mind, I could have become very wealthy, selling gorgeous sites, conserving old Portuguese homes and breathing eclectic new life into them, which I thoroughly enjoyed doing. But going professional no longer appealed to me. Pursuing wealth had never been a strong desire of mine. If anything, I had repeatedly shunned wealth-making opportunities throughout my life. I had watched other people make their fortunes from dreams and projects I had initiated—Hauz Khas Village was a glaring example. This was to be part of my chosen journey.

I derived pleasure from my little jaunts, locating interesting properties for friends. I had the gift of nosing out unique places, and as soon as I spotted a beauty, I was quick to call friends and pass on the deals, sometimes making a little profit. Soon, property prices skyrocketed. Suddenly, many of Delhi's elite wanted to have a 'dreamy villa by the water' in Goa. The time-honoured, laid-back nature and habitat of Goa's people and the endearing sight of saffron sunsets behind swaying palms enticed them towards this beautiful state.

Reflecting on my choice of moving to Goa, I realize that I had arrived at a momentous time. The mountains and valleys I have journeyed through have enriched my soul as I come to terms with approaching the august years of my life. The Goan psyche has resonated with mine, notwithstanding the fact that in my earliest years, I was weaned on a parlance of commerce and wealth-building. Unbeknownst to me, in that domain of business talk, I was developing an aversion to the subject and idea of accumulating riches. The psychological impact had been made and most of my life's choices, good or bad, were guided by that early aversion.

Introspecting further, I realize that sacrificing not one, but two passionate romances in exchange for a loveless marriage burdened with financial struggles was driven by this confused intellect. I have deep regret for the untold pain I inflicted upon my beloveds and still question my flawed judgement. I'm gratified to know that both of them moved into happy marriages. Having said that, I believe I earned a gift in disguise from this bittersweet sting of my own making. The two ardour-filled romances unleashed a reservoir of passion in me. Of course, if I hadn't opted for the road less travelled, in the thorny marriage with Andy, I may never have had the chance to recognize the hidden power of my passion. It drove me to taste life in its many hues. With every dark cloud there has shone a silver lining on the horizon. Andy may not have been the right choice of husband, but he did teach me about many of life's harsh realities.

So I did not fulfil the role of the trophy wife and exemplary homemaker by the principles of my upbringing. My elders answered my questions about what life held for me; I chose the path where I questioned their answers. I had awakened the elixir of life from within. My yin and yang found a balance, and I became of force of energy when it was called for. My husband Georges and I passionately value each other's individuality and live each day nurturing our senses in myriad ways.

Reflecting on my legacy, I rejoice in the comfort of having my two loving daughters, Malini and Gitu, my wonderful son-in-law David Ruff and my two prized gifts in this life, my grandsons Kai and Kaspian. For this, I owe gratitude to Andy—we made our magic!

These blessings notwithstanding, I could never have made it this far without the love and unstinting support of my entire loving family and my wonderful friends, who are spread across the globe. A handful of them have been my true guardians. They know who they are. I want them back in my next life as well; if there is to be one.

In the end I can only say that there are still many lessons to be learnt. Each day brings a new beginning, because I want to live before I die.

Acknowledgements

I started writing this memoir five years ago during my days in Tihar Jail. Then, for lack of confidence, I shelved it, resuming only after three years at the prodding of some of my friends in the US and in India. I owe my deepest gratitude to them.

My daughters, Malini and Gitu, have had some reservations about me revealing my life's journey to the world; nevertheless, they have supported me in different ways through this journey.

I would also like to thank Bonnie Strauss, Christine Wizner, Leela Ellis, Veeni Advani, Jaswant Lalwani, Bhagwanti Mohan, Payal Jauhar, Dilshad Sheikh, Bhaichand Patel, Francesca Von Habsburg, Rajyalaxmi Rao, Aryaman Sundaram, Tarun Tejpal, Malvika Sanghvi, Rohit Chawla and Urvashi Kaur, who helped carve my literary path in one way or the other. Khushwant Singh's blessings shall eternally live with me. I wish to particularly acknowledge Neela Devi, wife of Late Shammi Kapoor, whose support means a lot to me. Ritu Nanda and Mrs Raj Kapoor (Bhabhi-ji) revived beautiful memories of the romantic Shammi Kapoor era of my life. Georges enriched my knowledge and inspired my writing. Several other friends who helped me pull together the memoir, whose names I have missed, deserve my sincere thanks.

Carol Neiman and Biraj Bose have aided me in structuring the book.

Special thanks to Rupa Publications for having unquestioning faith in me.